Dramat
Sourcebook

MW01279929

1992–93 EDITION

Dramatists Sourcebook

1992-93 Edition

Complete opportunities for
playwrights, translators, composers,
lyricists and librettists

**EDITED BY
M. Elizabeth Osborn**

Theatre Communications Group ● New York

TCG gratefully acknowledges public funds from the National Endowment for the Arts, the New York State Council on the Arts and the New York City Department of Cultural Affairs in addition to the generous support of the following foundations and corporations: Alcoa Foundation; Ameritech Foundation; ARCO Foundation; AT&T Foundation; Consolidated Edison Company of New York; Council of Literary Magazines and Presses; Nathan Cummings Foundation; Dayton Hudson Foundation; EMR Systems Communication; Ford Foundation; GTE; James Irvine Foundation; Jerome Foundation; Management Consultants for the Arts; Andrew W. Mellon Foundation; Metropolitan Life Foundation; National Broadcasting Company; Pew Charitable Trusts; Philip Morris Companies; Prudential Foundation; Scherman Foundation; Shubert Foundation; L. J. Skaggs and Mary C. Skaggs Foundation; Audrey Skirball-Kenis Theatre; Lila Wallace–Reader's Digest Fund.

Published by Theatre Communications Group, Inc.
355 Lexington Ave., New York, NY 10017

Cover design by G&H/SOHO, Ltd.

Manufactured in the United States of America

ISSN 0733-1606
ISBN 1-55936-057-7

Contents

Preface

When I wrote my first preface to this *Sourcebook* nine years ago, it was a time of rapid expansion. The number of listings was up 25 percent that year; there were 40 new theatre entries and 30 new contests; two other sections doubled in size.

As we all know, signs of growth are hard to come by these days. The recession continues; the arts are beseiged. Theatres have been forced to cut back, to close down. Fellowships and grants once awarded annually are now given every other year. Today it costs playwrights more to enter many contests, and those who win may get less.

In this time of cutbacks it is surprising and encouraging, therefore, that the number of entries in this *Sourcebook* remains stable. Some 80 new listings have replaced those we have lost. Opportunities new and not-so-new still abound, especially for those prepared to take wise advantage of them. As surprisingly few entries pass unchanged from one *Sourcebook* to the next, acquiring an up-to-date *DSB* is a fine first step.

No doubt difficult economic times have hurt most theatre writers at least as much as the average citizen. It's more important than ever that you study the listings in this book carefully, rationally select those possibilities your work is best suited for, then follow guidelines meticulously. Before you send anything out, study—or restudy—Tony Kushner's guide to script submission. One of the hottest playwrights in the English-speaking world just might be worth paying attention to.

Remember that we are asking people submitting listings to tell us what they are going to do months from now, and that some of what they currently intend is bound to change. If you write to request guidelines and entry forms well in advance, you'll be more likely to discover in time the sorts of shifts that seem designed to drive us all crazy. And when you write for these pieces of paper, enclose a self-addressed stamped envelope (SASE) for them to go in. More and more organizations just can't pay the postage to respond to your requests, and they certainly can't afford the cost of sending your work back to you. I'm sure no veteran *DSB*er would or could forget the First Law of Script Submission, but for the newcomers out there: Except for the few entries that specify "scripts will not be returned," you *must* enclose a SASE—or give explicit permission for your manuscript or tape to be thrown out.

Newcomers to this book also need to know that when an entry begins with a person's name, it is alphabetized under the surname, not the first name. Hence you will find the Susan Smith Blackburn Prize under B, the Mary Roberts Rinehart Fund under R, the James White Review under W.

When I was warily considering the possibility of editing this *Sourcebook*—no one who hasn't been part of such a project can imagine how much work it is—TCG's literary coordinator Gillian Richards assured me that I would find the task much easier than I used to in the years when I was doing most of the work myself. She was absolutely right. Gillian and her patient assistant Regina Raiford gathered the information. With Gillian's advice and consent, I edited it. Regina entered the new material into the computer. We all proofread and checked and re-checked. Thanks to Gillian and Regina—and to Steve Samuels, who untangled computer glitches—the project could hardly have gone better. I hope the work pays off, in one way or another, for each of you. You are who it's for.

M. Elizabeth Osborn
June 1992

Prologue

A Simple Working Guide for Playwrights
by Tony Kushner

A) *Format:* Most playwrights use a format in which character headings are placed centered above the line and capitalized:

LIONEL

I don't possess a mansion, a car, or a string of polo ponies...

Lines should be one-and-a-half spaced. Stage directions should be in-dented and single-spaced. If a character's line is interrupted at the end of the page, its continuance on the following page should be marked as such:

LIONEL (cont'd)

or a string of polo ponies...

There are denser, and thus more economical, formats; since Xeroxing is expensive, and heavy scripts cost more to ship, you may be tempted to use these, but a generously spaced format is much easier to read, and in these matters it doesn't pay to be parsimonious.

B) *Typing and reproducing:* Scripts should be typed neatly and reproduced clearly. Remember that everyone who reads your script will be reading many others additionally, and it will work to your serious disadvantage if the copy's sloppy, faded, or otherwise unappealing. If you use a computer printer, eschew old-fashioned dot-matrix and other robotic kinds of print. Also, I think it's best to avoid using incredibly fancy word-processing printing programs with eight different typefaces and decorative borders. Simple typescript, carefully done, is best. Check for typos. A playwright's punctuation may be idiosyncratic for purposes of expressiveness, but not too idiosyncratic, and spelling should be correct.

C) *Sending the script:*

1) The script should have a title page with the title, your name, address and phone number, or that of your agent or representative. Scripts are now automatically copyrighted at the moment of creation, but simply writing © and the date on the title page can serve as a kind of scarecrow for thievish magpies.

2) Never, never send an unbound script. Loose pages held together by a rubber band don't qualify as bound, nor do pages clamped together with a mega-paperclip. A heavy paper cover will protect the script as it passes from hand to hand.

3) Always, always enclose a self-addressed stamped envelope (SASE) or you will never see your script again. You may enclose a note telling the theatre to dispose of the copy instead of returning it; but you must have the ultimate fate of the script planned for in the eventuality of its not being selected for production. Don't leave this up to the theatre! If you want receipt of the script acknowledged, include a self-addressed, stamped postcard (SASP).

D) *Letter of inquiry and synopsis:* If a theatre states, in its entry in the *Sourcebook,* that it does not accept unsolicited scripts, believe it. Don't call and ask if there are exceptions; there aren't. A well-written and concise letter of inquiry, however, accompanied by a synopsis possessed of similar virtues *can* get you an invitation to submit your play. It's prudent, then, to spend time on both letter and synopsis. It is, admittedly, very hard for a writer to sum up his or her work in less than a page, but this kind of boiling-down can be of value beyond its necessity as a tool for marketing; use it to help clarify for yourself what's central and essential about your play. A good synopsis should *briefly* summarize the basic features of the plot without going into excessive detail; it should evoke both the style and the thematic substance of the play without recourse to clichéd description ("This play is about what happens when people lose their dreams..."); and it should convey essential information, such as cast size, gender breakdown, period, location, or anything else a literary manager deciding whether to send for the play might want to know. Make reference to other productions in your letter, but don't send thick packets of reviews and photos. And don't offer your opinion of the play's worth, which will be inferred as being positive from the fact that you are its parent.

E)   *Waiting:*   Theatres almost always take a long time to respond to playwrights about a specific play, frequently far in excess of the time given in their listings in the *Sourcebook.* This is due neither to spite nor indolence. Literary departments are usually understaffed and their workload is fearsome. Then, too, the process of selection invariably involves a host of people and considerations of all kinds. In my opinion you do yourself no good by repeatedly calling after the status of your script; you will become identified as a pest. It's terribly expensive to copy and mail scripts, but you must be prepared to shoulder the expense and keep making copies if they don't get returned. If, after a certain length of time past the deadline, you haven't heard from a theatre, send a letter inquiring politely about the play, reminding the appropriate people that you'd sent an SASE with the script; and then forget about it. In most cases, you will get a response and the script returned eventually.

One way to cut down on the expenses involved is to be selective about venues for submission. Reading *Sourcebook* entries and scrutinizing a copy of *Theatre Profiles* (see Useful Publications) will help you select the theatres most compatible with your work. If you've written a musical celebration of the life of Phyllis Schlafly, for example, you won't want to send it to theatres with an interest in radical feminist dramas. Or you won't necessarily want to send your play about the history of Western imperialism to a theatre that produces an annual season of musical comedy.

F)   *Produce yourself!*   In *Endgame,* Clov asks Hamm, "Do you believe in the life to come?" and Hamm responds, "Mine was always that." The condition of endless deferment is one that modern American playwrights share with Beckett's characters and other denizens of the postmodern world. Don't spend your life waiting. You may not be an actor, but that doesn't mean that action is forbidden you. Playwrights can, with very little expense, mount readings of their work; they can band together with

other playwrights for readings and discussions; and they can, if they want
to, produce their work themselves. Growth as a writer for the stage
depends on seeing your work on stage, and if no one else will put it
there, the job is up to you. At the very least, and above all else, while
waiting, waiting, waiting for responses and offers, keep reading, thinking
and writing.

Tony Kushner is a playwright and director, and former director of literary
services at TCG. His plays include *A Bright Room Called Day*, *The Illusion*, and
Angels in America. Millennium Approaches, the first part of this epic drama, is
currently playing at the Royal National Theatre in London, and appeared in
the pages of *American Theatre* magazine in the summer of 1992. The entire
work will be staged in Los Angeles and New York during the 1992–93 season,
and published in book form by TCG. Kushner is also working on an adaptation
of *The Dybbuk* for Hartford Stage.

1

Script Opportunities

- Production
- Prizes
- Publication
- Development

Production

What theatres are included in this section?

The overwhelming majority of the nonprofit professional theatres throughout the United States are represented here. In order to be included, a theatre must be a TCG member. (A handful of TCG theatres asked not to be listed, in most cases because they don't do new work or they create all of their own material.) To be eligible for TCG membership, a theatre must have been operating for at least two years and must meet professional standards of staffing, programming and budget. *Commercial and amateur producers are not included.*

How should I go about deciding where to submit my play?

Don't send it out indiscriminately. Take time to study the listings and select those theatres most likely to be receptive to your material. Find out all you can about each of the theatres you select. Look to TCG's *Theatre Profiles 10* for information on most of these theatres, including seasonal lists of plays each performed from 1989–91. Read *American Theatre* every month to see what plays the theatres are currently presenting and what are their other activities. (See Publications from TCG in the back of this book for more information.) Whenever possible, go to see the theatre's work.

When I submit my play, what can I do to maximize its chances?

First, read carefully the Simple Working Guide for Playwrights in the Prologue of this *Sourcebook* for good advice on script submission. Then follow each theatre's guidelines meticulously. Pay particular attention to the Special Interests section: If a theatre specifies "gay and lesbian themes only," do not send them your heterosexual romantic comedy, however witty and well-written it is. Also, bear in mind the following points about the various submission procedures:

1) "Accepts unsolicited scripts": Don't waste the theatre's time and yours by writing to ask permission to submit your play—just send it. If you want an acknowledgment of receipt, say so and enclose a self-addressed stamped postcard (SASP) for this purpose. *Always* enclose a self-addressed stamped envelope (SASE) for the return of the script.

2) "Synopsis and letter of inquiry": An increasing number of theatres require a synopsis rather than the script itself. Never send an unsolicited script to these theatres. Prepare a clear, cogent and *brief* synopsis of your play and send it along with any other materials requested in the listing. The letter of inquiry is a cover note asking for permission to submit the script; if there is something about your play or about yourself as a writer that you think may spark the theatre's interest, by all means mention it, but keep the letter brief. Unless the theatre specifies that it only responds if it wants to see the script, always enclose an SASP for the theatre's response.

3) "Professional recommendation": Send a script (not a letter of inquiry) accompanied by a letter of recommendation from a theatre professional. Wait until you can obtain such a letter before approaching these theatres.

4) "Agent submission": If you do not have an agent yet, do not submit to these theatres. Wait until you have had a production or two and have acquired a representative.

5) "Direct solicitation from playwright or agent": Do not submit to these theatres. If they are interested in your work you will hear from them!

Note that we've persuaded theatres requiring letters and synopses to give us two response times—one for letters and one for scripts they ask to see. All response times are average and approximate. Even if it takes the theatres longer to respond than they say it will, don't pester them; practice patience, and get on with your life and your art.

ACADEMY THEATRE
649A Ponders Ave; Atlanta, GA 30318; (404) 365-8088
Elliott J. Berman, *Literary Manager*

Submission procedure: accepts unsolicited scripts from SE playwrights only; others send synopsis, dialogue sample and letter of inquiry. **Types of material:** full-length plays. **Special interests:** nontraditional plays with elements of poetic language that present challenges; plays that deal with important issues in unique ways. **Facilities:** no permanent facility. **Production considerations:** prefers cast limit of 8, simple set. **Best submission time:** Jul–Mar. **Response time:** 1 month letter; 4 months script. **Special programs:** readings and workshops, primarily of plays by regional playwrights.

A CONTEMPORARY THEATRE
100 West Roy St; Seattle, WA 98119-3824; (206) 285-3220
Steven E. Alter, *Artistic Associate/Literary Manager*

Submission procedure: accepts unsolicited scripts from WA playwrights only; others send synopsis, up to 10 pages of dialogue and letter of inquiry. **Types of material:** full-length plays, translations, adaptations. **Special interests:** contemporary social and political issues; plays innovative in form and perspective; not keen on kitchen-sink realism. **Facilities:** A Contemporary Theatre, 450 seats, thrust stage. **Best submission time:** Sep–Apr. **Response time:** 1 month letter; 3 months script. **Special programs:** Young ACT Company tours WA schools annually.

ACTHEATER
Box 1454; Anniston, AL 36202; (205) 236-8342
Josephine E. Ayers, *Producing Artistic Director*

Submission procedure: no unsolicited scripts; synopsis and letter of inquiry. **Types of material:** full-length plays, adaptations. **Special interests:** southern writers; sociopolitical issues. **Facilities:** ACTheater, 100 seats, thrust stage. **Production considerations:** prefers cast limit of 10, minimal changes of location. **Best submission time:** year-round. **Response time:** 10 days letter; 2 months script.

THE ACTING COMPANY
Box 898, Times Square Station; New York, NY 10108; (212) 564-3510
Zelda Fichandler, *Artistic Director*
Margot Harley, *Executive Producer*

Submission procedure: no unsolicited scripts; recommendation from professional familiar with company's work and goals. **Types of material:** full-length plays, one-acts, translations, adaptations, musicals. **Special interests:** mainly classical repertory but occasionally produces new works suited to acting ensemble of approximately 11 men, 6 women, age range 24–45. **Facilities:** no permanent facility; touring company which plays in New York City for 1 or 2 weeks a year.

Production considerations: productions tour in repertory; simple, transportable proscenium-stage set. **Best submission time:** Nov–Jan. **Response time:** 12 months.

ACTORS ALLIANCE THEATRE COMPANY
30800 Evergreen Rd; Southfield, MI 48076; (313) 642-1326
Jeffrey M. Nahan, *Executive Artistic Director*

Submission procedure: no unsolicited scripts; professional recommendation. **Types of material:** full-length plays. **Special interests:** contemporary social issues; new forms of theatrical experience. **Facilities:** various local venues; also tours. **Production considerations:** 1 set or unit set. **Best submission time:** Jan–Mar. **Response time:** 3–4 months.

THE ACTORS' COMPANY OF PENNSYLVANIA
Box 1153; Lancaster, PA 17603; (717) 397-1251
Jeanne Clemson, *Producing Director*

Submission procedure: no unsolicited scripts; synopsis and letter of inquiry. **Types of material:** full-length plays, one-acts, translations, adaptations, plays for young audiences, musicals. **Facilities:** Fulton Opera House, 800 seats, proscenium stage; Steinman Theatre, 200 seats, thrust stage. **Production considerations:** simple production demands. **Best submission time:** summer. **Response time:** 6 months letter (if interested); 3 months script.

ACTORS THEATRE OF LOUISVILLE
316 West Main St; Louisville, KY 40202-4218; (502) 584-1265
Michael Bigelow Dixon, *Literary Manager*

Submission procedure: accepts unsolicited 10-page one-acts only; professional recommendation for all other plays. **Types of material:** full-length plays, one-acts, translations, adaptations. **Facilities:** Pamela Brown Auditorium, 637 seats, thrust stage; Victor Jory Theatre, 159 seats, 3/4-arena stage. **Best submission time:** year-round. **Response time:** 6–9 months (most scripts returned in fall). **Special programs:** National Ten-Minute Play Contest (see Prizes).

ACTORS THEATRE OF PHOENIX
815 North 1st Ave, Suite 3; Phoenix, AZ 85003; (602) 253-6701
Judy Rollings, *Artistic Director*

Submission procedure: no unsolicited scripts; synopsis, character breakdown, scenic requirements and letter of inquiry with SASP for response. **Types of material:** full-length plays, one-acts, translations, adaptations, musicals. **Facilities:** Herberger Theater Center's Stage West, 290 seats, proscenium-thrust stage. **Production considerations:** prefers small cast, 1 set, minimal technical requirements. **Best submission time:** year-round. **Response time:** 1 week letter; 1 month script. **Special programs:** Brown Bag Theater: minimal-budget lunchtime productions of new plays performed by local non-Equity actors on set of current mainstage production or in rehearsal hall.

A.D. PLAYERS
2710 West Alabama St; Houston, TX 77098; (713) 526-2721
Martha Doolittle, *Literary Manager*

Submission procedure: no unsolicited scripts; synopsis, resume and letter of inquiry. **Types of material:** full-length plays, one-acts, adaptations, plays for young audiences, musicals. **Special interests:** quality works with a Christian world view. **Facilities:** Grace Theater, 212 seats, proscenium stage. **Production considerations:** cast limit of 12, prefers less than 10; no more than 2 sets, maximum height 11′ 6″; no fly space; minimal lighting. **Best submission time:** year-round. **Response time:** 1 month letter; 4 months script. **Special programs:** Theater Arts Academy: includes playwriting classes; contact theatre for information.

ALABAMA SHAKESPEARE FESTIVAL
1 Festival Dr; Montgomery, AL 36117; (205) 272-1640
Kent Thompson, *Artistic Director*
Bob Vardaman, *Literary Associate*

Submission procedure: no unsolicited scripts; synopsis, dialogue sample and letter of inquiry. **Types of material:** full-length plays, translations, adaptations. **Special interests:** new translations of 17th-20th century international classics; new plays with southern or black themes. **Facilities:** Festival Stage, 750 seats, modified thrust stage; Octagon, 225 seats, flexible space. **Best submission time:** Jul–Dec. **Response time:** 3 weeks letter; 3–4 months script.

ALLEY THEATRE
615 Texas Ave; Houston, TX 77002; (713) 228-9341
Christopher Baker, *Literary Director*

Submission procedure: no unsolicited scripts; synopsis and letter of inquiry. **Types of material:** full-length plays, translations, adaptations, musicals. **Facilities:** Main Stage, 800 seats, thrust stage; Arena Stage, 300 seats, arena stage. **Best submission time:** year-round. **Response time:** 6 weeks letter; 2–6 months script.

ALLIANCE THEATRE COMPANY
1280 Peachtree St NE; Atlanta, GA 30309; (404) 898-1132
Walter Bilderback, *Dramaturg*

Submission procedure: no unsolicited scripts; synopsis and letter of inquiry (plus sample dialogue if possible). **Types of material:** full-length plays, musicals. **Special interests:** new musicals; southern themes; works that deal with moral/spiritual questions of life in multicultural America. **Facilities:** Alliance Theatre, 864 seats, proscenium stage; Studio Theatre, 200 seats, flexible stage. **Best submission time:** Mar–Sep. **Response time:** 2–4 weeks letter; 1–3 months script.

AMERICAN CONSERVATORY THEATER
450 Geary St; San Francisco, CA 94102-1285; (415) 749-2200
Literary Manager

Submission procedure: no unsolicited scripts; agents and theatre professionals only may send synopsis and letter of inquiry. **Types of material:** full-length plays, translations, adaptations. **Special interests:** theatre plans to work with selected playwrights on company projects and adaptations. **Facilities:** In 1993–94, Geary Theatre, 1100 seats, proscenium stage; Second Stage, details not yet known. **Best submission time:** year-round. **Response time:** 3 months letter; 3 months script.

THE AMERICAN PLACE THEATRE
111 West 46th St; New York, NY 10036; (212) 840-2960
Literary Department

Submission procedure: accepts unsolicited scripts from agents only; others send synopsis, first 20 pages of script and letter of inquiry. **Types of material:** full-length plays, adaptations, performance pieces. **Special interests:** works by living American playwrights only; works innovative in form and perspective; less interested in "sentimental naturalism" and commercial material. **Facilities:** Main Stage, 180–299 seats, flexible stage; Cabaret Space, 75 seats, flexible stage; First Floor Theatre, 75 seats, flexible stage. **Best submission time:** Sep–Jun. **Response time:** 2 months letter; 3–4 months script. **Special programs:** American Humorist Series: works by or about American humorists. Jubilee: annual festival celebrating the history and experience of minority and ethnic Americans (black, Hispanic, Irish, Polish, etc.). First Floor Theatre: program of new experimental writing and performance pieces.

AMERICAN REPERTORY THEATRE
64 Brattle St; Cambridge, MA 02138; (617) 495-2668
Robert Scanlan, *Literary Director*

Submission procedure: no unsolicited scripts; synopsis, 10-page maximum sample and letter of inquiry. **Types of material:** full-length plays, one-acts, translations, adaptations, cabaret/revues. **Special interests:** prefers plays "which lend themselves to poetic use of the stage." **Facilities:** Loeb Drama Center, 556 seats, flexible stage; 12 Holyoke Street, 350 seats, proscenium stage. **Production considerations:** cast limit of 15. **Best submission time:** Sep–Jun. **Response time:** 6 weeks letter; 4–5 months script.

AMERICAN STAGE
Box 1560; St. Petersburg, FL 33731; (813) 823-1600
Victoria L. Holloway, *Artistic Director*

Submission procedure: no unsolicited scripts; synopsis, first 10 pages of dialogue and letter of inquiry. **Types of material:** full-length plays, adaptations, one-acts for young audiences. **Special interests:** plays by American playwrights written in the last 10 years; plays for young audiences and families. **Facilities:** American Stage,

120 seats, flexible stage. **Production considerations:** cast limit of 10. **Best submission time:** Jul–Sep. **Response time:** 2 months letter; 4 months script.

AMERICAN STAGE FESTIVAL
Box 225; Milford, NH 03055-0225
Attn: New Scripts, EARLY STAGES

Submission procedure: no unsolicited scripts; synopsis, 10 pages of dialogue and letter of inquiry with SASE for response; cassette of 2–3 songs for musicals. **Types of material:** full-length plays, musicals. **Special interests:** material with strong emotional content that tells a compelling story; material that encourages new theatrical techniques and a new sense of theatrical reality. **Facilities:** American Stage Festival, 497 seats, proscenium stage. **Production considerations:** cast limit of 10 for plays; cast limit of 15 plus 5 musicians for musicals. **Best submission time:** Sep–Dec. **Response time:** 2–3 months letter; 4–6 months script.

AMERICAN THEATRE COMPANY
Box 1265; Tulsa, OK 74101; (918) 747-9494
Rebecca Bones, *Education Department*

Submission procedure: no unsolicited scripts; synopsis, 5–10 pages of dialogue, resume and letter of inquiry. **Types of material:** full-length plays, translations, adaptations, plays for young audiences, musicals. **Facilities:** Tulsa Performing Arts Center's John Williams Theatre, 429 seats, proscenium stage. **Production considerations:** cast limit of 10, simple set. **Best submission time:** fall–early spring. **Response time:** 2 weeks letter; 1 month script.

AMERICAN THEATRE WORKS
Box 519; Dorset, VT 05251; (802) 867-2223
Jill Charles, *Artistic Director*

Submission procedure: no unsolicited scripts; professional recommendation. **Types of material:** full-length plays, adaptations, musicals. **Special interests:** plays which have not received first-class or Off-Broadway production. **Facilities:** Dorset Playhouse, 220 seats, proscenium stage. **Production considerations:** prefers cast limit of 10. **Best submission time:** Sep–Dec. **Response time:** 3 months. **Special programs:** Dorset Colony for Writers (see Colonies and Residencies).

ARDEN THEATRE COMPANY
Box 801; Philadelphia , PA 19105; (215) 829-8900
Terrence J. Nolen, *Producing Artistic Director*
Aaron Posner, *Artistic Director*

Submission procedure: accepts unsolicited scripts; prefers tape with musicals. **Types of material:** full-length plays, translations, adaptations, musicals. **Special interests:** new adaptations of literary works. **Facilities:** Mainstage, 150–175 seats, flexible stage. **Best submission time:** year-round. **Response time:** 6 months.

ARENA PLAYERS REPERTORY THEATRE OF LONG ISLAND

296 Farmingdale Rd; East Farmingdale, NY 11735; (516) 293-0674
Audrey Perry, *Literary Manager*

Submission procedure: accepts unsolicited scripts. **Types of material:** full-length plays. **Facilities:** Main Stage, 240 seats, arena stage (4 sides); Second Stage, 100 seats, arena stage (2 sides). **Production considerations:** cast limit of 12 for Main Stage, 6 for Second Stage. **Best submission time:** year-round. **Response time:** 3 months.

ARENA STAGE

6th & Maine Ave SW; Washington, DC 20024; (202) 554-9066
Chiori Miyagawa, *Literary Manager*

Submission procedure: no unsolicited scripts; synopsis, 10-page sample and letter of inquiry. **Types of material:** full-length plays, translations, adaptations, musicals. **Special interests:** plays for a multicultural company; plays by writers of color. **Facilities:** The Arena, 827 seats, arena stage; The Kreeger Theater, 514 seats, modified thrust stage; The Old Vat Room, 160 seats, cabaret stage. **Best submission time:** early summer. **Response time:** 3 months letter; 5 months script. **Special programs:** Workshop/performance program producing new plays and translations. Commissioning program; participation by invitation only.

ARIZONA THEATRE COMPANY

40 East 14th St, Box 1631; Tucson, AZ 85702; (602) 884-8210
David Ira Goldstein, *Artistic Director*

Submission procedure: accepts unsolicited scripts from SW playwrights only; others send synopsis, 10 pages of dialogue, resume and letter of inquiry. **Types of material:** full-length plays, translations, adaptations, musicals. **Facilities:** Temple of Music and Art (in Tucson), 600 seats, proscenium stage; Herberger Theatre (in Phoenix), 800 seats, proscenium stage. **Best submission time:** spring–summer. **Response time:** 4–6 weeks letter; 4–6 months script. **Special programs:** New Play Reading Series: rehearsed readings followed by discussion with audience.

ARKANSAS REPERTORY THEATRE

Box 110; Little Rock, AR 72203-0110; (501) 378-0405
Brad Mooy, *Literary Manager*

Submission procedure: accepts unsolicited scripts; prefers synopsis and letter of inquiry. **Types of material:** full-length plays, one-acts, musicals, cabaret/revues. **Facilities:** Arkansas Repertory Theatre, 354 seats, proscenium stage; Second Stage, 99 seats, black box. **Production considerations:** prefers small cast. **Best submission time:** year-round. **Response time:** 3 months letter; 3 months script. **Special programs:** New Playreading Series.

ARROW ROCK LYCEUM THEATRE
Main St; Arrow Rock, MO 65320; (816) 837-3311
Michael Bollinger, *Artistic Producing Director*

Submission procedure: no unsolicited scripts; synopsis and letter of inquiry. **Types of material:** full-length plays, translations, adaptations, musicals. **Special interests:** plays dealing with the myth and/or reality of the American dream. **Facilities:** Arrow Rock Lyceum Theatre, 208 seats, proscenium stage. **Production considerations:** cast limit of 12; prefers 1 set. **Best submission time:** Sep–Dec. **Response time:** 2 months letter; 2 months script. **Special programs:** Arrow Rock Lyceum Theatre Playwrights Competition (see Prizes).

ARTREACH TOURING THEATRE
3074 Madison Rd; Cincinnati, OH 45209; (513) 871-2300
Kathryn Schultz Miller, *Artistic Director*

Submission procedure: accepts unsolicited scripts. **Types of material:** plays for young audiences. **Special interests:** intelligent, well-plotted plays. **Facilities:** touring company. **Production considerations:** cast limit of 3; plays must be 50–60 minutes in length and easy to tour. **Best submission time:** Jan–Mar. **Response time:** 1 month.

ASOLO THEATRE COMPANY
Asolo Center for the Performing Arts; 5555 North Tamiami Trail;
    Sarasota, FL 34243; (813) 351-9010
Margaret Booker, *Artistic Director*

Submission procedure: no unsolicited scripts; 1-page synopsis and letter of inquiry with SASE for response. **Types of material:** full-length plays, translations, adaptations, plays for young audiences. **Facilities:** The Harold E. and Esther M. Mertz Theatre, 499 seats, proscenium stage. **Best submission time:** year-round. **Response time:** 2 months letter; 6 months script.

BAILIWICK REPERTORY
1225 West Belmont; Chicago, IL 60657-3205; (312) 883-1090
David Zak, *Executive Director*

Submission procedure: send SASE for Manuscript Submission Guidelines. **Types of material:** full-length plays, translations, adaptations, plays for young audiences, musicals. **Special interests:** innovative or highly theatrical works with a specific political point of view. **Facilities:** South Theater in the Theater Building, 150 seats, thrust stage. **Best submission time:** year-round. **Response time:** 4 months. **Special programs:** note: all playwrights submitting to these programs must first obtain Manuscript Submission Guidelines (see above). New Directions Series: fully staged performances of experimental works or works-in-progress on set of mainstage productions. Director's Festival: annual directors' showcase of 50 one-acts staged in month-long festival; *deadline:* 1 Nov 1992. Pride Performance Series:

annual festival of full-length plays serving North Side gay community; workshop productions and performance poetry; *deadline:* 1 Nov 1992.

BARTER THEATRE
Box 867; Abingdon, VA 24210; (703) 628-2281
Rex Partington, *Producing Director*

Submission procedure: accepts unsolicited scripts. **Types of material:** full-length plays, translations, adaptations, plays for young audiences. **Special interests:** social issues and current events. **Facilities:** Barter Theatre, 380 seats, proscenium stage. **Production considerations:** cast of 4–12, 1 set or unit set. **Best submission time:** Mar, Sep. **Response time:** 6–9 months.

BERKELEY REPERTORY THEATRE
2025 Addison St; Berkeley, CA 94704; (415) 841-6108
Erik Ehn, *Literary Manager*

Submission procedure: no unsolicited scripts; agent submission. **Types of material:** full-length plays, translations, adaptations. **Facilities:** Mark Taper Mainstage, 400 seats, thrust stage. **Best submission time:** Sep–May. **Response time:** 6–8 months. **Special programs:** Parallel Season: productions of 2–3 new plays each season. Commissioning program. In-house readings.

THE BERKSHIRE PUBLIC THEATRE
Box 860; Pittsfield, MA 01202; (413) 445-4631
Frank Bessell, *Artistic Director*

Submission procedure: no unsolicited scripts; synopsis, dialogue sample and letter of inquiry with SASP for response. **Types of material:** full-length plays, adaptations, plays for young audiences, musicals, cabaret/revues. **Special interests:** substantive, innovative treatment of contemporary issues; plays for young audiences suitable for touring. **Facilities:** The Berkshire Public Theatre, 297 seats, proscenium stage. **Production considerations:** 1 set or unit set. **Best submission time:** year-round. **Response time:** 6 months letter; 12 months script. **Special programs:** touring program of plays for young performers.

BERKSHIRE THEATRE FESTIVAL
Box 797; Stockbridge, MA 01262; (413) 298-5536
Richard Dunlap, *Artistic Director*

Submission procedure: no unsolicited scripts; agent submission. **Types of material:** full-length plays, one-acts, musicals. **Special interests:** thought-provoking vacation entertainment; theatre on the "cutting edge." **Facilities:** Playhouse, 429 seats, proscenium stage; Unicorn Theatre, 99 seats, thrust stage. **Production considerations:** cast limit of 8 for plays; small orchestra for musicals; prefers simple set. **Best submission time:** Nov–Dec. **Response time:** 6 months.

BILINGUAL FOUNDATION OF THE ARTS
421 North Ave 19; Los Angeles, CA 90031; (213) 225-4044
Margarita Galban, *Artistic Director*

Submission procedure: accepts unsolicited scripts. **Types of material:** full-length plays, one-acts, translations, adaptations, plays for young audiences. **Special interests:** plays with Hispanic themes or by Hispanic playwrights only. **Facilities:** BFA's Little Theatre, 99 seats, thrust stage. **Production considerations:** cast limit of 10, simple set. **Best submission time:** year-round. **Response time:** 3 months.

BIRMINGHAM CHILDREN'S THEATRE
Box 1362; Birmingham, AL 35201; (205) 324-0470
James W. Rye, Jr., *Managing/Artistic Director*

Submission procedure: no unsolicited scripts; synopsis and letter of inquiry. **Types of material:** plays for young audiences. **Special interests:** plays for preschool–grade 2. **Facilities:** Birmingham-Jefferson Civic Center Theatre, 1073 seats, thrust stage; Studio Theatre, up to 250 seats, lab space. **Production considerations:** prefers cast of 5–10. **Best submission time:** Sep–Dec. **Response time:** 2 weeks letter; several months script.

BLACKFRIARS THEATRE
(formerly The Bowery Theatre)
Box 126957; San Diego, CA 92112-6957; (619) 232-4088
Ralph Elias, *Artistic Director*

Submission procedure: no unsolicited scripts; synopsis and letter of inquiry. **Types of material:** full-length plays, translations, adaptations. **Special interests:** the nature and roots of American consciousness and culture. **Facilities:** Bristol Court Playhouse, 78 seats, proscenium thrust stage. **Production considerations:** cast limit of 8, unit set; no traps or fly space. **Best submission time:** year-round. **Response time:** 3–6 months letter; 6 months script.

BLOOMSBURG THEATRE ENSEMBLE
Box 66; Bloomsburg, PA 17815; (717) 784-5530
David Moreland, *Play Selection Chair*

Submission procedure: no unsolicited scripts; synopsis, dialogue sample, letter of recommendation from theatre professional and letter of inquiry. **Types of material:** full-length plays, translations, adaptations. **Special interests:** new translations of classics; plays suitable for 8-member acting ensemble. **Facilities:** Alvina Krause Theatre, 369 seats, proscenium stage. **Production considerations:** small to mid-sized cast, 1 set or unit set. **Best submission time:** year-round. **Response time:** 3 months letter; 6 months script.

BOARSHEAD: MICHIGAN PUBLIC THEATER
425 South Grand Ave; Lansing, MI 48933; (517) 484-7800
John Peakes, *Artistic Director*

Submission procedure: no unsolicited scripts; synopsis, character breakdown, 10 pages of dialogue and letter of inquiry with SASP for response. **Types of material:** full-length plays, plays for young audiences. **Special interests:** plays that make use of theatrical conventions or create new ones; social issues; comedies. **Facilities:** Center for the Arts, 249 seats, thrust stage. **Best submission time:** year-round. **Response time:** 1 month letter; 3–6 months script. **Special programs:** staged readings of 7 new plays a year.

THE BODY POLITIC THEATRE
2261 North Lincoln Ave; Chicago, IL 60614; (312) 348-7901
Silvia González S., *Literary Zone Consultant*

Submission procedure: no unsolicited scripts; synopsis, dialogue sample, resume and letter of inquiry. **Types of material:** full-length plays. **Special interests:** plays suitable for ensemble company; language-oriented plays. **Facilities:** Upstairs Stage, 192 seats, 3/4-thrust stage. **Production considerations:** cast limit of 8, unit set. **Best submission time:** year-round. **Response time:** 6 months letter; 12 months script. **Special programs:** Unknown Playwrights Staged Readings: unusual plays presented anonymously, so only the work is evaluated.

BOSTON POST ROAD STAGE COMPANY
25 Powers Ct; Westport, CT 06880; (203) 227-1290
Burry Fredrik, *Literary Manager*

Submission procedure: accepts unsolicited scripts. **Types of material:** full-length plays. **Facilities:** Westport Country Playhouse, 190 seats, modified thrust stage. **Production considerations:** cast limit of 6. **Best submission time:** Jun–Aug. **Response time:** 1–3 months. **Special programs:** readings of 6 new plays a season.

BRISTOL RIVERSIDE THEATRE
Box 1250; Bristol, PA 19007; (215) 785-6664
Susan D. Atkinson, *Artistic Director*

Submission procedure: accepts unsolicited scripts. **Types of material:** full-length plays, musicals. **Facilities:** Bristol Riverside Theatre, 302 seats, proscenium stage. **Production considerations:** prefers small cast, 1 set. **Best submission time:** May–Sep. **Response time:** 1 year.

CLARENCE BROWN THEATRE COMPANY
UT Box 8450; Knoxville, TN 37996-4800; (615) 974-6011
Thomas P. Cooke, *Producing Director*

Submission procedure: no unsolicited scripts; direct solicitation from playwright or agent. **Types of material:** full-length plays. **Special interests:** contemporary

American plays. **Facilities:** Clarence Brown Theatre, 600 seats, proscenium stage; Carousel Theatre, 400 seats, arena stage.

PAUL BUNYAN PLAYHOUSE
Box 752; Bemidji, MN 56601; (218) 751-3812 (Sep–May),
    751-7270 (Jun–Aug)
Play Selection Committee

Submission procedure: accepts unsolicited scripts. **Types of material:** full-length plays, one-acts, translations, adaptations, plays for young audiences, musicals. **Special interests:** MN and Upper Midwest playwrights; works suitable for signing for hearing-impaired. **Facilities:** Paul Bunyan Playhouse, 335 seats, thrust stage. **Production considerations:** summer-stock theatre; modest production demands. **Best submission time:** fall. **Response time:** 2–4 months.

CALDWELL THEATRE COMPANY
Box 277; Boca Raton, FL 33429-0277; (407) 241-7380
Michael Hall, *Artistic Director*

Submission procedure: no unsolicited scripts; professional recommendation. **Types of material:** full-length plays. **Special interests:** prefers plays of interest to an older audience. **Facilities:** Caldwell Theatre, 305 seats, proscenium stage. **Production considerations:** cast limit of 8, 1 set. **Best submission time:** year-round. **Response time:** 3–4 months.

CALIFORNIA THEATRE CENTER
Box 2007; Sunnyvale, CA 94087; (408) 245-2979
Will Huddleston, *Resident Director*

Submission procedure: accepts unsolicited scripts. **Types of material:** plays for young audiences. **Special interests:** classics adapted for young audiences; comedies; historical material and social issues. **Facilities:** Sunnyvale Performing Arts Center, 200 seats, proscenium stage. **Production considerations:** cast limit of 13 for professional productions; minimum cast of 20 for conservatory productions; modest production demands. **Best submission time:** year-round. **Response time:** 3–4 months.

CAPITAL REPERTORY COMPANY
Box 399; Albany, NY 12201; (518) 462–4531
Bruce Bouchard, *Artistic Director*

Submission procedure: no unsolicited scripts; synopsis, first 15 pages of text and letter of inquiry. **Types of material:** full-length plays, translations, adaptations, music-theatre works. **Facilities:** Market Theatre, 299 seats, thrust stage. **Production considerations:** cast limit of 10, simple set; modest musical requirements. **Best submission time:** late spring. **Response time:** 4–6 months letter; 6–8 months script.

CENTER STAGE
700 North Calvert St; Baltimore, MD 21202; (410) 685-3200
David Olivenbaum, *Dramaturg*

Submission procedure: no unsolicited scripts; synopsis, sample pages and letter
of inquiry. **Types of material:** full-length plays, translations, adaptations, music-
theatre pieces. **Facilities:** Pearlstone Theater, 541 seats, modified thrust stage;
Head Theater, 100–400 seats, flexible space. **Best submission time:** year-round.
Response time: 3–5 weeks letter; 3–5 months script.

CENTER THEATER
1346 West Devon; Chicago, IL 60660; (312) 508-0200
Dale Calandra, *Literary Manager*

Submission procedure: no unsolicited scripts; synopsis, resume and letter of
inquiry with SASE for response. **Types of material:** full-length plays, translations,
adaptations, musicals. **Special interests:** comedies; plays creating a heightened
reality; language-oriented plays; dramas of substance; original musicals only.
Facilities: Mainstage, 75 seats, modified thrust stage; Studio, 35 seats, black box.
Production considerations: cast limit of approximately 12; limited wing space, no
fly loft. **Best submission time:** year-round. **Response time:** 3 months letter; 3
months script. **Special programs:** Playwrights Workshop Series: participation by
invitation.

CHELTENHAM CENTER FOR THE ARTS
439 Ashbourne Rd; Cheltenham, PA 19012; (215) 379-4660
Harriet Power, *Dramaturg*

Submission procedure: no unsolicited scripts; synopsis/description and letter of
inquiry. **Types of material:** full-length plays, translations, adaptations. **Facilities:**
Bernard H. Berger Theater, 140 seats, proscenium stage. **Production considerations:** cast limit of 10. **Best submission time:** Jul-Feb. **Response time:** 1 month
letter; 6 months script.

THE CHILDREN'S THEATRE COMPANY
2400 Third Ave S; Minneapolis, MN 55404; (612) 874-0500
Dianne Schmiesing, *Executive Assistant*

Submission procedure: accepts unsolicited scripts. **Types of material:** full-length
plays, one-acts, translations, adaptations, plays for young audiences, musicals.
Special interests: adaptations or original plays for young audiences. **Facilities:**
Children's Theatre Company, 745 seats, proscenium stage; Studio Theatre,
80–100 seats, black box. **Best submission time:** Oct-Apr. **Response time:** 5 months.

CHILDSPLAY

Box 517; Tempe, AZ 85280; (602) 350-8101
David Saar, *Artistic Director*

Submission procedure: accepts unsolicited scripts; include cassette for musicals. **Types of material:** plays for young audiences, including full-length plays, adaptations, musicals, performance pieces. **Special interests:** nontraditional plays; material that entertains and challenges both performers and audiences; new work; 2nd and 3rd productions prior to publication. **Facilities:** Tempe Performing Arts Center, 250 seats, black box; Scottsdale Center for the Arts, 800 seats, proscenium stage; Herberger Theater Center, 350–800 seats, proscenium stage. **Production considerations:** van-sized touring productions. **Best submission time:** Jun-Oct. **Response time:** 6 months. **Special programs:** 1–3 works commissioned each season; each receives minimum 1-year development.

CHILD'S PLAY TOURING THEATRE

2650 West Belden, Suite 201; Chicago, IL 60647; (312) 235-8911
Victor Podagrosi, *Artistic Director*

Submission procedure: accepts unsolicited scripts. **Types of material:** plays, poems, stories, essays. **Special interests:** plays, and nondramatic material to be adapted for performance by theatre, by writers aged 5–13 years only. **Facilities:** touring company. **Best submission time:** summer. **Response time:** 2–4 weeks.

CHOPSTICK THEATER

Box 1625, Charleston, SC 29402; (803) 556-8025
Steve Lepre, *Artistic Director*

Submission procedure: no unsolicited scripts; synopsis and letter of inquiry with SASE for response. **Types of material:** full-length plays, one-acts, translations, adaptations, plays for young audiences. **Special interests:** adaptations of classic plays or novels; tourable works for young audiences grades K–8. **Facilities:** no permanent space. **Best submission time:** Sep-Dec. **Response time:** 3 months letter; 3 months script.

CINCINNATI PLAYHOUSE IN THE PARK

Box 6537; Cincinnati, OH 45206-0537; (513) 345-2242
Susan Banks, *Literary Manager*

Submission procedure: no unsolicited scripts; agent submission. **Types of material:** full-length plays, translations, adaptations, musicals, cabaret/revues. **Facilities:** Robert S. Marx Theatre, 629 seats, thrust stage; Thompson Shelterhouse, 220 seats, thrust stage. **Best submission time:** Apr-Oct. **Response time:** 6 months. **Special programs:** Lois and Richard Rosenthal New Play Prize (see Prizes).

CIRCLE REPERTORY COMPANY

161 Ave of the Americas; New York, NY 10013; (212) 691-3210
Lynn M. Thomson, *Literary Manager*

Submission procedure: no unsolicited scripts; professional recommendation. **Types of material:** full-length plays. **Facilities:** Circle Repertory, 162 seats, flexible stage. **Best submission time:** year-round. **Response time:** 3–4 months. **Special programs:** Projects-in-Progress: staged readings with 2 weeks of rehearsal. Playwrights Lab: participation by invitation.

CIRCLE THEATRE

2015 South 60th St; Omaha, NE 68106; (402) 553-4715
Laura Marr, *Executive Director*

Submission procedure: accepts unsolicited scripts from NE playwrights only; others send synopsis and letter of inquiry with SASE for response. **Types of material:** full-length plays, one-acts, musicals. **Special interests:** new works by NE playwrights. **Facilities:** Diner Theatre, 75 seats, diner. **Best submission time:** year-round. **Response time:** 1 month letter; 6 months script. **Special programs:** Play Search Contest: open to NE playwrights only; submit play not produced within 100 miles of theatre; 2–3 winners given staged reading or full production in Play Search Festival; *deadline:* 1 May 1993; *notification:* 30 Sep 1993; *dates:* Jun 1994.

CITIARTS THEATRE

1950 Parkside Dr; Concord, CA 94519; (510) 671-3065
Richard Elliott, *Artistic Director*

Submission procedure: accepts unsolicited scripts. **Types of material:** full-length plays, translations, adaptations, musicals. **Special interests:** small-scale plays, musicals and revues with an edge that will appeal to both urban and suburban audience. **Facilities:** Willows Theatre, 203 seats, proscenium stage; Gasoline Alley Theatre, 150 seats, black box; Performing Arts Academy, 100 seats, studio. **Production considerations:** cast of 2–15; limit of 12 musicians for musical works; prefers simple set, unit set or environmental staging which uses theatre space as setting. **Best submission time:** 1 Nov–1 Feb. **Response time:** 3–6 months. **Special programs:** Magic Monday Series: staged readings, limited productions.

CITY THEATRE COMPANY

57 South 13th St; Pittsburgh, PA 15203; (412) 431-4400
Scott T. Cummings, *Resident Dramaturg*

Submission procedure: no unsolicited scripts; synopsis, dialogue sample and letter of inquiry. **Types of material:** full-length plays, translations, adaptations, chamber musicals. **Special interests:** comedies of substance; plays with strong storyline; American themes. **Facilities:** mainstage, 250 seats, proscenium-thrust stage; laboratory theatre, 99 seats, black box. **Best submission time:** year-round. **Response time:** 1 month letter; 3 months script. **Special programs:** staged readings.

CLARENCE BROWN THEATRE COMPANY

Listing alphabetized under B.

THE CLEVELAND PLAY HOUSE

Box 1989; Cleveland, OH 44106; (216) 795-7010
Roger T. Danforth, *Literary Manager*

Submission procedure: no unsolicited scripts; agent submission. **Types of material:** full-length plays, translations, adaptations, musicals. **Facilities:** Kenyon C. Bolton Theatre, 612 seats, proscenium stage; Francis E. Drury Theatre, 501 seats, proscenium stage; Charles S. Brooks Theatre, 156 seats, proscenium stage; Studio One, 99 seats, black box. **Best submission time:** year-round. **Response time:** 3–5 months. **Special programs:** Playwright's lab. DiscoveReads (see Development).

CLEVELAND PUBLIC THEATRE

6415 Detroit Ave; Cleveland, OH 44102; (216) 631-2727
James A. Levin, *Artistic Director*

Submission procedure: no unsolicited scripts (except for Festival of New Plays); synopsis and letter of inquiry. **Types of material:** full-length plays, one-acts. **Special interests:** experimental works; works relevant to progressive political thought. **Facilities:** Cleveland Public Theatre, 150–175 seats, adaptable stage (arena/proscenium). **Production considerations:** simple set. **Best submission time:** year-round. **Response time:** 6 weeks letter; 6 months script. **Special programs:** Festival of New Plays: staged readings of 10–12 full-length and one-act plays; submit script and $10 reading fee; *deadline:* 1 Oct 1992; *notification:* Dec 1992; *dates:* Jan 1993.

JEAN COCTEAU REPERTORY

330 Bowery; New York, NY 10012; (212) 677-0060
Robert Hupp, *Artistic Director*

Submission procedure: no unsolicited scripts; synopsis and letter of inquiry. **Types of material:** full-length plays, translations. **Special interests:** material of philosophical/intellectual/poetic content only; no naturalistic plays, "thesis" plays or family dramas. **Facilities:** Bouwerie Lane Theatre, 140 seats, proscenium stage. **Production considerations:** resident company performing plays in repertory. **Best submission time:** year-round. **Response time:** 3–4 weeks letter; 3–4 months script.

THE COLONY STUDIO THEATRE

1944 Riverside Dr; Los Angeles, CA 90039
Judy Newton, *Literary Manager*

Submission procedure: no unsolicited scripts; send SASE for submission guidelines. **Types of material:** full-length plays, adaptations. **Facilities:** Studio Theatre, 99 seats, thrust stage. **Production considerations:** cast of 2–10; plays cast from resident company. **Best submission time:** year-round. **Response time:** 3–6 months.

COMPANY ONE THEATER
30 Arbor St; Hartford, CT 06106; (203) 233-4588
Juanita Rockwell, *Artistic Director*

Submission procedure: no unsolicited scripts; synopsis, 10-page sample, resume and letter of inquiry. **Types of material:** full-length plays, radio plays. **Special interests:** highly theatrical plays that take formal risks. **Facilities:** Aetna Theater at Wadsworth Atheneum, 284 seats, proscenium stage. **Best submission time:** Jan–May. **Response time:** 2 months letter; 6 months script. **Special programs:** live studio-produced radio theatre; send SASE for submission guidelines. Script Teas: 4 rehearsed readings a year in Atheneum cafe; playwright receives remuneration; scripts selected through normal submission procedure.

CONEY ISLAND, USA
Boardwalk at West 12th St; Coney Island, NY 11224; (718) 372-5159
Dick D. Zigun, *Artistic Director*

Submission procedure: no unsolicited scripts; synopsis, resume, reviews of prior work and letter of inquiry. **Types of material:** company books in already existing productions of plays and performance art. **Special interests:** new and old vaudeville; pop music; pop culture; Americana bizarro. **Facilities:** Sideshows by the Seashore, 150 seats, arena stage; also open-air performances on streets, boardwalk, beach. **Best submission time:** year-round. **Response time:** 1 month letter; 6 months script.

CONTEMPORARY ARTS CENTER
Box 30498; New Orleans, LA 70190; (504) 523-1216

Submission procedure: no unsolicited scripts; synopsis, dialogue sample and letter of inquiry. **Types of material:** full-length plays. **Facilities:** Freeport MacMoRan Theater, 200–225 seats, flexible stage; Theater II, 100–150 seats, flexible stage. **Best submission time:** Jan. **Response time:** 2–3 weeks letter; 7 months script. **Special programs:** monthly staged readings. CAC New Play Competition (see Prizes). CAC Playwright's Forum (see Development).

THE COTERIE
2450 Grand Ave; Kansas City, MO 64108; (816) 474-6785
Jeff Church, *Artistic Director*

Submission procedure: accepts unsolicited scripts from established playwrights in youth-theatre field; others send brief synopsis, dialogue sample, resume and letter of inquiry. **Types of material:** works for young and family audiences, including adaptations and musicals. **Special interests:** plays of universal appeal; social issues; adaptations of classic or contemporary literature; musicals. **Facilities:** The Coterie Theatre, 240 seats, flexible stage. **Production considerations:** cast limit of 12, prefers limit of 5–7; no fly or wing space. **Best submission time:** year-round. **Response time:** 2 months letter; 4 months script.

CREEDE REPERTORY THEATRE
Box 269; Creede, CO 81130; (719) 658-2541
Richard Baxter, *Producing/Artistic Director*

Submission procedure: no unsolicited scripts; synopsis, dialogue sample, resume and letter of inquiry with SASE for response. **Types of material:** full-length plays, translations, adaptations, plays for young audiences, musicals. **Special interests:** works about the American West and Southwest; plays for young audiences (through high school). **Facilities:** Creede Repertory Theatre, 243 seats, proscenium stage. **Production considerations:** cast limit of 10; prefers minimal set; no fly space. **Best submission time:** Sep–Nov. **Response time:** 1 month letter; 12 months script.

THE CRICKET THEATRE
1407 Nicollet Ave; Minneapolis, MN 55403; (612) 871-3763
William Partlan, *Artistic Director*

Submission procedure: accepts unsolicited scripts. **Types of material:** full-length plays, long one-acts. **Special interests:** hard-hitting, issue-oriented plays; plays relevant to the Midwest; no one-acts under 1 hour in length. **Facilities:** The Loring Theatre, 215 seats, open proscenium stage. **Production considerations:** prefers cast limit of 8. **Best submission time:** Oct–Mar. **Response time:** 6–12 months.

CROSSROADS THEATRE COMPANY
7 Livingston Ave; New Brunswick, NJ 08901; (908) 249-5581
Sydné Mahone, *Director of Play Development*

Submission procedure: no unsolicited scripts; synopsis and letter of inquiry. **Types of material:** full-length plays, one-acts, translations, adaptations, musicals, cabaret/revues. **Special interests:** African-American, African and West Indian issue-oriented, experimental plays that examine the complexity of the human experience. **Facilities:** Crossroads Theatre, 264 seats, thrust stage. **Best submission time:** year-round. **Response time:** 1 month letter; 6–9 months script.

CSC REPERTORY LTD.—THE CLASSIC STAGE COMPANY
136 East 13th St; New York, NY 10003; (212) 677-4210
Lenora Champagne, *Artistic Associate*

Submission procedure: no unsolicited scripts; synopsis, dialogue sample and letter of inquiry. **Types of material:** translations, adaptations. **Special interests:** translations and adaptations of classics or modern European plays; adaptations of major nondramatic works; prefers highly theatrical work. **Facilities:** CSC, 180 seats, flexible stage. **Production considerations:** cast limit of 10. **Best submission time:** year-round. **Response time:** 2 months letter; 3 months script. **Special programs:** developmental program of rehearsed readings.

CUMBERLAND COUNTY PLAYHOUSE
Box 484; Crossville, TN 38557; (615) 484-2300, -4324
James Crabtree, *Producing Director*

Submission procedure: no unsolicited scripts; synopsis and letter of inquiry. **Types of material:** full-length plays, adaptations, plays for young audiences, musicals. **Special interests:** works for family audiences; works with southern or rural background; works about Tennessee history or culture. **Facilities:** Cumberland County Playhouse, 420–480 seats, proscenium stage; Theater-in-the-Woods, 200 seats, outdoor arena; Adventure Theater, 250–300 seats, flexible black box (opens 1993). **Best submission time:** Aug–Dec. **Response time:** 2 weeks letter (if interested); 6–12 months script.

DALLAS THEATER CENTER
3636 Turtle Creek Blvd; Dallas, TX 75219-5598; (214) 526-8210
Richard Hamburger, *Artistic Director*

Submission procedure: no unsolicited scripts; professional recommendation. **Types of material:** full-length plays, adaptations, translations. **Facilities:** Frank Lloyd Wright Theater, 466 seats, thrust stage; Arts District Theater, 530 seats, flexible stage; "in the basement," 150 seats, flexible stage. **Production considerations:** plays cast from resident company (currently 11m, 6f, aged 23–60). **Best submission time:** spring. **Response time:** 6 months.

DELAWARE THEATRE COMPANY
200 Water St; Wilmington, DE 19801-5030; (302) 594-1104
Cleveland Morris, *Artistic Director*

Submission procedure: accepts unsolicited scripts. **Types of material:** full-length plays, translations, adaptations. **Facilities:** Delaware Theatre Company, 300 seats, thrust stage. **Production considerations:** cast limit of 10. **Best submission time:** Feb–May. **Response time:** 6 months.

DELL'ARTE PLAYERS COMPANY
Box 816; Blue Lake, CA 95525; (707) 668-5663
Michael Fields, *Managing Director*

Submission procedure: no unsolicited scripts; synopsis and letter of inquiry. **Types of material:** full-length plays, translations, adaptations, plays for young audiences. **Special interests:** comedies; issue-oriented works in commedia dell'arte style; Christmas plays for young audiences. **Facilities:** Dell'Arte Players, 100 seats, flexible stage. **Production considerations:** 3–4 actors, production demands adaptable to touring. **Best submission time:** Jan–Mar. **Response time:** 3 weeks letter; 6 weeks script.

DENVER CENTER THEATRE COMPANY
1050 13th St; Denver, CO 80204; (303) 893-4200
Tom Szentgyorgyi, *Associate Artistic Director/New Play Development*

Submission procedure: accepts unsolicited scripts. **Types of material:** full-length plays. **Special interests:** issue-oriented plays. **Facilities:** The Stage, 642 seats, thrust stage; The Space, 450 seats, arena stage; The Ricketson Theatre, 196 seats, proscenium stage; The Source, 155 seats, thrust stage. **Best submission time:** 1 Jul–1 Dec. **Response time:** 6–8 weeks. **Special programs:** New Plays Festival: 4 full productions of world premieres each season presented concurrently with U S West TheatreFest staged readings. U S West TheatreFest (see Development).

DETROIT REPERTORY THEATRE
13103 Woodrow Wilson Ave; Detroit, MI 48238; (313) 868-1347
Barbara Busby, *Literary Manager*

Submission procedure: accepts unsolicited scripts. **Types of material:** full-length plays. **Special interests:** issue-oriented plays. **Facilities:** Detroit Repertory Theatre, 186 seats, proscenium stage. **Production considerations:** prefers cast limit of 12. **Best submission time:** Sep–Feb. **Response time:** 3–6 months.

EAST WEST PLAYERS
4424 Santa Monica Blvd; Los Angeles, CA 90029; (213) 666-1929
Brian Nelson, *Literary Manager/Dramaturg*

Submission procedure: accepts unsolicited scripts; prefers synopsis, cast list with character descriptions, and letter of inquiry. **Types of material:** full-length plays, one-acts, translations, adaptations, plays for young audiences, musicals. **Special interests:** particularly but not exclusively new works dealing with Asian, Pacific and Asian-American experiences; musicals and comedies with multicultural resonance. **Facilities:** East West Players, 99 seats, 3/4-thrust stage. **Best submission time:** year-round. **Response time:** 3–4 weeks letter; 4–6 months script. **Special programs:** David Henry Hwang Writers' Institute: series of 6-month classes designed to develop multiethnic writing for the stage; contact theatre for further information.

EL TEATRO CAMPESINO
Box 1240; San Juan Bautista, CA 95045; (408) 623-2444
Phil Esparza, *Producer*

Submission procedure: no unsolicited scripts; synopsis, character breakdown, resume and letter of inquiry. **Types of material:** full-length plays, one-acts, translations, adaptations, plays for young audiences, musicals, cabaret/revues. **Special interests:** socially relevant works; works that reflect a multiethnic world; contemporary adaptations of classics. **Facilities:** El Teatro Campesino Playhouse, 150 seats, flexible stage. **Best submission time:** Jan–Apr. **Response time:** 6 months letter; 12 months script.

THE EMELIN THEATRE

Library Lane; Mamaroneck, NY 10543; (914) 698-3045
Norman Kline, *Producing Director*

Submission procedure: no unsolicited scripts; professional recommendation.
Types of material: full-length plays, one-acts, translations, adaptations, musicals,
cabaret/revues, stand-up, performance art. **Facilities:** The Emelin Theatre, 280
seats, proscenium stage. **Production considerations:** small cast; no fly space. **Best
submission time:** year-round. **Response time:** 2 months.

THE EMMY GIFFORD CHILDREN'S THEATER

Listing alphabetized under G.

THE EMPTY SPACE THEATRE

Box 1748; Seattle, WA 98111-1748; (206) 587-3737
Kurt Beattie, *Artistic Director*

Submission procedure: accepts unsolicited scripts from regional playwrights (ID,
MT, OR, WA, WY); others send synopsis and letter of inquiry. **Types of material:**
full-length plays, one-acts, translations, adaptations, musicals. **Facilities:** The Empty
Space, 160 seats, endstage. **Best submission time:** year-round. **Response time:** 3
weeks letter; 4 months script.

ENSEMBLE STUDIO THEATRE

549 West 52nd St; New York, NY 10019; (212) 581-9603
Christopher Smith, *Associate Artistic Director*

Submission procedure: accepts unsolicited scripts. **Types of material:** full-length
plays, one-acts. **Facilities:** Ensemble Studio Theatre, 98 seats, flexible stage;
Workshop, 45 seats, proscenium stage. **Best submission time:** Sep–Apr. **Response
time:** 3–5 months. **Special programs:** One Act Marathon: spring festival of one-
acts; *deadline:* 15 Dec 1992. New Works: series of 2–3 workshop productions of
full-length plays each season. New Voices: staged readings of 4–6 unproduced
plays over a 2-week period. Cold Reading Series: readings of unproduced plays.
National Theatre Colony: developmental program conducted in Catskills, NY.

ENSEMBLE THEATRE OF CINCINNATI

1127 Vine St; Cincinnati, OH 45210; (513) 421-3555
David A. White III, *Artistic Director*

Submission procedure: no unsolicited scripts; agent submission. **Types of
material:** full-length plays, adaptations, plays for young audiences. **Special
interests:** issues that awaken audience's social conscience. **Facilities:** Ensemble
Theatre of Cincinnati, 126 seats, 3/4-arena stage. **Production considerations:** cast
limit of 6, simple set. **Best submission time:** Sep. **Response time:** 2 months.

EUREKA THEATRE COMPANY
340 Townsend St, Suite 519; San Francisco, CA 94107; (415) 243-9899
Deborah J. Ballinger, *Producing Artistic Director*

Submission procedure: no unsolicited scripts; synopsis, dialogue sample, resume and letter of inquiry. **Types of material:** full-length plays, music-theatre works/operas. **Special interests:** contemporary plays responsive to social, political and cultural forces affecting our world. **Facilities:** no permanent facility. **Production considerations:** small-cast musicals only. **Best submission time:** year-round. **Response time:** 3 months letter; 6 months script. **Special programs:** Discovery Series: regularly scheduled rehearsed readings of new plays presented for public.

THE FANTASY THEATRE
Box 19206; Sacramento, CA 95819-0206; (916) 442-5635
Buck Busfield, *Artistic Director*

Submission procedure: no unsolicited scripts; direct solicitation from playwright or agent. **Types of material:** plays for young audiences. **Facilities:** "B" Street Theatre, 100 seats, thrust stage; also tours. **Production considerations:** cast limit of 6, 1 set. **Best submission time:** year-round.

FIRST STAGE MILWAUKEE
929 North Water St; Milwaukee, WI 53202; (414) 273-7121
Rob Goodman, *Artistic Director*

Submission procedure: no unsolicited scripts; synopsis, resume and letter of inquiry. **Types of material:** works for young audiences, including translations, adaptations and musicals. **Facilities:** The Performing Arts Center's Todd Wehr Theater, 500 seats, thrust stage. **Best submission time:** spring–summer. **Response time:** 1 month letter; 3 months script.

FLORIDA STUDIO THEATRE
1241 North Palm Ave; Sarasota, FL 34236; (813) 366-9017
Steve Ramay, *Associate Director*

Submission procedure: no unsolicited scripts; synopsis and letter of inquiry. **Types of material:** full-length plays, one-acts, translations, adaptations, musicals, cabaret/revues. **Facilities:** Florida Studio Theatre, 165 seats, thrust stage; The Cabaret Club, 75 seats, cabaret space. **Production considerations:** cast limit of 8, simple set. **Best submission time:** Apr–Nov. **Response time:** 1–2 weeks letter; 6 months script. **Special programs:** Sarasota Festival of New Plays: 3-tier May festival includes Young Playwrights Festival: workshop productions of plays by playwrights grades 2–12; winning plays tour FL schools in fall; *deadline:* 1 Mar 1993; Florida Playwrights Festival: workshops, seminars, staged readings and cabaret performances in conjunction with workshop productions of 3 plays by FL playwrights; scripts selected through theatre's normal submission procedure; National Playwrights Festival: workshop productions of 3 new plays; playwright receives stipend, travel, housing; scripts selected through theatre's normal submission procedure. Fall and summer reading series.

FORD'S THEATRE
511 Tenth St NW; Washington, DC 20004; (202) 638-2941
Ann Jackman, *Literary Associate*

Submission procedure: no unsolicited scripts; synopsis, dialogue sample and letter of inquiry. **Types of material:** full-length plays, adaptations, translations, musicals. **Facilities:** Ford's Theatre, 699 seats, proscenium-thrust stage. **Best submission time:** late spring–summer. **Response time:** 3–5 weeks letter; 3–4 months script.

FREE STREET THEATER
441 West North Ave: Chicago, IL 60610; (312) 642-1234
David Schein, *Artistic Director*
John Nelson, *Executive Director*

Submission procedure: no unsolicited scripts; letter from writer with "a concept for a show or a brilliant teaching idea." **Types of material:** plays and performance pieces. **Special interests:** inner-city kids/teenagers; cultural empowerment of new populations; developing work with communities; new work by Chicago-area artists; enhancing literacy through the arts. **Facilities:** touring company; mobile outdoor stage. **Response time:** 2 months.

FULTON OPERA HOUSE
Box 1865; 12 North Prince St; Lancaster, PA 17603; (717) 394-7133
Kathleen Collins, *Artistic Director*

Submission procedure: no unsolicited scripts; synopsis and letter of inquiry. **Types of material:** full-length plays, musicals. **Special interests:** contemporary themes. **Facilities:** Fulton Opera House, 900 seats, proscenium stage. **Production considerations:** cast limit of 10, unit set. **Best submission time:** year-round. **Response time:** 3 weeks letter; 4 months script.

GALA HISPANIC THEATRE
Box 43209; Washington, DC 20010; (202) 234-7174
Hugo Medrano, *Producing Artistic Director*

Submission procedure: accepts unsolicited scripts; prefers synopsis/description and letter of inquiry. **Types of material:** full-length plays. **Special interests:** plays by Spanish, Latino or Hispanic-American writers in Spanish or English only; prefers Spanish-language works with accompanying English translation; works that reflect sociocultural realities of Hispanics in Latin America, the Caribbean or Spain, as well as the Hispanic-American experience. **Facilities:** Gala Hispanic Theatre, 200 seats, proscenium stage. **Production considerations:** cast of 6–8. **Best submission time:** Apr–May. **Response time:** 2 weeks letter; 1 month script. **Special programs:** poetry-on-stage.

GEORGE STREET PLAYHOUSE
9 Livingston Ave; New Brunswick, NJ 08901; (201) 846-2895
Wendy Liscow, *Associate Artistic Director*

Submission procedure: no unsolicited scripts; professional recommendation. **Types of material:** full-length plays, one-acts, musicals. **Special interests:** comedies and dramas that present a fresh perspective on our society and challenge our expectations of theatre; works by minority writers; social-issue one-acts suitable for touring to schools. **Facilities:** Mainstage, 367 seats, proscenium-thrust stage. **Production considerations:** prefers cast limit of 8 for plays, 12 for musicals. **Best submission time:** year-round. **Response time:** 6–8 months. **Special programs:** staged reading series.

GERMINAL STAGE DENVER
2450 West 44th Ave; Denver, CO 80211; (303) 455-7108
Edward Baierlein, *Director/Manager*

Submission procedure: no unsolicited scripts; synopsis, 5-page dialogue sample and letter of inquiry with SASP for response. **Types of material:** full-length plays, translations, adaptations. **Special interests:** adaptations that use both dialogue and narration. **Facilities:** Germinal Stage Denver, 100 seats, 3/4-thrust stage. **Production considerations:** cast limit of 10, minimal production requirements. **Best submission time:** year-round. **Response time:** 2 weeks letter; up to 6 months script.

GEVA THEATRE
75 Woodbury Blvd; Rochester, NY 14607; (716) 232-1366
Ann Patrice Carrigan, *Literary Director*

Submission procedure: accepts unsolicited scripts for REFLECTIONS '93 only (see below); synopsis and letter of inquiry for all other submissions. **Types of material:** full-length plays, translations, adaptations, musicals. **Facilities:** GeVa Theatre, 557 seats, modified thrust stage. **Best submission time:** Jan–Nov. **Response time:** 1 week letter; up to 6 months script. **Special programs:** REFLECTIONS '93: A New Plays Festival: 3 world premieres presented in repertory as last production of mainstage season. REFLECTIONS Playreading Series: readings of 4–6 new plays a season. The GeVa Playwright Award (see Prizes).

THE EMMY GIFFORD CHILDREN'S THEATER
3504 Center St; Omaha, NE 68105; (402) 345-4849
James Larson, *Artistic Director*

Submission procedure: no unsolicited scripts; professional recommendation. **Types of material:** plays for family audiences. **Special interests:** plays based on children's literature and contemporary issues. **Facilities:** Emmy Gifford Children's Theater, 500 seats, proscenium stage. **Production considerations:** cast limit of 15; prefers unit set. **Best submission time:** year-round. **Response time:** 6 months.

GLOUCESTER STAGE COMPANY

267 East Main St; Gloucester, MA 01930; (508) 281-4099
Israel Horovitz, *Artistic Director*

Submission procedure: no unsolicited scripts; synopsis, letter of recommendation from theatre professional and letter of inquiry. **Types of material:** full-length plays, translations, adaptations, plays for young audiences. **Special interests:** New England subjects; contemporary themes. **Facilities:** Gloucester Stage Company, 150 seats, black box. **Production considerations:** cast limit of 10, simple production demands. **Best submission time:** Nov–Mar. **Response time:** 2 months letter; 12 months script. **Special programs:** staged readings of 4 plays a year. Samuel Beckett Playwriting Internship (see Colonies and Residencies).

GOODMAN THEATRE

200 South Columbus Dr; Chicago, IL 60603-6491; (312) 443-3811
Tom Creamer, *Dramaturg*

Submission procedure: no unsolicited scripts; professional recommendation. **Types of material:** full-length plays, translations, musicals. **Special interests:** social or political themes. **Facilities:** Goodman Mainstage, 683 seats, proscenium stage; Goodman Studio, 135 seats, proscenium stage. **Best submission time:** year-round. **Response time:** 6 months.

GOODSPEED OPERA HOUSE

Box A; East Haddam, CT 06423; (203) 873-8664
Sue Frost, *Associate Producer*

Submission procedure: no unsolicited scripts; synopsis and letter of inquiry. **Types of material:** original musicals only. **Facilities:** Goodspeed Opera House, 400 seats, proscenium stage; Goodspeed-at-Chester, 200 seats, adaptable proscenium stage. **Best submission time:** Jan–Mar. **Response time:** 1 month letter; 9 months script.

GREAT AMERICAN HISTORY THEATRE

30 East 10th St; St. Paul, MN 55101; (612) 292-4323
Lance Belville, *Co-Artistic Director/Literary Manager*

Submission procedure: no unsolicited scripts; synopsis and letter of inquiry. **Types of material:** full-length plays, adaptations, musicals. **Special interests:** works dealing with people, events, issues, ideas and places in history; nonrealistic works preferred; no pageants; small musicals only. **Facilities:** Crawford Livingston Theatre, 597 seats, thrust stage. **Production considerations:** cast limit of 10, moderate production demands. **Best submission time:** winter–spring. **Response time:** 1 month letter; at least 2–6 months script.

GREAT LAKES THEATER FESTIVAL

1501 Euclid Ave, Suite 250; Cleveland, OH 44115; (216) 241-5490
Victoria Bussert, *Associate Director*

Submission procedure: no unsolicited scripts; professional recommendation. **Types of material:** full-length plays. **Facilities:** Ohio Theatre, 646 seats, proscenium stage. **Best submission time:** Oct–Apr. **Response time:** 6 months.

GRETNA PRODUCTIONS

Box 578; Mt. Gretna, PA 17064; (717) 964-3322
Al Franklin, *Producing Director*

Submission procedure: no unsolicited scripts; synopsis, 5 pages dialogue, character list and breakdown, production history and letter of inquiry; no tapes for musicals. **Types of material:** full-length plays, plays for young audiences, musicals. **Special interests:** plays suitable for conservative community; prefers comedy; small-cast musicals only. **Facilities:** Mt. Gretna Playhouse, 625 seats, proscenium stage. **Production considerations:** open-air facility; 14′ ceiling over stage. **Best submission time:** Aug–Apr. **Response time:** 4 weeks letter; 12 weeks script.

GROVE SHAKESPEARE FESTIVAL

12852 Main St; Garden Grove, CA 92640; (714) 636-7213
Barbara G. Hammerman, *Managing Director*

Submission procedure: no unsolicited scripts; professional recommendation. **Types of material:** full-length plays, translations, adaptations. **Facilities:** Festival Amphitheatre, 550 seats, amphitheatre; Gem Theatre, 172 seats, proscenium stage. **Production considerations:** prefers cast limit of 10, single set. **Best submission time:** Aug–Dec. **Response time:** 4–6 weeks.

THE GROWING STAGE THEATRE

Box 132; Chester, NJ 07930; (908) 879-4946
Michael T. Mooney, *Literary Manager*

Submission procedure: no unsolicited scripts; synopsis and letter of inquiry. **Types of material:** original plays and adaptations for young audiences. **Facilities:** TGS Theatre, 250 seats, proscenium-thrust stage; also tours. **Best submission time:** year-round. **Response time:** 2 weeks letter; 2 months script.

THE GUTHRIE THEATER

725 Vineland Pl; Minneapolis, MN 55403; (612) 347-1100
Jim Lewis, *Dramaturg/Literary Manager*

Submission procedure: no unsolicited scripts; synopsis, 10 pages of dialogue and letter of inquiry. **Types of material:** full-length plays, translations, adaptations. **Facilities:** Guthrie Theater, 1441 seats, thrust stage. **Best submission time:** year-round. **Response time:** 2–3 weeks letter; 2–3 months script.

HARTFORD STAGE COMPANY

50 Church St; Hartford, CT 06103; (203) 525-5601
John Dias, *Literary Associate*

Submission procedure: no unsolicited scripts; synopsis, 10 pages of dialogue and letter of inquiry. **Types of material:** full-length plays, translations, adaptations. **Facilities:** John W. Huntington Theatre, 489 seats, thrust stage. **Best submission time:** year-round. **Response time:** 7–10 days letter; 6–9 months script.

HILBERRY THEATRE

95 West Hancock; Detroit, MI 48202; (313) 577-3508
Anthony Schmitt, *Associate Director*

Submission procedure: accepts unsolicited scripts. **Types of material:** full-length plays. **Facilities:** Hilberry Theatre, 530 seats, open stage. **Production considerations:** plays cast from company of 14 men, 6 women and performed in rotating repertory; simple set. **Best submission time:** year-round. **Response time:** 4 months.

THE HIPPODROME STATE THEATRE

25 SE 2nd Pl; Gainesville, FL 32601; (904) 373-5968
Mary Hausch, *Producing Director*

Submission procedure: no unsolicited scripts; synopsis and letter of inquiry. **Types of material:** full-length plays, translations, adaptations, musicals. **Facilities:** Hippodrome Theatre, 266 seats, thrust stage; Hippodrome's Second Stage, 87 seats, flexible stage. **Production considerations:** prefers small cast, unit set. **Best submission time:** year-round. **Response time:** 1 month letter (if interested); 1 month script.

HOME FOR CONTEMPORARY THEATRE AND ART

61 East 8th St., Suite 315; New York, NY 10003; (212) 529-9218
Randy Rollison, *Artistic Director*

Submission procedure: accepts unsolicited scripts from New York City playwrights only; professional recommendation for others. **Types of material:** full-length plays, adaptations, musicals, multidisciplinary works, short radio pieces. **Special interests:** NYC premieres only; experimental works; short comic sketches for radio. **Facilities:** none at present, in residence at Public Theater. **Best submission time:** year-round. **Response time:** 3–5 months. Special programs: HOMEmade Radio. Playwrights-in-Residence program: by invitation only.

HONOLULU THEATRE FOR YOUTH

2846 Ualena St; Honolulu, HI 96819-1910; (808) 839-9885
Pamela Sterling, *Artistic Director*

Submission procedure: no unsolicited scripts; synopsis, resume and letter of inquiry. **Types of material:** one-acts, plays for young audiences. **Special interests:** plays for audiences up to high school age, with contemporary themes; adaptations of fairy tales or literary classics; new works based on Pacific Rim cultures. **Facilities:** Leeward Community College Theatre, 650 seats, proscenium stage; Kaimuki High School Theatre, 650 seats, proscenium stage; McCoy Pavilion, 300 seats, flexible stage. **Production considerations:** cast limit of 10, simple production demands. **Best submission time:** year-round. **Response time:** 1 month letter; 4–5 months script.

HORIZON THEATRE COMPANY
Box 5376, Station E; Atlanta, GA 30307; (404) 584-7450
Lisa Adler, *Co-Artistic Director*

Submission procedure: accepts unsolicited scripts from Atlanta-area playwrights only; others send synopsis, resume and letter of inquiry. **Types of material:** full-length plays, one-acts, translations, adaptations, musicals. **Special interests:** one-acts about teen issues only (see Teen Ensemble below); contemporary social and political issues; plays by women; southern urban themes; satires and comedies. **Facilities:** Horizon Theatre, 170–200 seats, flexible stage. **Production considerations:** plays cast from ensemble of up to 10 actors aged 20–40 years. **Best submission time:** May–Jun. **Response time:** 6 months letter; 12 months script. **Special programs:** Teen Ensemble: submit full-length plays and one-acts about teen issues to be performed by teens.

HORSE CAVE THEATRE
Box 215; Horse Cave, KY 42749; (502) 786-1200
Warren Hammack, *Artistic Director*

Submission procedure: no unsolicited scripts; professional recommendation. **Types of material:** full-length plays. **Special interests:** KY-based plays by KY playwrights. **Facilities:** Horse Cave Theatre, 347 seats, thrust stage. **Production considerations:** cast limit of 10, single set. **Best submission time:** Oct–Apr. **Response time:** varies.

HUNTINGTON THEATRE COMPANY
Boston University Theatre; 264 Huntington Ave; Boston MA 02115-4606;
(617) 266-7900
Peter Altman, *Producing Director*

Submission procedure: no unsolicited scripts; synopsis and letter of inquiry. **Types of material:** full-length plays, translations, adaptations. **Special interests:** New England playwrights; plays of regional relevance. **Facilities:** Huntington Theatre, 850 seats, proscenium stage. **Best submission time:** May–Sep. **Response time:** 2 months letter; 6 months script.

IDAHO SHAKESPEARE FESTIVAL
Box 9365; Boise, ID 83707; (208) 336-9221
Charles Fee, *Artistic Director*
Rick Foster, *Literary Manager*

Submission procedure: no unsolicited scripts; resume and letter of inquiry. **Types of material:** full-length plays, musicals. **Facilities:** Festival Stage, 300 seats, thrust stage. **Best submission time:** Sep–Jan. **Response time:** 6 months letter; 3 months script.

ILLINOIS THEATRE CENTER
400A Lakewood Blvd; Park Forest, IL 60466; (708) 481-3510
Steve S. Billig, *Artistic Director*

Submission procedure: no unsolicited scripts; synopsis and letter of inquiry with SASE for response. **Types of material:** full-length plays, musicals. **Facilities:** Illinois Theatre Center, 200 seats, proscenium-thrust stage. **Production considerations:** cast limit of 9 for plays, 14 for musicals. **Best submission time:** year-round. **Response time:** 1 month letter; 2 months script.

ILLUSION THEATER
528 Hennepin Ave, Suite 704; Minneapolis, MN 55403; (612) 339-4944
Michael Robins, *Executive Producing Director*

Submission procedure: no unsolicited scripts; professional recommendation. **Types of material:** full-length plays, one-acts, translations, adaptations, musicals. **Special interests:** writers to collaborate on new works with the company. **Facilities:** Illusion Theater, 250 seats, semi-thrust stage. **Best submission time:** Jul–Nov. **Response time:** 6 months. **Special programs:** Fresh Ink Series: 5–6 plays each presented with minimal set and costumes for 1 weekend; post-performance discussion with audience, who are seated onstage; scripts selected through theatre's normal submission procedure.

INDIANA REPERTORY THEATRE
140 West Washington St; Indianapolis, IN 46204-3465; (317) 635-5277
Janet Allen, *Associate Artistic Director*

Submission procedure: no unsolicited scripts; synopsis and letter of inquiry. **Types of material:** full-length plays, translations, adaptations, plays for young audiences. **Special interests:** adaptations of classics; plays on social issues; plays for young audiences. **Facilities:** Mainstage, 600 seats, modified thrust stage; Upperstage, 250 seats, modified proscenium stage. **Production considerations:** cast limit of 8–10. **Best submission time:** Dec–Jan, Apr–May. **Response time:** 1–2 months letter; 3–4 months script. **Special programs:** Juniorworks: plays for young audiences grades 4–8 presented each season.

INTAR HISPANIC AMERICAN ARTS CENTER
Box 788; New York, NY 10108; (212) 695-6134, -6135
Max Ferra, *Artistic Director*

Submission procedure: accepts unsolicited scripts. **Types of material:** full-length plays, one-acts, translations, adaptations, musicals. **Special interests:** new plays by Hispanic-American writers and translations and adaptations of Hispanic works only. **Facilities:** INTAR on Theatre Row, 99 seats, proscenium stage; INTAR Stage Two, 75 seats, proscenium stage. **Production considerations:** prefers cast limit of 8; no wing space. **Best submission time:** year-round (season chosen late summer–early fall). **Response time:** 3–6 months. **Special programs:** Mini-Workshop Series leading to mainstage production.

INTIMAN THEATRE COMPANY
Box 19790; Seattle, WA 98109; (206) 626-0775
Susan Fenichell, *Associate Artistic Director*

Submission procedure: no unsolicited scripts; synopsis and letter of inquiry. **Types of material:** translations, adaptations. **Special interests:** new translations and adaptations of classics. **Facilities:** Intiman Theatre, 424 seats, thrust stage. **Production considerations:** cast limit of 12. **Best submission time:** year-round. **Response time:** 6 months letter; 8 months script.

INVISIBLE THEATRE
1400 North First Ave; Tucson, AZ 85719; (602) 882-9721
Deborah Dickey, *Literary Manager*

Submission procedure: no unsolicited scripts; synopsis and letter of inquiry. **Types of material:** full-length plays, one-acts, musicals. **Special interests:** mainly but not exclusively works with contemporary settings; works with strong female roles; social and political issues; small-cast musicals only. **Facilities:** Invisible Theatre, 78 seats, black box. **Production considerations:** cast limit of 10, simple set, minimal props. **Best submission time:** Jul–Sep. **Response time:** 1–3 months letter; 6 months script. **Special programs:** annual play contest open to AZ residents only; winner(s) receive honorarium and staged reading; type of material and guidelines vary; early winter deadline (Nov–Jan); contact theatre for information.

IRONDALE ENSEMBLE PROJECT
782 West End Ave, Suite 74; New York, NY 10025; (212) 633-1292
Steven Osgood, *Dramaturg*

Submission procedure: no unsolicited scripts; letter of inquiry from playwright interested in developing work with ensemble through ongoing workshop process. **Types of material:** full-length plays, one-acts, adaptations, plays for young audiences, musicals. **Special interests:** works with political or social relevance. **Facilities:** no permanent facility. **Production considerations:** cast limit of 8–9, unit set. **Best submission time:** year-round. **Response time:** 4 weeks.

JEAN COCTEAU REPERTORY

Listing alphabetized under C.

JEWISH REPERTORY THEATRE
344 East 14th St; New York, NY 10003; (212) 674-7200
Edward M. Cohen, *Associate Director*

Submission procedure: accepts unsolicited scripts. **Types of material:** full-length
plays, one-acts, musicals. **Special interests:** works that address some aspect of
Jewish life. **Facilities:** Jewish Repertory Theatre, 100 seats, proscenium stage.
Production considerations: small cast; no fly space. **Best submission time:**
Sep–May. **Response time:** 4 weeks. **Special programs:** Jewish Repertory Theatre
Writer's Lab: readings of new plays.

LAGUNA PLAYHOUSE
606 Laguna Canyon Rd; Laguna Beach, CA 92651; (714) 494-8022
Andrew Barnicle, *Artistic Director*

Submission procedure: no unsolicited scripts; synopsis and letter of inquiry. **Types
of material:** full-length plays, plays for young audiences, musicals. **Special
interests:** works by southern CA playwrights. **Facilities:** Moulton Theater, 418
seats, proscenium stage. **Best submission time:** year-round. **Response time:** 1
month letter; 6 months script. **Special programs:** staged readings.

LA JOLLA PLAYHOUSE
Box 12039; La Jolla, CA 92039; (619) 534-6760
Robert Blacker, *Associate Director/Dramaturg*
Elissa Adams, *Literary Manager*

Submission procedure: no unsolicited scripts; professional recommendation.
Types of material: full-length plays, translations, musicals. **Special interests:**
material pertinent to the lives we are leading at the end of this century. **Facilities:**
Mandell Weiss Center for the Performing Arts, 500 seats, proscenium stage; Weiss
Forum, 400 seats, thrust stage. **Best submission time:** year-round. **Response time:**
4 months.

LAMB'S PLAYERS THEATRE
Box 26; National City, CA 91951; (619) 474-3385
Kerry Meads, *Associate Director/Literary Manager*

Submission procedure: no unsolicited scripts; professional recommendation.
Types of material: full-length plays, translations, adaptations, plays for young
audiences, musicals, cabaret/revues. **Facilities:** Lamb's Players Theatre, 180 seats,
arena stage. **Best submission time:** year-round. **Response time:** 6 months.

L.A. THEATRE WORKS
681 Venice Blvd; Venice, CA 90291; (213) 827-0808
Susan Albert Loewenberg, *Producing Director*
Kirsten Dahl, *Literary Manager*

Submission procedure: no unsolicited scripts; agent submission. **Types of material:** full-length plays, one-acts, adaptations. **Special interests:** highly theatrical, nonrealistic new plays; contemporary adaptations of classic themes. **Facilities:** no permanent facility. **Best submission time:** year-round. **Response time:** 6–12 months. **Special programs:** Radio Theatre Series for New Plays: bimonthly performances. Writers Dialogue: series of advanced playwriting workshops; contact theatre for information.

LINCOLN CENTER THEATER
150 West 65th St; New York, NY 10023; (212) 362-7600
Anne Cattaneo, *Dramaturg*

Submission procedure: no unsolicited scripts; agent submission. **Types of material:** full-length plays, one-acts, musicals. **Facilities:** Vivian Beaumont, 1000 seats, thrust stage; Mitzi E. Newhouse, 300 seats, thrust stage. **Best submission time:** year-round. **Response time:** 2–4 months.

LIVE OAK THEATRE
311 Nueces; Austin, TX 78701; (512) 472-5143
Mari Marchbanks, *Executive Director, New Play Development*

Submission procedure: no unsolicited scripts; synopsis, 10-page dialogue sample, resume and letter of inquiry. **Types of material:** full-length plays, one-acts, translations, adaptations, plays for young audiences, musicals. **Special interests:** contemporary works; works with southern themes. **Facilities:** Live Oak Theatre, 210 seats, proscenium stage. **Production considerations:** no fly space. **Best submission time:** Sep–Feb. **Response time:** 1 month letter; 6 months script. **Special programs:** occasional stage readings and developmental productions. Live Oak Theatre New Play Awards (see Prizes).

LONG WHARF THEATRE
222 Sargent Dr; New Haven, CT 06511; (203) 787-4284
John Tillinger, *Literary Consultant*

Submission procedure: no unsolicited scripts; professional recommendation. **Types of material:** full-length plays, translations, adaptations. **Special interests:** plays about human relationships, social concerns, ethical and moral dilemmas; will also consider farces and comedies of manners. **Facilities:** Long Wharf Theatre, 484 seats, thrust stage; Stage II, 199 seats, flexible stage. **Best submission time:** year-round. **Response time:** 6 months. **Special programs:** Stage II Workshops (see Development). In-house readings of new plays.

LOVE CREEK PRODUCTIONS
c/o Granville; 42 Sunset Dr; Croton, NY 10520-2821
Cynthia Granville, *Literary Manager*

Submission procedure: accepts unsolicited scripts. **Types of material:** full-length plays, one-acts. **Special interests:** full-length plays with 8 or more characters, one-acts with 2 or more; plays that express a humanist philosophy; experimental works. **Facilities:** Nat Horne Theatre, 80 seats, proscenium stage. **Production considerations:** no fly space. **Best submission time:** Nov–Jan. **Response time:** 6 months. **Special programs:** Love Creek One-Act Festivals (see Prizes). Also hosts Off-Off Broadway Original Short Play Festival (see Prizes).

MABOU MINES
150 First Ave; New York, NY 10009; (212) 473-0559
Allison Astor, *Company Manager*

Submission procedure: no unsolicited scripts; professional recommendation. **Types of material:** full-length plays, one-acts, translations, adaptations. **Special interests:** contemporary works on contemporary issues. **Facilities:** no permanent facility. **Best submission time:** year-round. **Response time:** 6 months.

MADISON REPERTORY THEATRE
122 State St, Suite 201; Madison, WI 53703; (608) 256-0029
Joseph Hanreddy, *Artistic Director*

Submission procedure: no unsolicited scripts; synopsis and letter of inquiry. **Types of material:** full-length plays, one-acts, translations, adaptations, musicals. **Special interests:** works with midwestern themes. **Facilities:** Isthmus Playhouse, 335 seats, 3/4-thrust stage. **Production considerations:** cast limit of 15; no fly space. **Best submission time:** summer. **Response time:** 3–4 months letter; 3–4 months script.

MAD RIVER THEATER WORKS
Box 248; West Liberty, OH 43357; (513) 465-6751
Jeffrey Hooper, *Producing Director*

Submission procedure: no unsolicited scripts; synopsis and letter of inquiry. **Types of material:** full-length plays, one-acts, adaptations. **Special interests:** midwestern or rural subject matter. **Facilities:** Center Stage, 150 seats, flexible stage. **Production considerations:** cast limit of 10, simple set and costumes. **Best submission time:** year-round. **Response time:** 2 weeks letter; 3–4 months script.

MAGIC THEATRE
Fort Mason Center, Bldg D; San Francisco, CA 94123; (415) 441-8001
Mary DeDanan, *Literary Manager*

Submission procedure: no unsolicited scripts; synopsis, first 10–20 pages of the play, resume or artistic bio and letter of inquiry. **Types of material:** full-length plays. **Special interests:** new plays that are well beyond the ordinary: nonlinear, poetic, absurd, innovative; plays that are honest, risk-taking, theatrical, transforming; 2nd and 3rd productions considered. **Facilities:** Magic Theatre Southside, 170 seats, proscenium stage; Magic Theatre Northside, 155 seats, thrust stage. **Production considerations:** prefers cast limit of 6, simple set. **Best submission time:** year-round. **Response time:** 1–3 months letter; 3–7 months script. **Special programs:** commissioning program; participation by invitation. Magic Theatre Developmental Programs (see Development). Also hosts Bay Area Playwrights Festival (see Development).

MAIN STREET THEATER
2540 Times Blvd; Houston, TX 77005; (713) 524-3662
Rebecca Greene Udden, *Artistic Director*

Submission procedure: accepts unsolicited scripts. **Types of material:** full-length plays, one-acts, translations, adaptations, plays for young audiences, musicals. **Special interests:** good plays for young audiences. **Facilities:** Main Street Theater, 95 seats, arena-thrust stage. **Production considerations:** cast limit of 20. **Best submission time:** year-round. **Response time:** 4–6 months.

MANHATTAN CLASS COMPANY
120 West 28th St; New York, NY 10001; (212) 727-7722
Mary Samson, *Literary Manager*

Submission procedure: no unsolicited scripts; recommendation from theatre professional known to company. **Types of material:** full-length plays, one-acts, musicals. **Special interests:** New York City premieres only; American writers; writers of color; plays by or for the physically challenged. **Facilities:** MCC Theatre, 99 seats, flexible space. **Best submission time:** year-round. **Response time:** 3–4 months. **Special programs:** Performance Lab: approximately 40 ideas for plays, musicals, songs, poems or dances explored each year through 20-minute tryouts; unsolicited material, 15 minutes or less in length, accepted for this program only (specify that work is submitted for lab). Class1Acts Festival: annual festival of 4–6 one-acts. Shake a Leg: annual summer production of original play in cooperation with facility for rehabilitation of people with spinal-cord injuries, using both able and disabled performers.

MANHATTAN THEATRE CLUB
453 West 16th St; New York, NY 10011; (212) 645-5590
Kate Loewald, *Director of Script Department*

Submission procedure: no unsolicited scripts; synopsis, dialogue sample, resume and letter of inquiry. **Types of material:** full-length plays, translations, adaptations, musicals, cabaret/revues. **Facilities:** The Space at City Center, 299 seats, proscenium-thrust stage; Stage II, 150 seats, flexible stage. **Production considerations:** prefers small cast, 1 set or unit set. **Best submission time:** year-round. **Response time:** 1 month letter; 6 months script. **Special programs:** workshop productions of new plays. "First-hearing" readings: in-house readings of new plays or first drafts; scripts selected through theatre's normal submission procedure. Van Lier Playwriting Fellowships (see Fellowship and Grants).

MARIN THEATRE COMPANY
397 Miller Ave; Mill Valley, CA 94941; (415) 388-5200
Lee Sankowich, *Artistic Director*

Submission procedure: no unsolicited scripts; direct solicitation from playwright or agent. **Types of material:** full-length plays, translations, adaptations, plays for young audiences, musicals, cabaret/revues. **Facilities:** Marin Theatre, 250 seats, proscenium stage; second theatre, 125 seats, black box.

MARK TAPER FORUM
Listing alphabetized under T.

McCARTER THEATRE CENTER FOR THE PERFORMING ARTS
91 University Pl; Princeton, NJ 08540; (609) 683-9100
Janice Paran, *Literary Manager*

Submission procedure: no unsolicited scripts; agent submission. **Types of material:** full-length plays, musicals. **Facilities:** McCarter Theatre, 1077 seats, proscenium stage. **Best submission time:** year-round. **Response time:** 2 months.

MERRIMACK REPERTORY THEATRE
Box 228; Lowell, MA 01853; (508) 454-6324
David G. Kent, *Artistic Director*

Submission procedure: no unsolicited scripts; synopsis and letter of inquiry. **Types of material:** full-length plays, translations, adaptations, plays for young audiences, musicals. **Special interests:** well-crafted stories with a poetic and human focus; tapestries of American life and love. **Facilities:** Liberty Hall, 386 seats, thrust stage. **Production considerations:** moderate cast size, simple set. **Best submission time:** summer. **Response time:** 1 month letter; 6 months script.

MERRY-GO-ROUND PLAYHOUSE
Box 506; Auburn, NY 13021; (315) 255-1305
Edward Sayles, *Producing Director*

Submission procedure: accepts unsolicited scripts. **Types of material:** full-length plays, translations, adaptations, plays for young audiences, musicals. **Special interests:** participatory plays for young audiences with cast limit of 3–4; plays for grades K–12. **Facilities:** Merry-Go-Round Playhouse (adaptable), 325 seats, proscenium stage or 100 seats, thrust stage. **Best submission time:** Mar–May. **Response time:** 1 month.

METRO THEATER COMPANY

524 Trinity Ave; St. Louis, MO 63130; (314) 727-3552
Carol North Evans, *Producing Director*

Submission procedure: no unsolicited scripts; professional recommendation. **Types of material:** plays and musicals for young audiences. **Special interests:** no works longer than 60 minutes; plays with music and musicals which are not dramatically limited by traditional concepts of "children's theatre." **Facilities:** touring company. **Production considerations:** works cast from ensemble of 5; sets suitable for touring. **Best submission time:** year-round. **Response time:** 2–3 months. **Special programs:** commissioning program; interested writers send letter of inquiry with recommendations from theatres who have produced writer's work.

METTAWEE RIVER COMPANY

463 West St, #D405; New York, NY 10014; (212) 929-4777
May–Aug: RD2, Salem, NY 12865; (518) 854-9357
Ralph Lee, *Artistic Director*

Submission procedure: no unsolicited scripts; synopsis, dialogue sample and letter of inquiry. **Types of material:** multimedia theatre pieces. **Special interests:** primarily interested in theatre pieces created collaboratively with company and based on myths and legends; works combining dialogue with storytelling, lyrics, music, masks, puppetry and strong visual elements. **Facilities:** touring company. **Production considerations:** company of 6 performers; works performed outdoors in summer, often later adapted for indoor performance. **Best submission time:** year-round. **Response time:** 4 weeks letter; 8 weeks script.

MILL MOUNTAIN THEATRE

1 Market Square SE, Suite 6; Roanoke, VA 24011-1437; (703) 342-5730
Jo Weinstein, *Literary Manager*

Submission procedure: accepts unsolicited one-acts only; synopsis, 10 pages of dialogue and letter of inquiry for all other submissions. **Types of material:** full-length plays, one-acts, musicals. **Special interests:** plays with racially mixed casts. **Facilities:** Mill Mountain Theatre, 400 seats, flexible proscenium stage; Theatre B, 125 seats, flexible space. **Production considerations:** cast limit of 15 for plays, 24 for musicals; prefers unit set. **Best submission time:** year-round. **Response time:** 6 weeks letter; 6–8 months script. **Special programs:** Centerpieces: monthly lunchtime staged readings of one-acts by emerging playwrights; unpublished one-acts 25–35 minutes in length. Mill Mountain Theatre New Play Competition: The Norfolk Southern Festival of New Works (see Prizes).

MILWAUKEE CHAMBER THEATRE

152 West Wisconsin Ave, Suite 731; Milwaukee, WI 53203; (414) 276-8842
Montgomery Davis, *Artistic Director*

Submission procedure: no unsolicited scripts; professional recommendation. **Types of material:** full-length plays, one-acts, translations, adaptations. **Special**

interests: strong, well-crafted plays; plays about Shaw for annual Shaw Festival. Facilities: Steimke Theater, 200 seats, black box. Production considerations: 1 set or unit set. Best submission time: summer. Response time: 2 months.

MILWAUKEE PUBLIC THEATRE
Box 07147; Milwaukee, WI 53207; (414) 271-8484
Michael Moynihan, *Artistic/Producing Director*

Submission procedure: no unsolicited scripts; synopsis and letter of inquiry with SASE for response. Types of material: full-length plays, one-acts, translations, adaptations, plays for young audiences, cabaret/revues, clown/vaudeville shows. Special interests: works with cast of 1–3 playing multiple roles; political satire; social-political and regional or local themes; interart works; new clown/vaudeville shows; works for young and family audiences. Facilities: no permanent facility. Production considerations: simple production demands; productions tour. Best submission time: Sep only. Response time: 3 months letter; 6 months script. Special programs: outdoor park performances.

MILWAUKEE REPERTORY THEATER
108 East Wells St; Milwaukee, WI 53202; (414) 224-1761
John Dillon, *Artistic Director*

Submission procedure: contact the new artistic director, due to be appointed fall 1992, for procedure. Types of material: full-length plays, translations, adaptations, musicals, cabaret/revues. Facilities: Powerhouse Theatre, 720 seats, 3/4-thrust stage; Steimke Theatre, 200 seats, black box; Stackner Cabaret, 100 seats, cabaret stage.

MISSOURI REPERTORY THEATRE
4949 Cherry St; Kansas City, MO 64110-2499; (816) 363-4541
Felicia Londré, *Dramaturg*

Submission procedure: no unsolicited scripts; synopsis and letter of inquiry. Types of material: full-length plays, translations, adaptations. Facilities: Helen F. Spencer Theatre, 740 seats, modified thrust stage. Best submission time: academic year. Response time: 1 month letter; script varies. Special programs: Second Stage: develops scripts through a series of readings leading to production; contact Mary Guaraldi, Director.

MIXED BLOOD THEATRE COMPANY
1501 South 4th St; Minneapolis, MN 55454; (612) 338-0937
David Kunz, *Script Czar*

Submission procedure: no unsolicited scripts; synopsis and letter of inquiry. Types of material: full-length plays, translations, plays for young audiences, musicals, cabaret/revues. Facilities: Main Stage, 200 seats, flexible stage. Production considerations: prefers cast limit of 10. Best submission time: year-round.

Response time: 1 month letter; 2–6 months script. **Special programs:** Mixed Blood Versus America (see Prizes).

MUSIC-THEATRE GROUP

29 Bethune St; New York, NY 10014; (212) 924-3108
Jun–Aug: Box 1396; Stockbridge, MA 01262
Lyn Austin, *Producing Director*
Diane Wondisford, *Managing Director*

Submission procedure: no unsolicited scripts; direct solicitation from playwright or agent. **Types of material:** music-theatre works, operas, cabaret/revues. **Special interests:** experimental musical works; collaborations between music-theatre, dance and the visual arts. **Facilities:** no permanent facility.

NATIONAL JEWISH THEATER

5050 West Church St; Skokie, IL 60077; (708) 675-2200
Fran Brumlik, *Managing Director*

Submission procedure: no unsolicited scripts; synopsis and letter of inquiry with SASE for response. **Types of material:** full-length plays, translations, adaptations, musicals. **Special interests:** American Jewish experience from early immigration to contemporary problems. **Facilities:** Mainstage, 250 seats, open stage. **Production considerations:** prefers cast limit of 10–12; no more than 2 sets; no fly space. **Best submission time:** year-round. **Response time:** 1 month letter; 2 months script.

NEBRASKA REPERTORY THEATRE

215 Temple Bldg; 12th and R Sts; Lincoln, NE 68588-0201; (402) 472-2072
Robert Hall, *Artistic Director*

Submission procedure: no unsolicited scripts; synopsis and letter of inquiry. **Types of material:** full-length plays, musicals. **Facilities:** Howell Theatre, 380 seats, proscenium stage; Studio Theatre, 180 seats, black box. **Production considerations:** simple set for studio theatre. **Best submission time:** Aug–Apr. **Response time:** 2 weeks letter; 2 months script.

NEBRASKA THEATRE CARAVAN

6915 Cass St; Omaha, NE 68132; (402) 553-4890
Carolyn Rutherford, *Managing Director*

Submission procedure: no unsolicited scripts; synopsis and letter of inquiry. **Types of material:** full-length plays, translations, adaptations, plays for young audiences, musicals. **Facilities:** touring company. **Production considerations:** cast limit of 12, 1 set. **Best submission time:** year-round. **Response time:** 1 month letter; 3 months script.

NEW AMERICAN THEATER

118 North Main St; Rockford, IL 61101; (815) 963-9454
J.R. Sullivan, *Producing Director*

Submission procedure: accepts unsolicited scripts; prefers synopsis and letter of inquiry. **Types of material:** full-length plays, one-acts, translations, adaptations. **Facilities:** New American Theater, 282 seats, thrust stage; Lab Theatre, 90 seats, black box. **Best submission time:** Sep–Dec. **Response time:** 3 months letter; 12 months script.

NEW CITY THEATER AND ART CENTER

1634 Eleventh Ave; Seattle, WA 98122; (206) 323-6801
John Kazanjian, *Artistic Director*

Submission procedure: no unsolicited scripts; professional recommendation. **Types of material:** full-length plays, translations, adaptations. **Special interests:** contemporary nonnaturalistic works. **Facilities:** New City Theater, 100 seats, flexible stage. **Production considerations:** 11' ceiling; modest production demands. **Best submission time:** year-round. **Response time:** 5 months. **Special programs:** Playwright's Festival: annual month-long fall showcase for Seattle playwrights, directors and actors; one-acts given 1 performance, then 5 best run in repertory for 1 week; playwright finds director, mounts production, submits project and is responsible for costs, including $80 application fee; all projects accepted; write for information and early-fall deadline date.

THE NEW CONSERVATORY CHILDREN'S THEATRE COMPANY AND SCHOOL

New Conservatory Theatre Center; 25 Van Ness; San Francisco, CA 94102;
    (415) 861-4914
Ed Decker, *Artistic Director*

Submission procedure: accepts unsolicited scripts; prefers letter of inquiry. **Types of material:** works for young and family audiences, including full-length plays, translations, adaptations and musicals. **Special interests:** works dealing with contemporary problems and issues affecting young and family audiences. **Facilities:** New Conservatory Theatre Center, 60 seats, flexible stage. **Production considerations:** all roles played by actors aged 4–19 years; small cast, simple set. **Best submission time:** year-round. **Response time:** 1 month letter; several months script.

NEW DRAMATISTS

See Membership and Service Organizations.

NEW FEDERAL THEATRE
466 Grand St; New York, NY 10002; (212) 598-0400
Woodie King, Jr., *Producer*
Linda Herring, *Company Manager*

Submission procedure: no unsolicited scripts; professional recommendation. **Types of material:** full-length plays. **Special interests:** social issues; plays about blacks, Jews, Puerto Ricans, Chinese and other minorities. **Facilities:** Theatre of the Riverside Church, 250 seats, proscenium stage. **Production considerations:** small cast, no more than 2 sets. **Best submission time:** year-round. **Response time:** 5 months.

NEW JERSEY SHAKESPEARE FESTIVAL
Drew University; Rte 24; Madison, NJ 07940; (201) 408-3278
Bonnie J. Monte, *Artistic Director*

Submission procedure: no unsolicited scripts; synopsis and letter of inquiry. **Types of material:** full-length plays, translations, adaptations. **Special interests:** translations and/or adaptations of classic works only. **Facilities:** Festival Theatre, 238 seats, thrust stage. **Production considerations:** modest technical demands; limited wing space. **Best submission time:** early fall. **Response time:** 2 months letter; 1 month script.

NEW MEXICO REPERTORY THEATRE
Box 789; Albuquerque, NM 87103; (505) 243-4577
Coleen A. Turney, *Operations Manager*

Submission procedure: no unsolicited scripts; synopsis and letter of inquiry. **Types of material:** full-length plays, translations, adaptations, musicals. **Special interests:** Hispanic drama. **Facilities:** New Mexico Repertory Theatre (in Santa Fe), 340 seats, proscenium stage; KiMo Theatre (in Albuquerque), 750 seats, proscenium stage. **Best submission time:** year-round. **Response time:** 3 weeks letter; 4–6 months script.

NEW STAGE THEATRE
Box 4792; Jackson, MS 39296-4792; (601) 948-3533
Jane Reid-Petty, *Producing Artistic Director*

Submission procedure: no unsolicited scripts; synopsis and letter of inquiry. **Types of material:** full-length plays. **Facilities:** Meyer Crystal Auditorium, 364 seats, proscenium stage; Hewes Room Theatre, 100 seats, flexible stage. **Production considerations:** small cast; no fly space in Hewes Room Theatre. **Best submission time:** summer–fall. **Response time:** 2–4 weeks letter; 3–5 months script. **Special programs:** Eudora Welty New Plays Series: readings every season; full production of 1 new play in alternate seasons.

THE NEW TUNERS THEATRE
1225 West Belmont Ave; Chicago, IL 60657; (312) 929-7287
Allan Chambers, *Literary Manager*

Submission procedure: accepts unsolicited scripts. **Types of material:** full-length musicals. **Special interests:** traditional or innovative musicals for adult audiences. **Facilities:** North Theatre, 148 seats, proscenium stage; South Theatre, 148 seats, proscenium/thrust stage; West Theatre, 148 seats, thrust stage. **Production considerations:** prefers cast limit of 15. **Best submission time:** year-round. **Response time:** 6 months. **Special programs:** Making Tuners: 3-level developmental workshop for composers, librettists and lyricists; each group meets for 4 8-hour weekend sessions over 6-month period; participants pay $175 fee for each level; write for application and further information; *deadline:* 1 Aug; *dates:* Sep–Feb.

NEW YORK SHAKESPEARE FESTIVAL
425 Lafayette St; New York, NY 10003; (212) 598-7129
Jason Fogelson, *Literary Manager*

Submission procedure: accepts unsolicited scripts; also accepts synopsis, 10-page sample scene and letter of inquiry; cassette of 3–5 songs for musicals and operas. **Types of material:** full-length plays, translations, adaptations, musicals, operas. **Facilities:** Newman Theater, 299 seats, proscenium stage; Anspacher Theater, 275 seats, thrust stage; Martinson Hall, 200 seats, proscenium stage; LuEsther Hall, 150 seats, flexible stage; Shiva Theater, 100 seats, flexible stage. **Best submission time:** year-round. **Response time:** 3 weeks letter; 4 months script.

NEW YORK STATE THEATRE INSTITUTE
1400 Washington Ave, PAC 266; Albany, NY 12222; (518) 442-5399
James Farrell, *Literary Manager*

Submission procedure: accepts unsolicited scripts. **Types of material:** full-length plays, adaptations, musicals. **Special interests:** works for family audiences. **Facilities:** Main Theatre, 883 seats, flexible thrust stage; Studio Theatre, 450 seats, thrust stage. **Best submission time:** Jun–Sep. **Response time:** 3–4 months. **Special programs:** New Works: developmental workshops, staged readings or workshop productions; playwright receives negotiable remuneration, travel, housing.

NEW YORK THEATRE WORKSHOP
220 West 42nd St, 18th Floor; New York, NY 10036; (212) 302-7737
Christopher Grabowski, *Artistic Associate*

Submission procedure: no unsolicited scripts; synopsis, 10-page sample scene and letter of inquiry. **Types of material:** full-length plays, one-acts, translations, music-theatre pieces, proposals for performance projects. **Special interests:** large issues; socially relevant and/or minority issues; innovative form and language. **Facilities:** 79 East 4th Street Theatre, 125 seats, proscenium stage. **Best submission time:** fall–spring. **Response time:** 4 weeks letter; 3–5 months script. **Special programs:**

Mondays at Three: reading series, developmental workshops and symposiums. Playwrights Circle. Summer writing residency.

NORTHLIGHT THEATRE
600 Davis St; Evanston, IL 60201; (708) 869-7732
Literary Department

Submission procedure: no unsolicited scripts; synopsis and letter of inquiry. **Types of material:** full-length plays, translations, adaptations, musicals. **Special interests:** the public world and public issues; plays of ideas; Chicago and regional topics and settings; translations and adaptations of "lost" plays; stylistic exploration and complexity; no domestic realism. **Facilities:** Coronet Theatre, 377 seats, proscenium stage. **Production considerations:** no orchestra pit for musicals. **Best submission time:** Sep–Feb. **Response time:** 1 month letter; 2–4 months script.

NOVEL STAGES
7001 McCallum St; Philadelphia, PA 19119-3038; (215) 843-6152
Clista Townsend, *Artistic Associate*

Submission procedure: no unsolicited scripts; synopsis and letter of inquiry with SASP for response. **Types of material:** full-length plays, one-acts, translations, adaptations, plays for young audiences. **Facilities:** Stage III at 1619 Walnut St, 130 seats, endstage. **Production considerations:** simple set; no fly space, very little wing space. **Best submission time:** year-round. **Response time:** 1–2 months letter; 6 months script.

OAKLAND ENSEMBLE THEATRE
1615 Broadway, Suite 800; Oakland, CA 94612; (510) 763-7774
Sharon Walton, *Producing Director*

Submission procedure: no unsolicited scripts; synopsis and letter of inquiry. **Types of material:** full-length plays, musicals, cabaret/revues. **Special interests:** plays about black American life that reflect ethnic diversity and deal with pluralism in America as seen through the eyes of black Americans. **Facilities:** Alice Arts Center, 400 seats, flexible space. **Production considerations:** cast limit of 12. **Best submission time:** year-round. **Response time:** 10 months letter; script varies.

ODYSSEY THEATRE ENSEMBLE
2055 South Sepulveda Blvd; Los Angeles, CA 90025; (310) 477-2055
Jan Lewis, *Literary Manager/Dramaturg*

Submission procedure: no unsolicited scripts; synopsis, 8–10 pages of dialogue, play's production history (if any), resume and letter of inquiry. **Types of material:** full-length plays, translations, adaptations, musicals. **Special interests:** works with innovative form or provocative subject matter; works exploring the enduring questions of human existence and the possibilities of the live-theatre experience; works with political or sociological impact. **Facilities:** Odyssey 1, 99 seats, flexible stage; Odyssey 2, 99 seats, thrust stage; Odyssey 3, 99 seats, endstage. **Best submission time:** year-round. **Response time:** 2–4 weeks letter; 6 months script.

OLD GLOBE THEATRE
Box 2171; San Diego, CA 92112-2171; (619) 231-1941
Mark Hofflund, *Literary Manager*

Submission procedure: no unsolicited scripts; synopsis and letter of inquiry. **Types of material:** full-length plays, translations, adaptations, musicals. **Special interests:** well-crafted plays; strongly theatrical material. **Facilities:** Old Globe Theatre, 581 seats, modified thrust stage; Cassius Carter Centre Stage, 225 seats, arena stage; Lowell Davies Festival Stage, 620 seats, outdoor stage. **Production considerations:** prefers cast limit of 15. **Best submission time:** year-round. **Response time:** 2–3 weeks letter; 3–10 months script. **Special programs:** Play Discovery Program: 4–6 new plays given readings each season; developmental workshops for selected additional scripts, as needed.

OLNEY THEATRE
Box 550; Olney, MD 20820; (310) 924-4485
Vicki Sussman, *General Manager*

Submission procedure: no unsolicited scripts; professional recommendation. **Types of material:** full-length plays, translations, adaptations. **Facilities:** Mainstage, 700 seats, proscenium stage. **Production considerations:** cast limit of 8. **Best submission time:** year-round. **Response time:** 6 months.

OMAHA MAGIC THEATRE
1417 Farnam St; Omaha, NE 68102; (402) 346-1227
Megan Terry, *Dramaturg*

Submission procedure: accepts unsolicited scripts with $50 critique fee. **Types of material:** experimental plays, performance art. **Special interests:** only the most avant of the avant-garde; works regarded as unproducible by other theatres; works that push form and/or content to new dimensions; prefers works 60–90 minutes long. **Facilities:** 1st theatre, 150 seats, flexible space; 2nd theatre, 100 seats, flexible space; also uses nontraditional outdoor and alternative spaces. **Best submission time:** year-round. **Response time:** 1 year. **Special programs:** Play Events: limited-run full productions of new works-in-progress.

THE OPEN EYE: NEW STAGINGS
270 West 89th St; New York, NY 10024; (212) 769-4143
Amie Brockway, *Artistic Director*

Submission procedure: accepts unsolicited scripts. **Types of material:** full-length plays, one-acts, translations, adaptations. **Special interests:** multicultural themes; plays with music; ensemble plays; plays for family audiences. **Facilities:** The Open Eye, 115 seats, 20' x 25' open stage. **Production considerations:** minimal set. **Best submission time:** Apr–Jul. **Response time:** 3–6 months. **Special programs:** NEW

STAGINGS LAB: rehearsed readings. Eye on Directors: workshop productions of one-acts. The Joseph Campbell Memorial Fund Award: annual or biennial award to playwright, director or choreographer for development of new play "that strives to illuminate mythology or folklore relating to human experience"; recipient chosen through theatre's normal submission procedure.

OPEN STAGE OF HARRISBURG
Box 3805; Harrisburg, PA 17105-3805; (717) 652-7529
Donald L. Alsedek, *Artistic Director*

Submission procedure: no unsolicited scripts; synopsis and letter of inquiry. **Types of material:** full-length plays, translations, adaptations, radio plays. **Facilities:** Open Stage of Harrisburg at Strawberry Square, 99 seats, flexible stage. **Production considerations:** cast limit of 6, 1 set or unit set. **Best submission time:** year-round. **Response time:** 2 months letter; 4–6 months script. **Special programs:** Playwright Series: readings, studio productions and full productions of new plays.

OREGON SHAKESPEARE FESTIVAL
Box 158; Ashland, OR 97520; (503) 482-2111
Cynthia White, *Literary Manager*

Submission procedure: no unsolicited scripts; synopsis, 10 pages of dialogue and letter of inquiry. **Types of material:** full-length plays, translations. **Facilities:** Angus Bowmer Theatre, 600 seats, thrust stage; Elizabethan Theatre, 1194 seats, outdoor Elizabethan stage; Black Swan, 140 seats, black box; Portland Center for the Performing Arts Intermediate Theatre, 900 seats, proscenium stage. **Production considerations:** prefers small cast for Black Swan. **Best submission time:** year-round. **Response time:** varies.

OREGON STAGE COMPANY
17705 NW Springville Rd; Portland, OR 97229-1744; (503) 690-7328
Gary O'Brien, *Artistic Director*

Submission procedure: no unsolicited scripts; synopsis and letter of inquiry. **Types of material:** full-length plays, musicals. **Special interests:** Pacific Northwest playwrights. **Facilities:** Forum Theatre, 215 seats, proscenium stage. **Production considerations:** cast limit of 6, 1 set or unit set. **Best submission time:** year-round. **Response time:** 1 month letter; 6 months script.

ORGANIC THEATER COMPANY
3319 North Clark St; Chicago, IL 60657; (312) 327-2427
Sarah Tucker, *Literary Manager*

Submission procedure: no unsolicited scripts; synopsis, 10 pages of dialogue and letter of inquiry. **Types of material:** full-length plays, long one-acts, adaptations. **Special interests:** unproduced works only; adventurous, challenging scripts; plays that truly explore the theatrical medium; scripts by women and minorities; writers willing to work a year or more to bring script from initial idea through series of workshops to limited or full production. **Facilities:** Mainstage, 390 seats, flexible stage; Organic Greenhouse, 90 seats, proscenium stage; South Hall, up to 60 seats, flexible space; North Hall, up to 40 seats, flexible space. **Best submission time:** year-round. **Response time:** 1–3 weeks letter; 3–6 months script. **Special programs:** Greenhouse project: ongoing script-development program.

PAN ASIAN REPERTORY THEATRE
47 Great Jones St; New York, NY 10012; (212) 505-5655
Tisa Chang, *Artistic/Producing Director*

Submission procedure: accepts unsolicited scripts with resume. **Types of material:** full-length plays, translations, adaptations, musicals. **Special interests:** Asian or Asian-American themes only. **Facilities:** 46th Street Playhouse, 150 seats, 38' x 40' open stage. **Production considerations:** prefers cast limit of 8. **Best submission time:** summer. **Response time:** 9 months. **Special programs:** staged readings and workshops.

PAUL BUNYAN PLAYHOUSE

Listing alphabetized under B.

PEGASUS PLAYERS
1145 West Wilson; Chicago, IL 60640; (312) 878-9761
Arlene Crewdson, *Artistic Director*

Submission procedure: no unsolicited scripts; synopsis and letter of inquiry. **Types of material:** full-length plays, translations, adaptations, musicals. **Facilities:** The O'Rourke Center for the Performing Arts, 250 seats, proscenium stage. **Best submission time:** year-round. **Response time:** 1 month letter; 4–6 months script. **Special programs:** Chicago Young Playwrights Festival: annual June festival of plays by Chicago-area high school students; write for information.

PENDRAGON THEATRE
18 Park Ave; Saranac Lake, NY 12983; (518) 891-1854
Susan Neal, *Artistic Director*

Submission procedure: no unsolicited scripts; synopsis, dialogue sample and letter of inquiry. **Types of material:** full-length plays, translations, adaptations, plays for young audiences. **Facilities:** Pendragon Theatre, 80 seats, proscenium stage. **Production considerations:** small cast, simple sets; no fly space. **Best submission time:** year-round. **Response time:** 1 month letter; 3 months script.

PENGUIN REPERTORY COMPANY
Box 91; Stony Point, NY 10980; (914) 786-2873
Joe Brancato, *Artistic Director*

Submission procedure: no unsolicited scripts; synopsis, 10 pages of dialogue and letter of inquiry. **Types of material:** full-length plays, musicals. **Facilities:** Penguin

Repertory Theatre, 108 seats, proscenium stage. **Production considerations:** cast limit of 7. **Best submission time:** Dec–Mar. **Response time:** 1 month letter; 2 months script.

PENNSYLVANIA STAGE COMPANY
837 Linden St; Allentown, PA 18101; (215) 434-6110
Dennis Delaney, *Literary Manager*

Submission procedure: no unsolicited scripts; synopsis, cast list, 10 pages of dialogue and letter of inquiry. **Types of material:** full-length plays, musicals. **Facilities:** J.I. Rodale Theatre, 274 seats, proscenium stage. **Production considerations:** cast limit of 10 for musicals, 7 for plays; prefers 1 set. **Best submission time:** year-round. **Response time:** 1 month letter; 3 months script. **Special programs:** New Evolving Works Program: staged reading series.

THE PENUMBRA THEATRE COMPANY
The Martin Luther King Bldg; 270 North Kent St; St. Paul, MN 55102;
    (612) 224-4601
Lou Bellamy, *Artistic Director*

Submission procedure: accepts unsolicited scripts with resume. **Types of material:** full-length plays, one-acts, translations, adaptations, plays for young audiences, musicals. **Special interests:** works that address the African-American experience. **Facilities:** Hallie Q. Brown Theater, 250 seats, proscenium/thrust stage. **Best submission time:** year-round. **Response time:** 6–9 months. **Special programs:** Cornerstone Competition (see Prizes).

THE PEOPLE'S LIGHT AND THEATRE COMPANY
39 Conestoga Rd; Malvern, PA 19355-1798; (215) 647-1900
Alda Cortese, *Literary Manager*

Submission procedure: no unsolicited scripts; synopsis, cast list, 10 pages of dialogue and letter of inquiry. **Types of material:** full-length plays, one-acts, translations, adaptations. **Facilities:** People's Light and Theatre, 350 seats, flexible stage; Steinbright Stage, 99–150 seats, flexible stage. **Production considerations:** prefers cast limit of 12, 1 set or unit set. **Best submission time:** year-round. **Response time:** 2 weeks letter; 8–10 months script.

PERIWINKLE NATIONAL THEATRE FOR YOUNG AUDIENCES
19 Clinton Ave; Monticello, NY 12701; (914) 794-1666
Sunna Rasch, *Artistic Director*

Submission procedure: no unsolicited scripts; synopsis and letter of inquiry. **Types of material:** plays for young audiences. **Special interests:** plays dealing with needs and problems of youth; social issues for young audiences. **Facilities:** touring company. **Production considerations:** plays 45–60 minutes long; simple production demands for touring. **Best submission time:** spring. **Response time:** 2 weeks letter; 6–8 months script.

PERSEVERANCE THEATRE
914 3rd St; Douglas, AK 99824; (907) 364-2421, -2151
Molly Smith, *Artistic Director*

Submission procedure: accepts unsolicited scripts from AK playwrights only; others send synopsis, resume, list of previous productions and letter of inquiry. **Types of material:** full-length plays, one-acts. **Special interests:** new plays by AK playwrights; plays about ethnic experiences, gender, sexual orientation, disabilities, etc. **Facilities:** Mainstage, 150 seats, thrust stage; Phoenix Stage, 50–75 seats, flexible space; Voices Stage, 100 seats, flexible space. **Best submission time:** year-round. **Response time:** 1 month letter; 6 months script.

PETERBOROUGH PLAYERS
Box 1; Peterborough, NH 03458; (603) 924-7585
Ellen Dinerstein, *Producing Director*

Submission procedure: no unsolicited scripts; synopsis and letter of inquiry. **Types of material:** full-length plays, one-acts, adaptations. **Facilities:** Hadley Barn, 230 seats, flexible stage. **Best submission time:** Sep–Jan. **Response time:** 2 months letter; 6 months script. **Special programs:** staged readings.

PHILADELPHIA DRAMA GUILD
Robert Morris Bldg; 100 North 17th St; Philadelphia, PA 19103; (215) 563-7530
Victoria Abrash, *Dramaturg*

Submission procedure: no unsolicited scripts; synopsis, resume and letter of inquiry. **Types of material:** full-length plays, translations, adaptations. **Special interests:** new American plays. **Facilities:** Annenberg Center's Zellerbach Theatre, 900 seats, thrust stage. **Best submission time:** year-round. **Response time:** 3 weeks letter; 3 months script.

PHILADELPHIA FESTIVAL THEATRE FOR NEW PLAYS
3900 Chestnut St; Philadelphia, PA 19104-3105; (215) 222-5000
Michael Hollinger, *Literary Manager*

Submission procedure: no unsolicited scripts; synopsis, resume and letter of inquiry. **Types of material:** full-length plays, one-acts. **Special interests:** plays not previously given full production only; plays which reflect larger social issues through strong character relationships. **Facilities:** Harold Prince Theatre, 200 seats, proscenium or 3/4-arena stage. **Best submission time:** year-round; by 15 Jan 1993 for production Oct–Dec 1993; by 15 Jun 1993 for production Jan–Jun 1994. **Response time:** 4–5 months after each deadline. **Special programs:** Previewers: fall series of script-in-hand readings; scripts selected through theatre's normal submission procedure. The Dennis McIntyre Playwriting Award (see Prizes).

THE PHILADELPHIA THEATRE COMPANY
The Bourse Bldg, Suite 790; 21 South 5th St; Philadelphia, PA 19106;
(215) 592-8333
Sara Garonzik, *Producing Artistic Director*

Submission procedure: no unsolicited scripts; professional recommendation.
Types of material: full-length plays. **Special interests:** new American plays;
social/humanistic themes; sense of theatricality; minority playwrights; will consider
plays with music. **Facilities:** Plays and Players Theater, 324 seats, proscenium stage.
Best submission time: year-round. **Response time:** 4–6 months. **Special programs:**
STAGES: program of staged readings.

PIONEER THEATRE COMPANY
University of Utah; Salt Lake City, UT 84112; (801) 581-6356
Charles Morey, *Artistic Director*

Submission procedure: no unsolicited scripts; synopsis and letter of inquiry. **Types
of material:** full-length plays, translations, adaptations, musicals. **Facilities:** Pioneer
Memorial Theatre, 1000 seats, proscenium stage. **Best submission time:** fall.
Response time: 1 month letter; 6 months script.

PITTSBURGH PUBLIC THEATER
Allegheny Sq; Pittsburgh, PA 15212-5349; (412) 323-8200
Producing Director

Submission procedure: no unsolicited scripts; professional recommendation.
Types of material: full-length plays, translations, adaptations, musicals. **Facilities:**
Theodore L. Hazlett, Jr. Theater, 449 seats, arena or thrust stage. **Best submission
time:** year-round. **Response time:** 12 months.

PLAYERS THEATRE COLUMBUS
Box 18185; Columbus, OH 43218-0185; (614) 644-5300
Ed Graczyk, *Artistic Director*

Submission procedure: no unsolicited scripts; synopsis and letter of inquiry. **Types
of material:** full-length plays, translations, adaptations, plays for young audiences,
musicals. **Special interests:** the midwestern experience. **Facilities:** Mainstage, 750
seats, thrust stage; Second Stage, 250 seats, modified thrust stage; Studio Space,
100 seats, arena stage. **Best submission time:** year-round. **Response time:** 3 weeks
letter; 3–4 months script.

PLAYHOUSE ON THE SQUARE
51 South Cooper St; Memphis, TN 38104; (901) 725-0776
Jackie Nichols, *Executive Director*

Submission procedure: accepts unsolicited scripts. **Types of material:** full-length
plays, musicals. **Facilities:** Playhouse on the Square, 250 seats, proscenium stage;
Circuit Playhouse, 136 seats, proscenium stage. **Best submission time:** year-round.

Response time: 3–5 months. **Special programs:** Midsouth Playwrights' Competition (see Prizes).

PLAYMAKERS REPERTORY COMPANY

CB# 3235 Graham Memorial Bldg; Chapel Hill, NC 27599-3235; (919) 962-1122
David Hammond, *Artistic Director*

Submission procedure: no unsolicited scripts; professional recommendation. **Types of material:** full-length plays, translations, adaptations. **Facilities:** Paul Green Theatre, 498 seats, thrust stage. **Best submission time:** Apr–Sep. **Response time:** 6 months.

THE PLAYWRIGHTS' CENTER

See Membership and Service Organizations.

PLAYWRIGHTS HORIZONS

416 West 42nd St; New York, NY 10036; (212) 564-1235
Tim Sanford, *Literary Manager*
Nicholas Martin, *Associate Artistic Director (Musicals)*

Submission procedure: prefers unsolicited scripts with resume and cover letter; also accepts synopsis, dialogue sample and letter of inquiry; for musicals, send script and cassette (no synopses). **Types of material:** full-length plays, musicals. **Special interests:** works by American writers only; works with strong sense of language that take theatrical risks; works by minority writers. **Facilities:** Mainstage, 145 seats, proscenium stage; Studio Theater, 72 seats, black box. **Best submission time:** year-round. **Response time:** 3 weeks letter; 4 months script. **Special programs:** Theatre School: includes playwriting classes; write for information to 412 West 42nd St.

PORTLAND REPERTORY THEATER

2 World Trade Center; 25 SW Salmon St; Portland, OR 97204; (503) 224-4491
Geoffrey Sherman, *Artistic Director*

Submission procedure: no unsolicited scripts; synopsis, dialogue sample, resume and letter of inquiry. **Types of material:** full-length plays, translations, adaptations. **Facilities:** Portland Repertory Theater, 230 seats, proscenium stage; PRT Rehearsal Hall, 90 seats, proscenium stage. **Production considerations:** cast limit of 8, simple set. **Best submission time:** year-round. **Response time:** 2 months letter; 6–12 months script. **Special programs:** play reading series.

PORTLAND STAGE COMPANY

Box 1458; Portland, ME 04104; (207) 774-1043
Greg Leaming, *Artistic Director*

Submission procedure: no unsolicited scripts; synopsis, dialogue sample and letter of inquiry. **Types of material:** full-length plays, translations, adaptations. **Facilities:**

Performing Arts Center Theatre, 290 seats, proscenium stage; PSC Rehearsal Hall, 90 seats, flexible space (readings only). **Best submission time:** year-round. **Response time:** 2 months letter; 3–6 months script. **Special programs:** in-house play readings.

POTOMAC THEATRE PROJECT
4 Nedde Lane; Middlebury, VT 05753
Alyssa Gallin, *Assistant to the Producing Director*

Submission procedure: no unsolicited scripts; synopsis, resume and letter of inquiry. **Types of material:** full-length plays, one-acts. **Special interests:** highly political, socially conscious material only; prefers one-acts. **Facilities:** no permanent facility. **Production considerations:** casts combine resident ensemble of 4–5 AEA actors with students; minimal production demands. **Best submission time:** Dec–Feb. **Response time:** 2–3 months letter; 6–12 months script.

QUAIGH THEATRE
205 West 89th St; New York, NY 10024-1868; (212) 787-0862
Dennis Rickabee, *Literary Manager*

Submission procedure: accepts unsolicited scripts with synopsis and character breakdown. **Types of material:** full-length plays, one-acts. **Facilities:** Quaigh Theatre, 100 seats, proscenium stage. **Best submission time:** year-round. **Response time:** 3–6 months one-acts; 6–9 months full-length plays. **Special programs:** Lunchtime Series: workshop productions of new one-acts presented twice monthly Oct–May.

RED BARN ACTORS STUDIO
Box 707; Key West, FL 33040; (305) 296-9911
Mimi McDonald, *Business Manager*

Submission procedure: no unsolicited scripts; synopsis, character breakdown and letter of inquiry. **Types of material:** full-length plays, one-acts, adaptations, plays for young actors and young audiences, musicals, cabaret/revues. **Facilities:** Red Barn Theatre Main Stage, 94 seats, proscenium stage. **Production considerations:** cast limit of 8; no fly space. **Best submission time:** 1 Mar–1 Jul. **Response time:** 1 month letter; 6–9 months script.

REMAINS THEATRE
1800 North Clybourn; Chicago, IL 60614; (312) 335-9595
Larry Sloan, *Artistic Director*

Submission procedure: no unsolicited scripts; synopsis and letter of inquiry. **Types of material:** full-length plays, adaptations, plays for young audiences, musicals, cabaret/revues. **Special interests:** political plays; plays of local interest; adaptations. **Facilities:** Remains Theatre, 250 seats, flexible space. **Production considerations:** works cast from resident ensemble (7m, 4f, ages 20–38). **Best submission time:** year-round. **Response time:** 3 weeks letter; 3 months script.

REPERTORIO ESPAÑOL
138 East 27th St; New York, NY 10016; (212) 889-2850
Rene Buch, *Artistic Director*

Submission procedure: accepts unsolicited scripts. **Types of material:** full-length plays, adaptations, plays for young audiences, operas. **Special interests:** plays dealing with Hispanic themes. **Facilities:** Gramercy Arts Theatre, 140 seats, proscenium stage. **Production considerations:** prefers cast limit of 10, 1 set. **Best submission time:** year-round. **Response time:** 6 months. **Special programs:** Young Artist Development Program: 1–2 new full-length plays by Hispanic playwrights written in Spanish or English developed each year; playwright receives royalty if play is produced; scripts selected through theatre's normal submission process.

THE REPERTORY THEATRE OF ST. LOUIS
Box 191730; St. Louis, MO 63119; (314) 968-7340
Susan Gregg, *Associate Artistic Director*

Submission procedure: no unsolicited scripts; synopsis and letter of inquiry. **Types of material:** full-length plays. **Special interests:** nonnaturalistic plays; contemporary social and political issues. **Facilities:** Main Stage, 750 seats, thrust stage; Studio Theatre, 130 seats, black box. **Production considerations:** small cast, modest production demands. **Best submission time:** year-round. **Response time:** 4 weeks letter; 6 months script. **Special programs:** developmental workshop for new plays; scripts selected through theatre's normal submission process.

RIVER ARTS REPERTORY
Box 1166; Woodstock, NY 12498; (914) 679-5899, -2100
Lawrence Sacharow and Michael Cristofer, *Co-Artistic Directors*

Submission procedure: no unsolicited scripts; agent submission. **Types of material:** full-length plays, translations, adaptations. **Special interests:** new translations of classics; social issues; plays with poetic dimension. **Facilities:** Bearsville Theatre, 250 seats, proscenium stage; Second Stage (readings only), 100 seats, flexible space. **Production considerations:** cast limit of 8. **Best submission time:** Nov–Mar. **Response time:** 4 months. **Special programs:** International Writers Program: by invitation only. The Playwrights in Residence New Works Program: writer in residence Jul–Aug in Woodstock to develop script for staged reading or full production; writer receives stipend; plays unproduced in New York City; submit letter of inquiry between Oct 1992 and Mar 1993 to Lawrence Sacharow; *notification:* 1 May 1993.

RIVERSIDE THEATRE
Box 3788; Vero Beach, FL 32964; (407) 231-5860
Brian Spitler, *Production Manager*

Submission procedure: no unsolicited scripts; synopsis and letter of inquiry. **Types of material:** full-length plays, translations, adaptations, plays for young audiences, musicals. **Facilities:** Riverside Theatre, 633 seats, proscenium stage; Agnes

Wahlstrom Youth Playhouse, 200 seats, flexible stage. **Production considerations:** cast limit of 10. **Best submission time:** fall. **Response time:** 3 weeks letter; 2–3 months script.

RIVERSIDE THEATRE
Box 1651; Iowa City, IA 52244; (319) 338-7672
Ron Clark, *Artistic Director*

Submission procedure: no unsolicited scripts; synopsis and letter of inquiry. **Types of material:** full-length plays, one-acts, translations, adaptations, cabarets/revues. **Facilities:** Riverside Theatre, 110 seats, flexible stage. **Production considerations:** small cast, simple set. **Best submission time:** year-round. **Response time:** 1 month letter; 3–5 months script.

THE ROAD COMPANY
Box 5278 EKS; Johnson City, TN 37603-5278; (615) 926-7726
Christine Murdock, *Literary Manager*

Submission procedure: no unsolicited scripts; synopsis and letter of inquiry. **Types of material:** full-length plays, one-acts, adaptations, cabaret/revues. **Special interests:** southern playwrights; experimental work. **Facilities:** Memorial Theater, 600 seats, proscenium stage; The Down Home, 175 seats, cabaret. **Production considerations:** small cast, simple sets. **Best submission time:** year-round. **Response time:** 1 month letter (if interested); 6–12 months script. **Special programs:** salaried writer-in-residence each season.

ROADSIDE THEATER
306 Madison St; Whitesburg, KY 41858; (606) 633-0108
Dudley Cocke, *Director*

Submission procedure: no unsolicited scripts; synopsis, dialogue sample and letter of inquiry. **Types of material:** full-length plays. **Special interests:** plays about the Appalachian region only. **Facilities:** Appalshop Theater, 150 seats, thrust stage. **Production considerations:** small cast, simple sets suitable for touring. **Best submission time:** year-round. **Response time:** 2 weeks letter; 1 month script. **Special programs:** reading and workshop series. Playwright residencies initiated by theatre; playwright may not apply.

ROUNDABOUT THEATRE COMPANY
1530 Broadway; New York, NY 10036; (212) 719-9393
Todd Haimes, *Producing Director*

Submission procedure: no unsolicited scripts; synopsis and letter of inquiry. **Types of material:** full-length plays, translations, adaptations. **Special interests:** adaptations of classics; subjects of literary interest. **Facilities:** Roundabout Theatre, 499 seats, proscenium stage. **Production considerations:** medium-size cast (8–15). **Best submission time:** year-round. **Response time:** 1–3 months letter; 3–5 months script.

ROUND HOUSE THEATRE
12210 Bushey Dr; Silver Spring, MD 20902; (301) 217-6770
Jerry Whiddon, *Artistic Director*

Submission procedure: no unsolicited scripts; professional recommendation.
Types of material: full-length plays, translations, adaptations, plays for young
audiences, musicals. **Special interests:** contemporary social and political issues;
new translations of lesser-known classics; experimental works. **Facilities:** Round
House Theatre, 216 seats, modified thrust stage. **Production considerations:** cast
limit of 10; prefers 1 set. **Best submission time:** year-round. **Response time:** at
least 12 months.

SACRAMENTO THEATRE COMPANY
1419 H St; Sacramento, CA 95814; (916) 446-7501
Tim Ocel, *Associate Artistic Director*

Submission procedure: no unsolicited scripts; synopsis, resume and letter of
inquiry with SASE for response. **Types of material:** full-length plays, adaptations,
cabaret/revues. **Special interests:** contemporary social and political issues;
craftsmanship; theatricality; vital language; characters an audience will care about.
Facilities: McClatchy Mainstage, 301 seats, proscenium stage; Stage II, 86 seats,
black box. **Best submission time:** year-round. **Response time:** 3 months letter; 6
months script.

THE SALT LAKE ACTING COMPANY
168 West 500 N; Salt Lake City, UT 84103; (801) 363-0526
Aden Ross, *Literary Manager*

Submission procedure: no unsolicited scripts; synopsis, 10-page dialogue sample,
resume and letter of inquiry. **Types of material:** full-length plays, translations,
adaptations, musicals. **Special interests:** experimental, unconventional, provocative
works; works exploring social issues and larger questions of the human condition.
Facilities: The Salt Lake Acting Company Theater, 150–200 seats, proscenium-
thrust stage; The Readers' Theater, 35–75 seats, black box. **Best submission time:**
year-round. **Response time:** 1 month letter; 6 months script. **Special programs:**
reading series.

SAN DIEGO REPERTORY THEATRE
79 Horton Plaza; San Diego, CA 92101; (619) 231-3586
Literary Manager

Submission procedure: no unsolicited scripts; synopsis and letter of inquiry. **Types
of material:** full-length plays, translations, adaptations, musicals, literary cabaret,
mixed-media events. **Special interests:** multiethnic work; hard-hitting social and
political work; offbeat hip musicals; dramatic work with unusual incorporation of
music; women's issues; sharp-edged comedy; poetic visions; Hispanic plays suitable
for presentation in both Spanish and English. **Facilities:** Lyceum Stage, 550 seats,
modified thrust stage; Lyceum Space, 225 seats, flexible stage; Sixth Avenue

Playhouse, 190 seats, proscenium stage. **Production considerations:** no fly loft. **Best submission time:** year-round. **Response time:** 3 months letter; 12 months script. **Special programs:** readings and workshop productions.

SANTA MONICA PLAYHOUSE
1211 4th St; Santa Monica, CA 90401; (310) 394-9779
Chris DeCarlo, *Co-Artistic Director*

Submission procedure: no unsolicited scripts; synopsis and letter of inquiry. **Types of material:** full-length plays, one-acts, translations, adaptations, plays for young audiences, musicals. **Facilities:** Santa Monica Playhouse, 88 seats, arena/thrust stage. **Production considerations:** cast limit of 8, simple production demands. **Best submission time:** year-round. **Response time:** 2 months letter; 6 months script.

ZACHARY SCOTT THEATRE CENTER
Box 244; Austin, TX 78767-0244; (512) 476-0594
Alice Wilson, *Artistic Director*

Submission procedure: no unsolicited scripts; synopsis, dialogue sample, resume and letter of inquiry. **Types of material:** full-length plays, plays for young audiences. **Facilities:** Mainstage 1, 200 seats, thrust stage; Mainstage 2, 130 seats, arena stage. **Production considerations:** plays for young audiences tour. **Best submission time:** Jul–Aug. **Response time:** 6 weeks letter; 4–6 months script.

SEACOAST REPERTORY COMPANY OF PAPA
125 Bow St; Portsmouth, NH 03801; (603) 433-4793
Roy M. Rogosin, *Producing Artistic Director*

Submission procedure: accepts unsolicited scripts with synopsis and resume. **Types of material:** full-length plays, one-acts, plays for young audiences, musicals. **Special interests:** new American plays; small-scale musicals; plays for young audiences. **Facilities:** Seacoast Repertory Company of the Portsmouth Academy of Performing Arts, 240 seats, 3/4-thrust stage. **Best submission time:** year-round. **Response time:** 3–6 months.

SEASIDE MUSIC THEATER
Box 1310; Daytona Beach, FL 32115; (904) 252-3394
Lester Malizia, *General Manager*

Submission procedure: no unsolicited scripts; synopsis, cassette of music and letter of inquiry. **Types of material:** musicals for young and adult audiences, cabaret/revues. **Facilities:** Winter Dinner Theater, 159 seats, thrust stage; Summer Repertory Theater, 500 seats, proscenium stage; Theater for Children, 150 seats, modified thrust stage. **Production considerations:** cast limit of 8 for Winter Dinner Theater, 30 for Summer Repertory Theater, 10 for Theater for Children; small musical combo for Theater for Children and winter productions, 25-member orchestra in summer; no fly space except in summer theatre. **Best submission time:** Sep–Nov. **Response time:** 1 month letter; 3 months script.

SEATTLE CHILDREN'S THEATRE
305 Harrison St; Seattle, WA 98109; (206) 443-0807
Linda Hartzell, *Artistic Director*

Submission procedure: no unsolicited scripts; synopsis, 10 pages of dialogue and letter of inquiry. **Types of material:** works for young audiences, including full-length plays, one-acts, translations, adaptations and musicals. **Special interests:** sophisticated work for young audiences only; scripts dealing with contemporary life and concerns which do not "talk down" to young audiences. **Facilities:** Poncho Theatre, 280 seats, proscenium stage. **Best submission time:** Dec–Feb. **Response time:** 2 months letter; 6 months script.

SEATTLE GROUP THEATRE
3940 Brooklyn Ave NE; Seattle, WA 98105; (206) 685-4969
Nancy Griffiths, *Dramaturg/Literary Manager*

Submission procedure: no unsolicited scripts; synopsis, 10–15 pages of dialogue, resume and letter of inquiry. **Types of material:** full-length plays, translations, adaptations. **Special interests:** plays suitable for multiethnic casts; serious plays on social/cultural issues; satires or comedies with bite. **Facilities:** The Ethnic Theatre, 200 seats, modified thrust stage. **Production considerations:** cast limit of 10; prefers unit set or simple sets. **Best submission time:** year-round; submit by 1 Nov 1992 for 1993–94 season. **Response time:** 6 months letter; script varies. **Special programs:** MultiCultural Playwrights' Festival (see Development).

SEATTLE REPERTORY THEATRE
155 Mercer St; Seattle, WA 98109; (206) 443-2210
Douglas Hughes, *Associate Artistic Director*

Submission procedure: no unsolicited scripts; professional recommendation. **Types of material:** full-length plays, translations, adaptations, musicals. **Facilities:** Seattle Repertory Theatre, 856 seats, proscenium stage; Poncho Forum, 142 seats, arena stage. **Best submission time:** year-round. **Response time:** 2–3 months. **Special programs:** New Plays in Process Project: program of workshop productions; playwright receives travel and per diem.

SECOND STAGE THEATRE
Box 1807, Ansonia Station; New York, NY 10023; (212) 787-8302
Erin Sanders, *Literary Manager/Dramaturg*

Submission procedure: no unsolicited scripts; synopsis, 5–10 pages of dialogue and letter of inquiry. **Types of material:** full-length plays, adaptations, musicals. **Special interests:** new and previously produced American plays (include production history with script); "heightened" realism; sociopolitical issues; plays by women and minority writers. **Facilities:** McGinn/Cazale Theatre, 110 seats, endstage. **Best submission time:** year-round. **Response time:** 1 month letter; 3–4 months script. **Special programs:** annual series of 6–8 readings of new and previously produced plays.

7 STAGES
1105 Euclid Ave NE; Atlanta, GA 30307; (404) 522-0911
Andrew C. Ordover, *Literary Manager*

Submission procedure: no unsolicited scripts; synopsis, dialogue sample, resume and letter of inquiry. **Types of material:** full-length plays. **Special interests:** nontraditional plays and performance texts focusing on social, political or spiritual themes, especially by young black writers and women. **Facilities:** 7 Stages, 250 seats, thrust stage; Back Door, 100 seats, flexible stage. **Best submission time:** year-round. **Response time:** 4 months letter; 8–10 months script. **Special programs:** Workshop Program: year-round development of nontraditional, process-oriented pieces that involve collaboration with other theatre artists (dancers, musicians, designers, etc.); send letter of inquiry.

SHADOWLAND THEATER
157 Canal St; Ellenville, NY 12428; (914) 647-5511
Ronald Marquette, *Artistic Director*
Eileen Haworth Weil, *Literary Manager*

Submission procedure: accepts unsolicited scripts. **Types of material:** full-length plays, one-acts, plays for young audiences. **Special interests:** new American plays that are traditional in form. **Facilities:** Main Stage, 399 seats, proscenium/thrust stage; Second Stage, 150 seats, thrust stage. **Production considerations:** cast limit of 8, 1 set or unit set. **Best submission time:** year-round. **Response time:** 3–5 months. **Special programs:** staged reading series.

THE SHAKESPEARE THEATRE
301 East Capitol St SE; Washington, DC 20003; (202) 547-3230
Michael Kahn, *Artistic Director*

Submission procedure: no unsolicited scripts; professional recommendation. **Types of material:** translations, adaptations. **Special interests:** translations and adaptations of classics only. **Facilities:** Lansburgh Theatre, 447 seats, thrust stage. **Best submission time:** summer. **Response time:** 2 months.

THE SHALIKO COMPANY
151 Second Ave, Suite 1E; New York, NY 10003; (212) 475-6313
Karen P. Fricker, *Administrator*

Submission procedure: no unsolicited scripts; synopsis and letter of inquiry with SASE for response. **Types of material:** full-length plays, one-acts, translations, adaptations, plays for young audiences, musicals, cabaret/revues. **Facilities:** no permanent facility. **Production considerations:** cast limit of 10. **Best submission time:** spring. **Response time:** 1 month letter; 1 month script.

SIDEWALKS THEATRE
40 West 27th St; New York, NY 10001; (212) 481-3077
Literary Manager

Submission procedure: accepts unsolicited scripts; also accepts synopsis and letter of inquiry. **Types of material:** full-length plays. **Special interests:** plays with strong theatrical values about meaningful issues. **Facilities:** Sidewalks Theatre, 72 seats, flexible stage. **Production considerations:** small cast, 1 set. **Best submission time:** year-round. **Response time:** 4 months letter; 6 months script.

SOCIETY HILL PLAYHOUSE
507 South 8th St; Philadelphia, PA 19147; (215) 923-0210
Walter Vail, *Director, Script Development*

Submission procedure: no unsolicited scripts; synopsis and letter of inquiry with SASE for response. **Types of material:** full-length plays, translations, adaptations, plays for young audiences, musicals. **Facilities:** Society Hill Playhouse, 223 seats, proscenium stage; Second Space, 90 seats, flexible stage. **Production considerations:** prefers small cast for musicals. **Best submission time:** year-round. **Response time:** 1 month letter; 6 months script.

SOURCE THEATRE COMPANY
1835 14th St NW; Washington, DC 20009; (202) 462-1073
Keith Parker, *Literary Manager*

Submission procedure: accepts unsolicited scripts with synopsis and resume; include cassette for musicals. **Types of material:** full-length plays, one-acts, musicals. **Facilities:** Source Theatre Company, 107 seats, 3/4-thrust stage. **Best submission time:** 1 Sep–15 Feb. **Response time:** theatre responds in May, Jun, Aug, Sep only. **Special programs:** Washington Theatre Festival: 4-week series of staged readings and workshop productions of unproduced plays; scripts selected through competition (see below) or from submissions to festival; playwright occasionally brought in for production; *deadline:* 1 Feb 1993; *dates:* Jul–Aug 1993. SourceWorks: play reading series. Source Workshops: developmental series. Source Theatre Company National Playwriting Competition (see Prizes).

SOUTH COAST REPERTORY
Box 2197; Costa Mesa, CA 92628; (714) 957-2602
Jerry Patch, *Dramaturg*
John Glore, *Literary Manager*

Submission procedure: no unsolicited scripts; synopsis, optional dialogue sample, and letter of inquiry. **Types of material:** full-length plays, one-acts, translations, adaptations, musicals. **Facilities:** Mainstage, 507 seats, modified thrust stage; Second Stage, 161 seats, thrust stage. **Best submission time:** year-round. **Response time:** 1–3 weeks letter; 2–4 months script. **Special programs:** COLAB (Collaboration Laboratory) New Play Program: developmental program involving readings, staged readings, workshop and full productions; participation and all commissions offered by David Emmes and Martin Benson, artistic directors; playwright receives grant, commission and/or royalties depending on nature of project. California Playwrights Competition (see Prizes). Hispanic Playwrights Project (see Development).

SOUTH JERSEY REGIONAL THEATRE
738 Bay Ave; Somers Point, NJ 08244; (609) 653-0553
Joanna Papada, *Artistic Director*

Submission procedure: no unsolicited scripts; synopsis and letter of inquiry with SASE for response. **Types of material:** full-length plays, adaptations, musicals, revues. **Facilities:** Primary Space, 299 seats, proscenium stage. **Production considerations:** cast limit of 8, unit set or minimal sets; no fly space. **Best submission time:** year-round. **Response time:** 3 weeks letter; 3–6 months script.

SPOKANE INTERPLAYERS ENSEMBLE
Box 1961; Spokane, WA 99210; (509) 455-7529
Robert A. Welch, *Managing Director*

Submission procedure: no unsolicited scripts; synopsis with cast list, set requirements and play's production history and reviews (if any), dialogue sample and letter of inquiry. **Types of material:** full-length plays, bills of related one-acts, translations, adaptations, cabaret/revues. **Facilities:** Spokane Interplayers Ensemble, 255 seats, thrust stage. **Production considerations:** prefers cast limit of 8, 1 set. **Best submission time:** year-round. **Response time:** 3 months letter (if interested); 3–6 months script.

STAGE ONE: THE LOUISVILLE CHILDREN'S THEATRE
425 West Market St; Louisville, KY 40202-3300; (502) 589-5946
Moses Goldberg, *Producing Director*

Submission procedure: accepts unsolicited scripts. **Types of material:** plays for young audiences. **Special interests:** plays about young people in the real world; good, honest treatments of familiar titles. **Facilities:** Moritz von Bomard Theater, 610 seats, thrust stage; Boyd Martin Experimental Theater, 200 seats, arena stage. **Production considerations:** prefers cast limit of 12; some productions tour. **Best submission time:** Oct–Dec. **Response time:** 3 months.

STAGES
11902 Gorham Ave; Los Angeles, CA 90049; (213) 463-5356
Paul Verdier, *Artistic Director*

Submission procedure: no unsolicited scripts; synopsis and letter of inquiry. **Types of material:** full-length plays, one-acts, translations, adaptations. **Special interests:** plays by foreign writers both in original language and in translation; theatre regularly produces plays in Spanish, French and English but can also find actors fluent in other languages; challenging, experimental work. **Facilities:** Mainstage, 49 seats, proscenium stage; Lab, 25 seats, classroom; Amphitheatre, 99 seats, outdoor flexible stage. **Production considerations:** prefers cast limit of 5. **Best submission time:** year-round. **Response time:** 1 month letter; 3 months script.

STAGES REPERTORY THEATRE
3201 Allen Pkwy, Suite 101; Houston, TX 77019; (713) 527-0220
Peter Bennett, *Artistic Director*

Submission procedure: accepts unsolicited scripts with synopsis. **Types of material:** full-length plays, one-acts, plays for young audiences, cabaret/revues. **Special interests:** new plays by TX writers (not necessarily on regional themes). **Facilities:** Stage 2, 248 seats, arena stage; Stage 1, 195 seats, thrust stage. **Production considerations:** prefers small cast, simple set; plays for young audiences tour schools. **Best submission time:** year-round. **Response time:** 6 months. **Special programs:** Women Playwrights Repertory: festival of readings and full productions. Texas Playwrights Festival: festival of readings and full productions; negotiable remuneration for full productions; contact theatre for information.

STAGE WEST
Box 2587; Fort Worth, TX 76113; (817) 332-6265
Jerry Russell, *Artistic Director*

Submission procedure: no unsolicited scripts; synopsis and letter of inquiry. **Types of material:** full-length plays, translations, adaptations, musicals, cabaret/revues. **Special interests:** plays with universal themes; contemporary issues. **Facilities:** Stage West, 210 seats, flexible space. **Production considerations:** prefers cast limit of 9. **Best submission time:** Jan–Mar. **Response time:** 1 month letter; 3 months script.

STAGEWEST
One Columbus Center; Springfield, MA 01103; (413) 781-4470
Eric Hill, *Artistic Director*

Submission procedure: no unsolicited scripts; synopsis and letter of inquiry. **Types of material:** full-length plays, translations, adaptations. **Special interests:** new translations or adaptations of neglected classic and 20th-century European plays; adaptations of nondramatic material. **Facilities:** Mainstage, 480 seats, thrust stage; Studio, 99 seats, flexible stage. **Best submission time:** year-round. **Response time:** 3 months letter; 3 months script. **Special programs:** staged readings.

STAMFORD THEATRE WORKS
95 Atlantic St; Stamford, CT 06901; (203) 359-4414
Jane Desy, *Literary Manager*

Submission procedure: accepts unsolicited scripts; include cassette for musicals. **Types of material:** full-length plays, translations, adaptations, musicals. **Special interests:** plays that are innovative and thought-provoking, socially and culturally relevant, challenging and entertaining. **Facilities:** Center Stage, 150 seats, modified thrust stage. **Production considerations:** prefers small cast, unit set. **Best**

submission time: year-round. **Response time:** 6 months. **Special programs:** Plays-In-Process Series: 3 staged readings a year of unproduced plays or musicals for purpose of developing future STW productions.

STEPPENWOLF THEATRE COMPANY
1650 North Halsted St; Chicago, IL 60614; (312) 335-1888
Randall Arney, *Artistic Director*

Submission procedure: no unsolicited scripts; professional recommendation. **Types of material:** full-length plays, adaptations. **Facilities:** mainstage, 500 seats, proscenium stage; second stage, 100 seats, black box. **Production considerations:** cast limit of 8, 1 set. **Best submission time:** Oct–Dec. **Response time:** 6 months.

ST. LOUIS BLACK REPERTORY COMPANY
634 North Grand, Suite 10-F; St. Louis, MO 63103; (314) 534-3807
Ron Himes, *Producing Director*

Submission procedure: accepts unsolicited scripts. **Types of material:** full-length plays, plays for young audiences, musicals. **Special interests:** works by African-American and Third World playwrights. **Facilities:** 23rd Street Theater, 250 seats, proscenium stage. **Best submission time:** Jan–Aug. **Response time:** 2 months. **Special programs:** touring company presenting works for young audiences.

THE STREET THEATER
228 Fisher Ave, Room 226; White Plains, NY 10606; (914) 761-3307
Gray Smith, *Executive Director*

Submission procedure: no unsolicited scripts; synopsis and letter of inquiry. **Types of material:** one-acts, plays for young audiences. **Special interests:** ensemble pieces; plays for youth audiences (not children's theatre). **Facilities:** touring company. **Production considerations:** actors' theatre; minimal production demands; company plays in community rooms and on school stages. **Best submission time:** Nov–Feb. **Response time:** 2–4 weeks letter; 2–4 weeks script. **Special programs:** possibility of commissioning playwrights to write for or collaborate with Youth Company and Touring Company; write for information.

STUDIO ARENA THEATRE
710 Main St; Buffalo, NY 14202-1990; (716) 856-8025
Gavin Cameron-Webb, *Artistic Director*

Submission procedure: no unsolicited scripts; agent submission. **Types of material:** full-length plays, translations, adaptations. **Special interests:** plays of a theatrical nature; American history and culture; ethnic cultures, including plays about minorities. **Facilities:** Studio Arena Theatre, 637 seats, thrust stage. **Production considerations:** cast limit of 12; no fly system, limited wing space. **Best submission time:** year-round. **Response time:** 3 months.

THE STUDIO THEATRE
1333 P St NW; Washington, DC 20005; (202) 232-7267
Maynard Marshall, *Dramaturg*

Submission procedure: no unsolicited scripts; professional recommendation. **Types of material:** full-length plays, translations, adaptations, musicals. **Special interests:** American lyric realism; ethnic American themes; translations of new European and Asian plays. **Facilities:** The Studio Theatre, 200 seats, modified thrust stage; Secondstage, 50 seats, flexible stage. **Best submission time:** Aug–Sep, Dec–Jan. **Response time:** 2 months.

SUMMER THEATRE AT MOUNT HOLYOKE COLLEGE
South Hadley, MA 01075; (413) 538-2632
Michael Walker, *Producing Director*

Submission procedure: accepts unsolicited scripts from MA playwrights for Massachusetts Playwrights Project only (see below); others send synopsis and letter of inquiry. **Types of material:** full-length plays. **Special interests:** comedies. **Facilities:** Mainstage (tent theatre), 390 seats, arena stage. **Production considerations:** 18' x 18' arena stage. **Best submission time:** Jul–Nov. **Response time:** 1 month letter; 2–6 months script. **Special programs:** Massachusetts Playwrights Project: 1–2 full-length comedies by MA playwrights given 1-week workshop, culminating in public reading; possible production; playwright receives stipend, travel and expenses; submit scripts 1 Jul–30 Nov only.

SYRACUSE STAGE
820 East Genesee St; Syracuse, NY 13210; (315) 443-4008
Submissions to: 1014 Medinah Dr; Winter Haven, FL 33884
Howard Kerner, *Literary Manager*

Submission procedure: accepts unsolicited scripts; also accepts synopsis and letter of inquiry; submit to Howard Kerner at FL address. **Types of material:** full-length plays, translations. **Facilities:** John D. Archbold Theatre, 499 seats, flexible stage; The Experimental Theatre, 199 seats, proscenium stage. **Production considerations:** prefers cast limit of 8. **Best submission time:** May–Jul for unsolicited scripts; year-round for inquiries. **Response time:** 2 weeks letter; 2–4 weeks script.

TACOMA ACTORS GUILD
1323 South Yakima Ave; Tacoma, WA 98405; (206) 272-3107
Bruce K. Sevy, *Artistic Director*

Submission procedure: no unsolicited scripts; synopsis and letter of inquiry. **Types of material:** full-length plays, translations, adaptations. **Facilities:** Tacoma Actors Guild, 298 seats, modified thrust stage. **Production considerations:** prefers small cast; 1 set or unit set. **Best submission time:** spring–summer. **Response time:** 1–2 months letter; 6–12 months script.

TADA!
120 West 28th St; New York, NY 10001; (212) 627-1732
Janine Nina Trevens, *Artistic Director*

Submission procedure: accepts unsolicited scripts with a view to commissioning new works from selected playwrights. **Types of material:** plays and musicals for young audiences. **Special interests:** ensemble pieces to be performed by children aged 6–17 only; no adult characters. **Facilities:** The TADA! Theater, 95 seats, black box. **Best submission time:** Jan–Apr. **Response time:** 3 months. **Special programs:** Spring Staged Readings Series (see Prizes).

MARK TAPER FORUM
135 North Grand Ave; Los Angeles, CA 90012; (213) 972-7353
Frank Dwyer, *Literary Manager*

Submission procedure: no unsolicited scripts; description (not synopsis) of play, 5–10 sample pages and letter of inquiry. **Types of material:** full-length plays, one-acts, translations, adaptations, plays for young audiences, literary cabaret, performance art. **Facilities:** Mark Taper Forum, 742 seats, thrust stage; Taper, Too, 80–90 seats, flexible stage; Itchey Foot Ristorante, 100 seats, literary cabaret. **Best submission time:** year-round. **Response time:** 1–2 weeks letter; 8–10 weeks script. **Special programs:** Mark Taper Forum Developmental Programs (see Development).

TAPROOT THEATRE COMPANY
Box 31116; Seattle, WA 98103; (206) 781-9705
Scott L. Nolte, *Producing Artistic Director*

Submission procedure: no unsolicited scripts; 1-page synopsis, sample scene and letter of inquiry; include music sample for musical. **Types of material:** full-length plays, one-acts, plays for young audiences, musicals. **Special interests:** the application of "traditional Christian values" to contemporary social issues; Christmas plays; tourable one-acts for schools program only (see below). **Facilities:** Thrust Stage, 230 seats, thrust stage; Dinner Theatre, 180 seats, proscenium stage. **Production considerations:** prefers cast of 5–10. **Best submission time:** year-round. **Response time:** 2 weeks letter; 4–6 weeks script. **Special programs:** Touring Theatre: tours one-acts dealing with chemical dependency and other social issues to elementary, middle and senior high schools; cast limit of 2 men, 2 women; plays selected through theatre's normal submission process.

TENNESSEE REPERTORY THEATRE
427 Chestnut St; Nashville, TN 37203; (615) 244-4878
Don Jones, *Associate Artistic Director*

Submission procedure: no unsolicited scripts; synopsis, dialogue sample and letter of inquiry; include sample of music and lyrics for musical. **Types of material:** full-length plays, one-acts, translations, adaptations, musicals. **Special interests:** new

American musicals. **Facilities:** Polk Theatre, 1050 seats, proscenium stage. **Best submission time:** Jun–Sep. **Response time:** 4–6 weeks letter; 9–12 months script.

THALIA SPANISH THEATRE
Box 4368; Sunnyside, NY 11104; (718) 729-3880
Silvia Brito, *Artistic/Executive Director*

Submission procedure: accepts unsolicited scripts. **Types of material:** full-length plays, translations, adaptations. **Special interests:** plays in Spanish only. **Facilities:** Thalia Spanish Theatre, 74 seats, proscenium stage. **Production considerations:** cast limit of 6, 1 set. **Best submission time:** Dec–Jan. **Response time:** 3 months.

THEATER AT LIME KILN
Box 663; Lexington, VA 24450; (703) 463-7088
Don Baker, *Artistic Director*

Submission procedure: no unsolicited scripts; synopsis and letter of inquiry. **Types of material:** full-length plays, adaptations, musicals, cabaret/revues. **Special interests:** issues, language and music indigenous to VA and region; nontraditional staging. **Facilities:** The Kiln, 299 seats, outdoor theatre. **Production considerations:** prefers cast limit of 9; unit set. **Best submission time:** year-round. **Response time:** 1 month letter; 5 months script.

THE THEATER AT MONMOUTH
Box 385; Monmouth, ME 04259; (207) 933-2952
Richard Sewell, *Artistic Director*

Submission procedure: no unsolicited scripts; synopsis and letter of inquiry. **Types of material:** full-length plays, plays for young audiences. **Special interests:** traditional plays for young audiences. **Facilities:** Cumston Hall, 275 seats, raked thrust stage. **Production considerations:** simple set. **Best submission time:** Nov. **Response time:** 4–6 weeks letter; 4–6 months script.

THEATER BY THE BLIND
306 West 18th St; New York, NY 10011; (212) 243-4337
Ike Schambelan, *Artistic Director*

Submission procedure: accepts unsolicited scripts. **Types of material:** full-length plays, one-acts, translations, adaptations, plays for young audiences, musicals. **Special interests:** plays dealing with blindness. **Facilities:** no permanent facility. **Best submission time:** year-round. **Response time:** 6 weeks.

THE THEATRE CLUB OF THE PALM BEACHES
262 South Ocean Blvd; Manalapan, FL 33462; (407) 585-3404
Louis Tyrrell, *Producing Director*

Submission procedure: no unsolicited scripts; agent submission. **Types of material:** full-length plays. **Special interests:** contemporary issues and ideas.

Facilities: Lois Pope Theatre, 250 seats, thrust stage. **Production considerations:** cast of 2–6, 1 set. **Best submission time:** year-round. **Response time:** 3–4 months.

THEATRE DE LA JEUNE LUNE
Box 582176; Minneapolis, MN 55458; (612) 332-3968
Barbara Berlovitz Desbois, *Co-Artistic Director*

Submission procedure: no unsolicited scripts; synopsis and letter of inquiry. **Types of material:** full-length plays, translations, adaptations, musicals, cabaret/revues. **Special interests:** large-cast plays dealing with universal themes. **Facilities:** Hennepin Center for the Arts, 380 seats, modified thrust stage; second stage (in Minneapolis Van & Warehouse Company building), 500 seats, flexible stage. **Best submission time:** year-round. **Response time:** 8–10 weeks letter; 4 months script.

THEATER FACTORY ST. LOUIS
4977 Fyler Ave; St. Louis, MO 63139; (314) 832-1919
Hope Wurdack, *Artistic Director*

Submission procedure: accepts unsolicited scripts (include cassette for musicals). **Types of material:** full-length plays, translations, adaptations, plays for young audiences, musicals. **Special interests:** musicals; historical dramas. **Facilities:** Washington University's Edison Theatre, 400 seats, proscenium-thrust stage. **Production considerations:** modest production requirements. **Best submission time:** fall. **Response time:** 2 months.

THEATRE FOR A NEW AUDIENCE
220 East 4th St, 4th Floor; New York, NY 10009; (212) 505-8345

Submission procedure: no unsolicited scripts; direct solicitation from playwright. **Types of material:** full-length plays, one-acts. **Special interests:** works on social issues by women and playwrights of color. **Facilities:** Theatre at St. Clement's, 151 seats, proscenium stage. **Special programs:** commissioning program; participation by invitation only.

THEATER FOR THE NEW CITY
155 First Ave; New York, NY 10003; (212) 254-1109
Crystal Field and George Bartenieff, *Artistic Directors*

Submission procedure: accepts unsolicited scripts. **Types of material:** full-length plays, one-acts, cabaret/revues. **Special interests:** experimental American works; plays with poetry, music and dance; social issues. **Facilities:** Joyce and Seward Johnson Theater, 200 seats, flexible space; 2nd theatre, 66 seats, flexible space; 3rd theatre, 75 seats, flexible space; also cabaret space. **Best submission time:** summer. **Response time:** 9–12 months.

THEATRE IV

114 West Broad St; Richmond, VA 23220; (804) 783-1688
Bruce Miller, *Artistic Director*

Submission procedure: no unsolicited scripts; synopsis and letter of inquiry. **Types of material:** full-length plays, translations, adaptations, plays for young audiences. **Special interests:** plays for young audiences. **Facilities:** Empire Theatre, 604 seats (150 for adult-audience productions), proscenium stage; Little Theatre, 79 seats, endstage. **Production considerations:** moderate budget for all productions. **Best submission time:** year-round. **Response time:** 1 month letter; 6 months script.

THEATRE GROTTESCO

Box 32658; Detroit, MI 48232; (313) 961-5880
John Flax, *Co-Artistic Director*

Submission procedure: no unsolicited scripts; synopsis, dialogue sample and letter of inquiry. **Types of material:** full-length plays. **Special interests:** plays with broad themes, sparse text and emphasis on visual imagery for actors' theatre. **Facilities:** touring company. **Production considerations:** limit of 5 major roles, no set. **Best submission time:** May–Aug. **Response time:** 1–3 weeks letter; 3 months script.

THEATRE IN THE SQUARE

11 Whitlock Ave; Marietta, GA 30064; (404) 422-8369
Abigail Donahower, *Administrative Assistant*

Submission procedure: no unsolicited scripts; synopsis and letter of inquiry. **Types of material:** full-length plays, one-acts, translations, musicals. **Special interests:** world and southeastern premieres. **Facilities:** Mainstage, 225 seats, proscenium stage; Alley Stage, up to 80 seats, flexible stage. **Production considerations:** cast limit of 9, unit set; no fly space. **Best submission time:** Jan–Feb. **Response time:** 1 month letter (if interested); 6 months script.

THEATER OF THE FIRST AMENDMENT

Institute of the Arts; George Mason University; Fairfax, VA 22030-4444;
(703) 993-2195
Rick Davis, *Producing Artistic Director*

Submission procedure: no unsolicited scripts; synopsis, sample pages, resume and letter of inquiry. **Types of material:** full-length plays, one-acts, translations, adaptations. **Special interests:** cultural history made dramatic as distinct from history dramatized; large battles joined; hard questions asked; word and image stretched. **Facilities:** TheaterSpace, 150–200 seats, flexible space; LabSpace, 50–100 seats, flexible space. **Production considerations:** roles for younger actors welcome as TFA works with training program. **Best submission time:** Aug–Jan. **Response time:** 2 weeks letter; 3 months script. **Special programs:** readings, workshops and other development activities tailored to work under serious consideration for production.

THEATRE RHINOCEROS
2926 16th St; San Francisco, CA 94103; (415) 552-4100
Doug Holsclaw, *Literary Manager*

Submission procedure: no unsolicited scripts; synopsis and letter of inquiry. **Types of material:** full-length plays, one-acts, translations, adaptations, musicals, performance art. **Special interests:** works with gay and lesbian themes and characters only. **Facilities:** Mainstage, 112 seats, endstage; Studio, 57 seats, proscenium stage. **Best submission time:** year-round. **Response time:** 4–6 weeks letter; 3 months script.

THEATRE VIRGINIA
2800 Grove Ave; Richmond, VA 23221-2466; (804) 367-0840
William Gregg, *Artistic Director*

Submission procedure: no unsolicited scripts; synopsis, dialogue sample and letter of inquiry. **Types of material:** full-length plays, musicals. **Facilities:** Main Stage, 500 seats, proscenium stage. **Best submission time:** year-round. **Response time:** 2–3 weeks letter (if interested); 3–8 months script.

THEATRE WEST
3333 Cahuenga Blvd W; Los Angeles, CA 90068; (213) 851-4839
Jan Harris, *Workshop Moderator*

Submission procedure: no unsolicited scripts; scripts developed in weekly workshops open to member playwrights only; submit script, resume and letter of intent; dues of $34 per month upon acceptance. **Types of material:** full-length plays, one-acts, translations, adaptations, plays for young audiences, musicals. **Facilities:** Theatre West, 180 seats, proscenium stage. **Best submission time:** year-round. **Response time:** 1 month.

THEATREWORKS
1305 Middlefield Rd; Palo Alto, CA 94301; (415) 323-8311
Jeannie Barroga, *Literary Consultant*

Submission procedure: accepts unsolicited full-length plays and musicals; also accepts synopsis, dialogue sample and letter of inquiry with SASP for response; for translations and adaptations, send only letter of inquiry with SASP for response. **Types of material:** full-length plays, translations, adaptations, musicals. **Special interests:** works offering opportunities for multicultural casting. **Facilities:** Mountain View Center, 625 seats, proscenium stage; Stage II, 117 seats, thrust stage. **Best submission time:** Aug–Nov. **Response time:** 1 month letter; 4 months script. **Special programs:** Discovery Project: 6 play readings annually Sep–May.

THEATREWORKS/COLORADO
See Playwrights' Forum Awards in Prizes.

THEATREWORKS/USA

890 Broadway, 7th Floor; New York, NY 10003; (212) 677-5959
Barbara Pasternack, *Literary Manager*

Submission procedure: no unsolicited scripts; synopsis, sample scene(s) and songs (include cassette and lyric sheet) and letter of inquiry. **Types of material:** musicals for young audiences. **Special interests:** historical/biographical themes; fairy tales; contemporary issues. **Facilities:** Promenade Theatre, 398 seats, proscenium stage; also tours. **Production considerations:** cast limit of 5 (can play multiple roles), sets suitable for touring. **Best submission time:** summer. **Response time:** 1 month letter; 6 months script. **Special programs:** Theatreworks/USA Commissioning Program (see Prizes).

THEATRE X

Box 92206; Milwaukee, WI 53202; (414) 278-0555
John D. Schneider, *Co-Artistic Director*

Submission procedure: no unsolicited scripts; recommendation from professional familiar with company's work. **Types of material:** full-length plays. **Special interests:** plays written for or with the company; performance art and avant-garde works. **Facilities:** Black Box, 99 seats, flexible stage. **Production considerations:** small cast. **Best submission time:** year-round. **Response time:** 6 months.

THEATRICAL OUTFIT

Box 7098; Atlanta, GA 30309; (404) 872-0665
Phillip DePoy, *Artistic Director*

Submission procedure: no unsolicited scripts; synopsis and letter of inquiry. **Types of material:** full-length plays, translations, adaptations, music-theatre works. **Special interests:** music-theatre; no mainstream works. **Facilities:** Theatrical Outfit, 200 seats, black box. **Best submission time:** winter–spring. **Response time:** 2 months letter; 2 months script.

THREE RIVERS SHAKESPEARE FESTIVAL

1617 CL, University of Pittsburgh; Pittsburgh, PA 15260; (412) 624-7288
Ellen Kelson, *Literary Manager*

Submission procedure: no unsolicited scripts; synopsis and letter of inquiry. **Types of material:** full-length plays, translations, adaptations. **Special interests:** new translations and adaptations of classics; intercultural adaptations of Shakespeare; new plays of classical aspiration and scope. **Facilities:** Stephen Foster Memorial Theatre, 600 seats, modified proscenium stage; Studio Theatre, 100 seats, flexible stage. **Best submission time:** fall. **Response time:** 3 months letter; 3 months script.

TOUCHSTONE THEATRE
321 East 4th St; Bethlehem, PA 18015; (215) 867-1689
Bridget George, *Producing Director*

Submission procedure: no unsolicited scripts; letter of inquiry. **Types of material:** proposals for works to be created in collaboration with company's ensemble only. **Facilities:** Touchstone Theatre, 74 seats, black box. **Production considerations:** 18' x 20' playing area. **Best submission time:** year-round. **Response time:** 1 month.

TRINITY REPERTORY COMPANY
201 Washington St; Providence, RI 02903; (401) 521-1100
Richard Jenkins, *Artistic Director*

Submission procedure: no unsolicited scripts; agent submission. **Types of material:** full-length plays, translations, adaptations. **Facilities:** Upstairs Theatre, 440 seats, thrust stage; Downstairs Theatre, 297 seats, thrust stage. **Best submission time:** year-round. **Response time:** 12 months.

TRUSTUS THEATRE
Box 11721; Columbia, SC 29211; (803) 254-9732
Jim Thigpen, *Artistic Director*

Submission procedure: accepts unsolicited scripts. **Types of material:** full-length plays, one-acts, plays for young audiences. **Facilities:** Mainstage, 106 seats, flexible stage. **Production considerations:** cast limit of 8; prefers 1 set. **Best submission time:** 1 Jan–1 Apr. **Response time:** 6 months. **Special programs:** South Carolina Playwrights' Festival (see Prizes). Late Night Alternative Space: pieces 1 hour maximum length.

UNDERMAIN THEATRE
Box 141166; Dallas, TX 75214; (214) 748-3082
Willie Bogie, *Literary Manager*

Submission procedure: no unsolicited scripts; synopsis, dialogue sample and letter of inquiry. **Types of material:** full-length plays, one-acts, musicals. **Special interests:** experimental or innovative plays; language-oriented plays. **Facilities:** Undermain Theatre, 75 seats, flexible thrust stage. **Production considerations:** cast limit of 8. **Best submission time:** May–Jul. **Response time:** 3 months letter; 6 months script.

UNICORN THEATRE
See Unicorn Theatre National Playwright Award in Prizes.

VICTORY GARDENS THEATER
2257 North Lincoln Ave; Chicago, IL 60614; (312) 549-5788
Sandy Shinner, *Associate Artistic Director*

Submission procedure: accepts unsolicited scripts from Chicago-area writers only; others send synopsis, 10 pages of dialogue and letter of inquiry. **Types of material:** full-length plays, adaptations, musicals. **Special interests:** Chicago and Midwest playwrights; plays by women and writers of color. **Facilities:** Mainstage, 195 seats, thrust stage; Studio, 70 seats, proscenium stage. **Production considerations:** prefers cast limit of 10; small-cast musicals only; simple set. **Best submission time:** Mar–Jun. **Response time:** 1 month letter; 6 months script. **Special programs:** Readers Theater: staged readings of works-in-progress by area writers twice a month. Studio mini-series. The Marianne and Michael O'Shaughnessy Playwright Development Fund; participation in program by invitation only.

VINEYARD THEATRE
108 East 15th St; New York, NY 10003; (212) 353-3366
Douglas Aibel, *Artistic Director*

Submission procedure: accepts unsolicited scripts; include cassette for musicals. **Types of material:** full-length plays, musicals. **Special interests:** works with a strongly poetic flavor; plays which incorporate music in a unique way; musicals with strong narrative. **Facilities:** Vineyard Theatre, 70 seats, thrust stage; Vineyard at Union Square, 150 seats, flexible stage. **Best submission time:** year-round. **Response time:** 6 months. **Special programs:** New Works at the Vineyard: play reading series. Developmental workshop for new musicals.

VIRGINIA STAGE COMPANY
Box 3770; Norfolk, VA 23514; (804) 627-6988

Submission procedure: accepts unsolicited scripts; include cassette for musicals. **Types of material:** full-length plays, musicals. **Special interests:** plays by VA writers; poetic drama and comedy; no "kitchen-sink" plays. **Facilities:** Mainstage, 700 seats, proscenium stage; laboratory theatre, 99 seats, flexible space. **Best submission time:** May–Jul only. **Response time:** 6 months.

WEST COAST ENSEMBLE
Box 38728; Los Angeles, CA 90038; (213) 871-8673
Les Hanson, *Artistic Director*

Submission procedure: accepts unsolicited scripts. **Types of material:** full-length plays, one-acts, translations, adaptations, plays for young audiences, musicals, cabaret/revues. **Special interests:** world premieres; musicals; translations and adaptations. **Facilities:** Theatre A, 65 seats, proscenium stage; Theatre B, 99 seats, flexible stage. **Production considerations:** simple set; no fly space. **Best submission time:** Jun–Dec. **Response time:** 6 months. **Special programs:** Playwrights Unit: member playwrights meet weekly; staged readings of new plays developed in unit; local playwrights apply by submitting script. One-Act Play Festival: 9 one-acts presented over 6-week period in May–Jun; see One-Act Play Competition below. West Coast Ensemble One-Act Play Competition: 9 winners receive full production in One-Act Play Festival; unproduced, unpublished one-act; submit script with SASE or SASP for acknowledgment; *deadline:* 15 Nov 1992; *notification:* within 6 months; *dates:* May–Jun 1993. West Coast Ensemble Contests (see Prizes).

WHITE RIVER THEATRE FESTIVAL
Box 336; White River Junction, VT 05001-0336; (802) 296-2033
Stephen Legawiec, *Artistic Director*

Submission procedure: no unsolicited scripts; synopsis and letter of inquiry. **Types of material:** full-length plays, translations, adaptations, musicals. **Special interests:** highly theatrical, nonrealistic plays; fresh adaptations of classics. **Facilities:** Briggs Opera House, 250 seats, thrust stage. **Production considerations:** no fly space. **Best submission time:** Dec–Feb. **Response time:** 1 month letter; 3 months script.

WILLIAMSTOWN THEATRE FESTIVAL
Box 517; Williamstown, MA 01267; (413) 458-3200
Peter Hunt, *Artistic Director*

Submission procedure: no unsolicited scripts; synopsis, dialogue sample and letter of inquiry. **Types of material:** full-length plays, adaptations, musicals. **Facilities:** Main Stage, 479 seats, proscenium stage; 2nd stage, 96 seats, thrust stage. **Production considerations:** cast limit of 10 for musicals. **Best submission time:** Nov–15 Mar. **Response time:** 1 month letter; several months script. **Special programs:** New Play Staged Readings Series.

THE WILMA THEATER
2030 Sansom St; Philadelphia, PA 19103; (215) 963-0249
Janet E. Finegar, *Literary Manager*

Submission procedure: no unsolicited scripts; synopsis, dialogue sample and letter of inquiry. **Types of material:** full-length plays, translations, adaptations, musicals. **Special interests:** new translations and adaptations from the international repertoire with emphasis on innovative, bold staging; world premieres; ensemble works; works with poetic dimension; plays with music; multimedia works; social issues. **Facilities:** Wilma Theater, 100 seats, proscenium stage. **Production considerations:** prefers cast limit of 10, limited scene changes; stage 30' x 22'. **Best submission time:** year-round. **Response time:** 8–10 weeks letter; 4–6 months script.

WISDOM BRIDGE THEATRE
1559 West Howard St; Chicago, IL 60626; (312) 743-0486
Jose Calleja, *Literary Manager*

Submission procedure: no unsolicited scripts; synopsis and letter of inquiry. **Types of material:** full-length plays, translations, adaptations, musicals. **Special interests:** contemporary social and political issues; plays by women and minorities. **Facilities:** Wisdom Bridge Theatre, 196 seats, proscenium stage. **Production considerations:**

prefers cast limit of 8. **Best submission time:** year-round. **Response time:** 1–3 weeks letter; 3 months script.

THE WOMEN'S PROJECT AND PRODUCTIONS
220 West 42nd St, 18th Floor; New York, NY 10036; (212) 382-2750
Susan Bougetz, *Literary Manager*

Submission procedure: no unsolicited scripts; synopsis, 10-page dialogue sample and letter of inquiry with SASE for response. **Types of material:** full-length plays. **Special interests:** plays by women only. **Facilities:** Judith Anderson Theatre, 99 seats, proscenium stage. **Best submission time:** year-round. **Response time:** 2–4 weeks letter; 3–6 months script. **Special programs:** developmental program including play readings, work-in-progress presentations and directors' forum; participation by invitation only. Commissioning program.

WOOLLY MAMMOTH THEATRE COMPANY
1401 Church St NW; Washington, DC 20005; (202) 393-3939
Greg Tillman, *Literary Manager*

Submission procedure: accepts unsolicited scripts. **Types of material:** full-length plays, translations, adaptations. **Special interests:** offbeat topics and styles; nonrealism. **Facilities:** Woolly Mammoth, 135 seats, thrust stage. **Production considerations:** small cast, minimal staging requirements. **Best submission time:** year-round. **Response time:** 4 months.

WORCESTER FOOTHILLS THEATRE COMPANY
074 Worcester Center; Worcester, MA 01608; (508) 754-3314
Marc P. Smith, *Artistic Director*

Submission procedure: no unsolicited scripts; synopsis and letter of inquiry. **Types of material:** full-length plays, translations, adaptations, musicals. **Special interests:** plays suited to multigenerational audiences. **Facilities:** Worcester Foothills Theatre, 349 seats, proscenium stage. **Production considerations:** prefers cast limit of 10, simple set; small-scale musicals only. **Best submission time:** year-round. **Response time:** 3–4 weeks letter; 1–4 months script.

YALE REPERTORY THEATRE
Box 1903A, Yale Station; New Haven, CT 06520-7434; (203) 432-1560
Resident Dramaturg

Submission procedure: no unsolicited scripts; synopsis and letter of inquiry. **Types of material:** full-length plays, translations, adaptations, music-theatre works. **Special interests:** new work; new translations of classics; contemporary foreign plays. **Facilities:** Yale Repertory Theatre, 487 seats, modified thrust stage; University Theatre, 654 seats, proscenium stage. **Best submission time:** year-round. **Response time:** 6 weeks letter; 3 months script.

YOUNG PLAYWRIGHTS FESTIVAL

See Prizes.

ZACHARY SCOTT THEATRE CENTER

Listing alphabetized under S.

Prizes

What competitions are included here?

All the playwriting contests we've heard of that offer prizes of at least $200 or, in the case of awards to playwrights under the age of 19, the equivalent in production or publication. Most awards for which the playwright cannot apply—the Joseph Kesselring Award, the Pulitzer Prize—are not listed. Exceptions are made when, as with the Susan Smith Blackburn Prize, the nominating process allows playwrights to encourage nomination of their work by theatre professionals who are familiar with it.

How can I give myself the best chance of winning?

Don't wait till the last minute. Write for guidelines and application forms several months ahead. Be aware that a few contests will change their rules or their deadlines after this book has been published. Follow the guidelines precisely. Send your script in well before the deadline, when the readers are fresh and enthusiastic rather than buried by an avalanche of submissions. Except in the few cases where sponsors note that scripts won't be returned, always send an SASE with your submission.

Should I enter contests that charge entry fees?

It's true that a number of listings in this section (and in other sections as well) require a payment of a fee. You need not conclude from this that the whole world is out to rip off playwrights. It is unfortunately the case that many contest sponsors do not secure sufficient funding to cover their costs, which are considerable. Some playwrights as a matter of principle will not pay fees, and are prepared to protest their imposition. Other writers are willing to add an entry fee to the costs of copying and postage as a part of doing business. It's up to you.

Aren't new playwriting contests being created all the time?

Yes. As soon as we hear about them, we publish details of major new contests in the "Opportunities" column of our monthly magazine *American Theatre*. See Membership and Service Organizations and Useful Publications for other sources of current contest news.

ACTORS' GUILD OF LEXINGTON NEW PLAY CONTEST
161 North Mill St; Lexington, KY 40507; (606) 233-7330
Vic Chaney, *Artistic Manager*

Types of material: full-length plays, one-acts. **Frequency:** annual. **Remuneration:** 3 awards of $400; production in regular season. **Guidelines:** unproduced, unpublished play; special interest in plays addressing contemporary social, political and personal dilemmas; prefers small cast, simple set; 2-submission limit; send SASE for information sheet. **Submission procedure:** script only. **Deadline:** *1st deadline:* 15 Nov 1992; *2nd deadline:* TBA (1 Jul in 1992). **Notification:** 15 Mar 1993; TBA (1 Nov in 1992).

ALLIANCE REPERTORY COMPANY
ANNUAL ONE-ACT PLAYWRITING CONTEST
3204 West Magnolia Blvd; Burbank, CA 91505; (818) 566-7935
Elkanah J. Burns, *Dramaturge*

Types of material: one-acts. **Frequency:** annual. **Remuneration:** $500; possible production in annual one-act series with royalty. **Guidelines:** play not produced professionally. **Submission procedure:** script only. **Deadline:** 1 Jan 1993.

AMERICAN INDEPENDENT SCREENPLAY COMPETITION
Box 16526; Hattiesburg, MS 39402; (601) 268-2058
Dixon McDowell, *President*

Types of material: screenplays. **Frequency:** annual. **Remuneration:** TBA (3 awards, 1 of $5000, 1 of $3000, 1 of $2000 in 1992). **Guidelines:** original screenplay 90–

120 pages long, not optioned, purchased or produced; write for entry form. **Submission procedure:** 2 copies of screenplay and 1-page synopsis; entry form, release agreement, $45 fee. **Deadline:** TBA (1 Jun in 1992). **Notification:** TBA (1 Sep in 1992).

AMERICAN MUSICAL THEATRE FESTIVAL COMPETITION
8025 Santa Monica Blvd, #1219; West Hollywood, CA 90046; (213) 663-1912
Mikel Pippi, *Executive Director*

Types of material: full-length musicals, including adaptations. **Frequency:** annual. **Remuneration:** $2000; possible production; runners-up eligible for series of directed readings. **Guidelines:** unproduced, unpublished work with completed score that has potential for commercial production and has not won major competition. **Submission procedure:** no unsolicited scripts; write for submission requirements and entry form; $15 fee. **Deadline:** 31 Dec 1992. **Notification:** 1 Apr 1993 for finalists; 1 Jun 1993 for winner.

AMERICAN TRANSLATORS ASSOCIATION AWARDS
Honors Division; 324 North Jordan; Indiana University; Bloomington, IN 47405;
     (812) 855-3555
Breon Mitchell, *Chair, ATA Honors and Awards*

Lewis Galantiere Literary Translation Prize

Biennial contest; next deadline 15 Mar 1994.

German Literary Translation Prize

Types of material: translations of full-length and one-act plays. **Frequency:** biennial. **Remuneration:** $1000. **Guidelines:** translation from German published in U.S. by American publisher in past 2 years as single volume or in collection. **Submission procedure:** translation nominated by publisher; 2 copies of book plus 10 consecutive pages of German original, extra jacket and any advertising copy; brief vita of translator. **Deadline:** 15 Mar 1993. **Notification:** Aug 1993.

ARROW ROCK LYCEUM THEATRE PLAYWRIGHTS COMPETITION
Main St; Arrow Rock, MO 65320; (816) 837-3311
Michael Bollinger, *Artistic Director*

Types of material: full-length plays. **Frequency:** biennial. **Remuneration:** $1000; production; travel to attend rehearsals. **Guidelines:** unpublished, unproduced play that deals with "the American dream"; write for guidelines. **Submission procedure:** script with synopsis and resume. **Deadline:** 31 Dec 1992. **Notification:** Apr 1993.

ASF TRANSLATION PRIZE
The American-Scandinavian Foundation; 725 Park Ave; New York, NY 10021;
  (212) 879-9779
Publishing Office

Types of material: translations. **Frequency:** annual. **Remuneration:** $2000; publication of excerpt in *Scandinavian Review.* **Guidelines:** unpublished translation from a Scandinavian language into English of work written by a Scandinavian author born after 1891; manuscript must be at least 50 pages long if prose, 25 pages if poetry, and must be conceived as part of a book; write for guidelines. **Submission procedure:** 4 copies of translation, 1 of original; permission letter from copyright holder. **Deadline:** 1 Jun 1993. **Notification:** fall 1993.

ASIAN AMERICAN PLAYWRIGHTS' CONTEST
Northwest Asian American Theatre; 409 Seventh Ave S; Seattle, WA 98104;
  (206) 340-1445
Kathy Hsieh, *Managing Director*

Types of material: TBA. **Frequency:** annual. **Remuneration:** $500; production; travel and housing to attend performance. **Guidelines:** Asian-American themes; play that has not received professional full production; type of material changes each year; write for guidelines. **Submission procedure:** see guidelines. **Deadline:** 15 Mar 1993. **Notification:** Jun 1993.

ATHE PLAYWRIGHTS WORKSHOP
Box 2250; Mississippi State, MS 39762; (601) 325-7952
Jeffery Scott Elwell, *Coordinator*

Types of material: one-acts, adaptations. **Frequency:** annual. **Remuneration:** cash award to winning playwright(s) of at least $200; staged reading at 1993 Playwrights' Theater Conference in Philadelphia. **Guidelines:** playwright must be enrolled college student and must attend reading; 1 submission; write for guidelines. **Submission procedure:** completed application with 2 copies of script and SASP. **Deadline:** 31 Dec 1992. **Notification:** Apr 1993. **Dates:** 4–7 Aug 1993.

BAKER'S PLAYS HIGH SCHOOL PLAYWRITING CONTEST
Baker's Plays; 100 Chauncy St; Boston, MA 02111; (617) 482-1280
Raymond Pape, *Associate Editor*

Types of material: full-length plays, one-acts, plays for young audiences. **Frequency:** annual. **Remuneration:** 1st prize $500 and publication in Baker's Plays' *Best Plays from the High School* series; 2nd prize $250; 3rd prize $100. **Guidelines:** high school student, sponsored by a high school drama or English teacher; play suitable for production on high school stages, preferably about "the high school experience," which has been produced or given public reading; write for guidelines. **Submission procedure:** script with signature of sponsoring teacher. **Deadline:** 31 Jan 1993. **Notification:** May 1993.

MARGARET BARTLE PLAYWRITING AWARD
Community Children's Theatre; 8021 East 129th Terr; Grandview, MO 64030;
   (816) 761-5775
Blanche Sellens, *Chairman, Playwriting Contest*

Types of material: plays and musicals for young audiences. **Frequency:** annual.
Remuneration: $500. **Guidelines:** unpublished, unproduced work suitable for
grades 1–6; 55–60 minutes; 8-character limit; all parts played by adult women.
Submission procedure: script only; include cassette for musicals. **Deadline:** 30 Jan
1993. **Notification:** Apr 1993.

BASIC ISSUES FORUM PLAYWRIGHT'S COMPETITION
Washington & Jefferson College; 45 South Lincoln; Washington, PA 15301;
   (412) 222-4400
William Cameron, *Director of Student Theater*

Biennial competition; deadline for 1993 forum, dealing with the existence of
natural evil, will probably be 2 Sep 1993, but could be earlier; send SASE for
information.

BAY AREA RADIO DRAMA (BARD) COMMISSIONS
Box 5615; Berkeley, CA 94705; (510) 849-3500
Erik Bauersfeld, *Director*

Types of material: radio plays; plays and monologues suitable for adaptation to
radio. **Frequency:** ongoing. **Remuneration:** commissioning fee, contingent on
funding (past commissioning grants $500 plus $500 if broadcast, or $1000 fee for
ready script); possible local broadcast with national distribution; possible
recommendation to overseas broadcasting companies. **Guidelines:** CA writer only;
90-minute maximum; monologues 5–60 minutes; material not written or adapted
for radio must be accompanied by statement indicating how writer would adapt
it; writer encouraged to participate in production process. **Submission procedure:**
script and resume. **Deadline:** ongoing.

BBC WORLD SERVICE DRAMA PLAYWRITING COMPETITION
Bush House; P.O. Box 76; Strand; London, England WC2B 4PH

Types of material: radio plays. **Frequency:** biennial. **Remuneration:** £1200 (about
$2200); radio production; possible publication; possible radio production and
publication for runners-up. **Guidelines:** writer resident outside U.K.; original,
unpublished radio play, approximately 1 hour long and not on offer for
publication or broadcasting in any other form or medium; limit of 6 central
characters; 1 submission; write for guidelines and entry form. **Submission
procedure:** completed entry form and script. **Deadline:** 30 Nov 1992.

BEVERLY HILLS THEATRE GUILD–
JULIE HARRIS PLAYWRIGHT AWARD
2815 North Beachwood Dr; Los Angeles, CA 90068; (213) 465-2703
Marcella Meharg, *Coordinator*

Types of material: full-length plays. **Frequency:** annual. **Remuneration:** $5000 1st prize plus $2000 to help finance production in Los Angeles area within 1 year; $1000 2nd prize; $500 3rd prize. **Guidelines:** U.S. citizen; 1 submission, not previously submitted, published, produced or optioned, or winner of major competition. **Submission procedure:** completed application and script; send SASE for application and guidelines. **Deadline:** 1 Nov 1992. **Notification:** Jun 1993.

BIENNIAL PROMISING PLAYWRIGHT AWARD
Colonial Players; 108 East St; Annapolis, MD 21401; (301) 268-7373
Award Coordinator

Types of material: full-length plays. **Frequency:** biennial. **Remuneration:** $750; possible production. **Guidelines:** play, not produced professionally, suitable for arena stage; 90-minute length; cast limit of 20, prefers 12 or fewer; send SASE for rules. **Submission procedure:** script only. **Deadline:** 31 Dec 1992. **Notification:** Aug 1993.

THE SUSAN SMITH BLACKBURN PRIZE
3239 Avalon Pl; Houston, TX 77019; (713) 522-8529
Emilie S. Kilgore, *Board of Directors*

Types of material: full-length plays. **Frequency:** annual. **Remuneration:** $5000 1st prize plus signed print, made especially for Blackburn Prize, of drawing by Willem de Kooning; $1000 2nd prize; $500 to other finalists. **Guidelines:** woman playwright of any nationality writing in English; unproduced play or play produced within one year of deadline. **Submission procedure:** no submission by playwright; professional artistic director, literary manager or dramaturg nominates play and submits 2 copies of script; playwright may bring script to attention of eligible nominator. **Deadline:** 20 Sep 1992. **Notification:** Jan 1993 for finalists; Feb 1993 for winner.

BLOOMINGTON PLAYWRIGHTS PROJECT CONTEST
310 West 7th St; Bloomington, IN 47404; (812) 334-1188
Gretchen Smith, *Literary Manager*

Types of material: full-length plays, musicals. **Frequency:** annual. **Remuneration:** $250; staged reading; production. **Guidelines:** unpublished, unproduced play suitable for production in small 75-seat theatre; simple set; write for guidelines. **Submission procedure:** script with cover letter and $5 reading fee; cassette for musicals. **Deadline:** 15 Oct 1992. **Notification:** Feb 1993.

WALDO M. AND GRACE C. BONDERMAN IUPUI PLAYWRITING COMPETITION FOR YOUNG AUDIENCES

(formerly IUPUI National Playwriting for Youth Competition and Symposium)
IUPUI University Theatre; 525 North Blackford St; Indianapolis, IN 46202;
(317) 274-2095
Mark McCreary, *Literary Manager*

Types of material: plays for young audiences. **Frequency:** biennial. **Remuneration:** 4 prizes of $1000; showcase reading at National Youth Theatre Playwriting Symposium; travel, room and board for residency. **Guidelines:** well-crafted play with strong storyline, compelling characters and careful attention to language; unpublished play not less than 45 minutes long and not previously produced by Equity company; writer must be available for week-long residency ending in symposium. **Submission procedure:** send SASE for entry form and guidelines. **Deadline:** 1 Sep 1992. **Notification:** Dec 1992. **Dates:** 21–27 Feb 1993.

CAC NEW PLAY COMPETITION

Contemporary Arts Center; Box 30498; New Orleans, LA 70190; (504) 523-1216

Types of material: full-length plays, musicals. **Frequency:** annual. **Remuneration:** $500 1st prize; staged reading for top 3 works. **Guidelines:** AL, AR, GA, LA or MS resident; unpublished full-length work, not produced professionally and not previously submitted; 2-submission limit. **Submission procedure:** send SASE for entry form. **Deadline:** 1 Nov 1992. **Notification:** Mar 1993.

CALIFORNIA PLAYWRIGHTS COMPETITION

South Coast Repertory; Box 2197; Costa Mesa, CA 92628-2197; (714) 957-2602
John Glore, *Project Director*

Types of material: full-length plays. **Frequency:** annual. **Remuneration:** $5000 1st prize, $3000 2nd prize; production with negotiable royalty or workshop/reading in theatre's spring California Play Festival; travel, housing and per diem to attend rehearsals. **Guidelines:** playwright whose principal residence is in CA; play not professionally produced or optioned; previous entries ineligible; 2-submission limit; write for guidelines. **Submission procedure:** completed application and script; synopsis of no more than 300 words; cast list; 1-paragraph bio including information on CA residency. **Deadline:** TBA (15 Dec in 1991).

CALIFORNIA YOUNG PLAYWRIGHTS CONTEST

Playwrights Project; Box 2068; San Diego, CA 92112; (619) 232-6188
Deborah Salzer, *Director*

Types of material: full-length plays, one-acts, musicals. **Frequency:** annual. **Remuneration:** cash prize ($100 in 1992), production or staged reading, travel and housing to attend rehearsals and 1-year Dramatists Guild membership to each of several winners (4 in 1991); entrants receive written evaluation of work. **Guidelines:** CA writer or collaborating writers under 19 years of age as of deadline date; 10-page minimum; previous submissions ineligible; write for guidelines. **Submission procedure:** script with cover letter and brief bio; script will not be returned. **Deadline:** 1 Apr 1993. **Notification:** late fall 1993.

CELEBRATION '94: A FESTIVAL OF DRAMA
Lodi Arts Commission; 125 South Hutchins St, Suite D; Lodi, CA 95240;
(209) 369-4952
Don Levy, *Commissioner*

Types of material: full-length plays, plays for young audiences, musicals. **Frequency:** biennial. **Remuneration:** $1000 for full-length play or musical, $500 for play for young audiences; production; travel, housing and board to attend rehearsals. **Guidelines:** unproduced, unpublished work; write for guidelines. **Submission procedure:** script and entry form. **Deadline:** 1 Apr 1993; no submissions before 1 Jan 1993. **Notification:** fall 1993.

JANE CHAMBERS PLAYWRITING AWARD
English Department; Box 1852; Brown University; Providence, RI 02912;
(401) 351-5294
Tori Haring-Smith, *Coordinator*

Types of material: full-length plays, one-acts, performance-art texts. **Frequency:** annual. **Remuneration:** $500; rehearsed rea
ding at national conference of Association for Theatre in Higher Education; travel to attend rehearsals; student submissions eligible for $100 Student Award. **Guidelines:** award sponsored by ATHE's Women and Theatre Program; 1 submission by a woman that reflects a feminist perspective and contains a majority of roles for women; experimentation with dramatic form encouraged; no one-woman shows; winner must be available to attend part of preconference in late Jul and reading in early Aug; write for guidelines. **Submission procedure:** script with synopsis; resume; if possible, letter of endorsement by theatre professional familiar with writer's work; optional SASP for acknowledgment of receipt. **Deadline:** 15 Feb 1993. **Notification:** 30 May 1993.

CHICANO/LATINO LITERARY CONTEST
Department of Spanish and Portuguese; University of California at Irvine;
Irvine, CA 92717; (714) 856-5702, -8429
Juan Bruce-Novoa, *Director*

Prize awarded for different genres (novel, short story, poetry, drama) in successive years; next deadline for drama 31 May 1994.

CLAUDER COMPETITION FOR EXCELLENCE IN PLAYWRITING
TheatreWorks, Box 635, Boston, MA 02117; (617) 497-1340
Kathleen Donohue, *Artistic Director*

Biennial contest; next deadline 29 Jun 1994.

COE COLLEGE NEW WORKS FOR THE STAGE COMPETITION

Department of Theatre Arts; 1220 First Ave NE; Cedar Rapids, IA 52402;
(319) 438-1029
Susan Wolverton, *Chair, Playwriting Festival*

Types of material: full-length plays, plays for young audiences. **Frequency:** annual, contingent on funding. **Remuneration:** $325; staged reading; travel, room and board for 1-week residency during Jan term. **Guidelines:** unproduced, unpublished play dealing with theme of Playwriting Festival and Symposia: "Main Street America: Rural and Small Town Life in the United States" (theme different each year); festival includes workshops and public discussions; no translations, adaptations or musicals; send SASE for guidelines. **Submission procedure:** script only. **Deadline:** 1 Sep 1992. **Notification:** 1 Nov 1992.

COLORADO CHRISTIAN UNIVERSITY
NEW CHRISTIAN PLAYS COMPETITION

Department of Theatre; Colorado Christian University; 180 South Garrison St;
Lakewood, CO 80226; (303) 238-5386
Patrick Rainville Dorn, *Theatre Coordinator*

Types of material: full-length plays, one-acts, musicals, plays for young audiences. **Frequency:** annual. **Remuneration:** $200; full or workshop production or staged reading for winner and 3 finalists. **Guidelines:** unpublished work, not produced professionally, of interest to Christian churches, colleges or drama groups; 4 submission categories are Biblical Adaptation, Holiday, History/Tradition and Contemporary. **Submission procedure:** send SASE for guidelines. **Deadline:** 31 Jan 1993. **Notification:** 1 Apr 1993.

CHRISTOPHER COLUMBUS SCREENPLAY DISCOVERY AWARDS

(formerly Screenplay Discovery Award)
433 North Camden Dr, Suite 600; Beverly Hills, CA 90210; (310) 288-1881
Carlos de Abreu and Janice Pennington, *Co-Founders*

Types of material: screenplays. **Frequency:** annual. **Remuneration:** options, from $1000–10,000. **Guidelines:** up to 12 screenplays a year selected on a monthly basis to be optioned and developed; writer receives written evaluation from professional story analyst and has personal or phone meeting with qualified film industry professional to discuss possible rewrites; 2nd draft of screenplay introduced to agents, producers and studios; "Discovery of the Month" screenplay submitted to panel of industry experts who select prizewinners; unproduced feature screenplay not under current option; write for guidelines. **Submission procedure:** screenplay with completed application and $45 fee. **Deadline:** 1 Jun 1993.

CORNERSTONE COMPETITION

The Penumbra Theatre Company; The Martin Luther King Bldg;
270 North Kent St; St. Paul, MN 55102; (612) 224-4601
Lou Bellamy, *Artistic Director*

Types of material: full-length plays. **Frequency:** annual. **Remuneration:** $2000;
workshop with playwright in residence; mainstage production. **Guidelines:** play
dealing with the Pan African and/or African-American experience which has not
received professional full production; write for guidelines. **Submission procedure:**
script and resume. **Deadline:** 1 Mar 1993. **Notification:** 1 Sep 1993.

THE CUNNINGHAM PRIZE FOR PLAYWRITING

Theatre School, DePaul University; 2135 North Kenmore;
    Chicago, IL 60614-4111; (312) 362-6150
Lisa A. Quinn

Types of material: full-length plays, plays for young audiences, musicals.
Frequency: annual. **Remuneration:** $5000. **Guidelines:** Chicago-area playwright
only; play which "affirms the centrality of religion, broadly defined, and the
human quest for meaning, truth and community"; write for guidelines.
Submission procedure: script and brief statement making connection to purpose
of prize. **Deadline:** 1 Sep 1992. **Notification:** 15 Dec 1992.

DAYTON PLAYHOUSE FUTUREFEST

1301 East Siebenthaler Ave; Dayton, OH 45414; (513) 277-0144
Jim Payne, *Managing Director*

Types of material: full-length plays. **Frequency:** annual. **Remuneration:** 3 plays
selected for full production, 3 for reading at Jul 1993 FutureFest weekend;
possible travel, room and board to attend rehearsals; judges view full productions
and select winner of $1000 1st prize; 2 runners-up receive $500; 1st-place
production given additional performances. **Guidelines:** unproduced, unpublished
play; send SASE for guidelines. **Submission procedure:** script with resume.
Deadline: 30 Sep 1992. **Notification:** Apr 1993.

DC ART/WORKS PLAYWRIGHTS COMPETITION

410 8th St NW, Suite 400; Washington, DC 20004; (202) 727-3412
Ulysses Garner, *Executive Director*

Types of material: full-length plays, one-acts. **Frequency:** no set dates. **Remuneration:** $1000–2000; production by organization's Performing Arts Ensemble, under
professional supervision; travel to attend production. **Guidelines:** unproduced,
unpublished play by playwright over age of 18 dealing with inner-city issues;
maximum length of 90 minutes; cast limit of 8; production requirements suitable
for touring. **Submission procedure:** 6 copies of script. **Deadline:** 15 Feb 1993.
Notification: 1 Apr 1993.

DEEP SOUTH WRITERS CONFERENCE

c/o English Department; Box 44691; University of Southwestern Louisiana;
   Lafayette, LA 70504-4691
John Fiero, *Director*

Miller Award

Types of material: full-length plays. **Frequency:** biennial. **Remuneration:** $1500.
Guidelines: unpublished play, readily adaptable for film or TV, dealing with some
aspect of the English Renaissance and/or the life of Edward de Vere, Earl of
Oxford. **Submission procedure:** script with brief bio; write for rules. **Deadline:** 15
Jul 1993. **Notification:** Sep 1993.

Paul T. Nolan One-Act Play Award

Types of material: one-acts for young and adult audiences. **Frequency:** annual.
Remuneration: $200 1st prize, $100 2nd prize; possible publication in DSWC
Chapbook. **Guidelines:** original, unpublished play not produced commercially;
prefers plays for adult audiences; publication rights to winning plays reserved
until 1 Jun 1994; 3-submission limit; write for guidelines. **Submission procedure:**
script with brief bio and $5 fee for each submission; script will not be returned.
Deadline: 15 Jul 1993. **Notification:** Sep 1993.

James H. Wilson Full-Length Play Award

Types of material: full-length plays for young and adult audiences. **Frequency:**
annual. **Remuneration:** $300 1st prize, $200 2nd prize. **Guidelines:** 1 original,
unpublished submission not produced commercially; prefers plays for adult
audiences; write for guidelines. **Submission procedure:** script with brief bio and
$15 fee. **Deadline:** 15 Jul 1993. **Notification:** Sep 1993.

DRURY COLLEGE ONE-ACT PLAY COMPETITION

Drury College; 900 North Benton Ave; Springfield, MO 65802; (417) 865-8234
Sandy Asher, *Writer-in-Residence*

Types of material: one-acts. **Frequency:** biennial. **Remuneration:** $300 1st prize,
$150 2nd prize; possible production; winners recommended to the Open Eye:
New Stagings in NYC. **Guidelines:** unproduced play; small cast, simple set; 1 submission; send SASE for guidelines. **Submission procedure:** script only. **Deadline:**
1 Dec 1992. **Notification:** 1 Apr 1993.

DUBUQUE FINE ARTS PLAYERS
NATIONAL ONE-ACT PLAYWRITING CONTEST

569 South Grandview Ave; Dubuque, IA 52003; (319) 582-5558
Sally Ryan, *Coordinator*

Types of material: one-acts. **Frequency:** annual. **Remuneration:** $300 1st prize,
$200 2nd prize, $100 3rd prize; possible production for all 3 plays. **Guidelines:**
unproduced, unpublished play not more than 40 minutes long; no submission

limit but playwright may not win more than 1 prize; send SASE for guidelines. **Submission procedure:** completed application and script; $5 entry fee per submission. **Deadline:** 31 Jan 1993; no submission before 1 Nov 1992. **Notification:** 30 Jun 1993.

DAVID JAMES ELLIS MEMORIAL AWARD
Theatre Americana; Box 245; Altadena, CA 91001; (818) 397-1740
Gina Walton, *Chair, Playreading Committee*

Types of material: full-length plays. **Frequency:** annual. **Remuneration:** $500 to best of 4 plays selected for production; color videotape of produced play. **Guidelines:** unpublished original play, not more than 2 hours in length; prefers American writers and plays on the American scene; 2-submission limit; write for guidelines. **Submission procedure:** script only. **Deadline:** 31 Jan 1993.

ELMIRA COLLEGE PLAYWRITING AWARD
Department of Theatre; Elmira College, Elmira, NY 14901; (607) 734-3911
Amnon Kabatchnik, *Artistic Director*

Biennial contest; next deadline TBA (1 Jun in 1992).

EMERGING PLAYWRIGHT AWARD
Playwright's Preview Productions; 1160 Fifth Ave, #304; New York, NY 10029; (212) 996-7287
Deborah Goodman, *Literary Manager*

Types of material: full-length plays, one-acts. **Frequency:** annual. **Remuneration:** $500; production; travel to attend rehearsals. **Guidelines:** play unproduced in New York; submissions by minority playwrights encouraged. **Submission procedure:** script with production history of play (if any); bio. **Deadline:** ongoing.

LAWRENCE S. EPSTEIN PLAYWRITING AWARD
280 Park Ave South, #22E; New York, NY 10010; (212) 979-0865
Lawrence S. Epstein, *Director*

Types of material: full-length plays, one-acts. **Frequency:** annual. **Remuneration:** $250. **Guidelines:** unproduced play on specified theme; send SASE for information. **Submission procedure:** script with $1 fee. **Deadline:** 31 Mar 1993; no submission before 1 Jan 1993. **Notification:** Dec 1993.

FAMILY ONE-ACT PLAY FESTIVAL
Theatre with a Message; Box 22551; Nashville, TN 37202-0125; (800) 767-7699
Don Breedwell, *Executive Director*

Types of material: one-acts, including plays for young audiences and musicals. **Frequency:** annual. **Remuneration:** $500; production; travel, housing and board to attend rehearsals. **Guidelines:** unproduced work, not more than 45 minutes long; family themes, situations or issues; "reasonable" cast size; write for guidelines. **Submission procedure:** script; cassette for musical; entry form. **Deadline:** 1 Dec 1992. **Notification:** Mar 1993.

FERNDALE REPERTORY THEATRE
NEW WORKS COMPETITION
Box 892; Ferndale, CA 95536-0892; (707) 725-4636
Clinton Rebik, *Artistic Director*

Types of material: full-length plays. **Frequency:** annual. **Remuneration:** production with $250 royalty; set of all photos and promotional materials. **Guidelines:** unpublished play which has not received full production; write for guidelines. **Submission procedure:** script with cast list and synopsis; resume; SASP. **Deadline:** 15 Oct 1992. **Notification:** 15 May 1993.

FESTIVAL OF FIRSTS PLAYWRITING COMPETITION
Sunset Center; Box 5066; Carmel, CA 93921; (408) 624-3996
Director

Types of material: full-length plays. **Frequency:** annual. **Remuneration:** up to $1000; possible production. **Guidelines:** unproduced play; send SASE for guidelines. **Submission procedure:** script with cast list and synopsis; completed entry form; $5 entry fee. **Deadline:** TBA (31 Aug in 1992).

FESTIVAL OF SOUTHERN THEATRE
PLAYWRITING COMPETITION
Department of Theatre Arts; University of Mississippi; University, MS 38677;
   (601) 232-5816
Scott McCoy, *Producing Director*

Types of material: full-length plays. **Frequency:** annual. **Remuneration:** up to 3 awards: $1000; production; travel, room and board to attend rehearsals; post-production critique by representatives of national critical press. **Guidelines:** southern playwright or markedly southern theme; playwright available for Jul residency; 1 submission, unpublished and not professionally produced. **Submission procedure:** script with bio. **Deadline:** 30 Nov 1992. **Notification:** 28 Feb 1993.

FMCT NATIONAL PLAYWRIGHTS COMPETITION
Fargo-Moorhead Community Theatre; Box 644; Fargo, ND 58107;
   (701) 235-1901
Contest Administrator

Biennial contest; next deadline 1 Nov 1993.

THE FRENCH-AMERICAN FOUNDATION TRANSLATION PRIZE
41 East 72nd St; New York, NY 10021; (212) 288-4400
Dana Arifi

Types of material: translations. **Frequency:** annual. **Remuneration:** $5000. **Guidelines:** book-length translation of prose from French to English; must have been published in U.S. between 1 Jan and 31 Dec 1992; write for guidelines. **Submission procedure:** two copies of book with French original. **Deadline:** 30 Apr 1993. **Notification:** Nov 1993.

GALLERY PLAYERS OF THE LEO YASSENOFF
JEWISH CENTER PLAYWRITING CONTEST
1125 College Ave; Columbus, OH 43209-2893; (614) 231-2731
Director of Performing Arts

Biennial contest; next deadline 1 Sep 1993.

JOHN GASSNER MEMORIAL PLAYWRITING AWARD
New England Theatre Conference; c/o Department of Theatre; 337 Ryder Hall; Northeastern University; Boston, MA 02115; (617) 424-9275

Types of material: one-acts, plays for young audiences. **Frequency:** annual. **Remuneration:** $500 1st prize, $250 2nd prize; staged reading by leading theatre group at NETC annual convention; possible publication. **Guidelines:** U.S. or Canadian citizen; unpublished play, 20–60 minutes long, that has not had professional full production and is not under consideration for publication or professional production; 2-submission limit; send SASE for complete guidelines. **Submission procedure:** 3 copies of script; each copy must include cast list with character descriptions, brief synopsis and statement that play has not been published or professionally produced and is not under consideration; $10 fee per entry, except for NETC members. **Deadline:** 15 Apr 1993. **Notification:** 1 Sep 1993.

GEVA THEATRE PLAYWRIGHT AWARD
(formerly The Davie Award for Playwrighting)
75 Woodbury Blvd; Rochester, NY 14607; (716) 232-1366
Anthony Zerbe, *REFLECTIONS Festival Director*
Ann Patrice Carrigan, *Literary Director*

Types of material: full-length plays. **Frequency:** annual. **Remuneration:** $5000 and production in REFLECTIONS '93 play festival (see theatre's entry in Production) for each of 3 winners. **Guidelines:** play that has not received professional full production. **Submission procedure:** script only. **Deadline:** 1 Oct 1992. **Notification:** Feb 1993.

GILMAN AND GONZALEZ-FALLA THEATRE FOUNDATION MUSICAL THEATRE AWARD
109 East 64th St; New York, NY 10021; (212) 734-8011
C. Kempler, *Coordinator*

Types of material: musicals. **Frequency:** annual. **Remuneration:** $25,000. **Guidelines:** writer(s) must have had a musical produced by commercial or nonprofit theatre; contact foundation for guidelines. **Submission procedure:** book and lyrics; cassette of music; resume. **Deadline:** 30 Dec 1992.

GILMORE CREEK PLAYWRITING COMPETITION
Campus Box 82; St. Mary's College of Minnesota; Winona, MN 55987;
      (507) 457-1606
Robert Pevitts, *Dean of School of Fine/Performing Arts*

Types of material: full-length plays, translations, adaptations, plays for young audiences, musicals. **Frequency:** biennial. **Remuneration:** $3500; production; $2500 stipend to cover travel, room and board for 4-week residency. **Guidelines:** full-length work not produced professionally. **Submission procedure:** completed application and script. **Deadline:** 15 Jan 1993. **Notification:** 15 May 1993.

GOLDEN GATE NATIONAL PLAYWRIGHTS CONTEST
American Theatre Ventures; 580 Constanzo St; Stanford, CA 94305;
      (415) 326-0336
Roberta Roth-Patterson, *Contest Administrator*

Types of material: full-length plays, bills of related one-acts. **Frequency:** annual. **Remuneration:** $1000; staged reading; possible production; all entrants sent written evaluation of work. **Guidelines:** unproduced play at least 60 minutes in length by U.S. resident; send SASE for guidelines. **Submission procedure:** script with completed application and $20 reading fee. **Deadline:** mid-Aug 1993 (16 Aug in 1992). **Notification:** Mar 1994.

GOSHEN COLLEGE PEACE PLAYWRITING CONTEST
Communication Dept; Goshen College; 1700 South Main St; Goshen, IN 46526;
      (219) 535-7393
Lauren Friesen, *Director of Theatre*

Biennial contest; next deadline 31 Dec 1993.

GREAT PLATTE RIVER PLAYWRIGHTS' FESTIVAL
University of Nebraska-Kearney Theatre; Kearney, NE 68849-5260;
      (308) 234-8406
Jack Garrison, *Coordinator*

Types of material: full-length plays, one-acts, plays for young audiences, musicals. **Frequency:** annual. **Remuneration:** $500 1st prize, $300 2nd prize, $200 3rd prize; production; travel and housing to attend rehearsals. **Guidelines:** unproduced, unpublished original work; submission of works-in-progress for possible development encouraged. **Submission procedure:** script with cover letter; include cassette for musical. **Deadline:** 15 Mar 1993. **Notification:** 1 May 1993.

HENRICO THEATRE COMPANY PLAYWRITING COMPETITIONS
The County of Henrico; Division of Recreation and Parks; Box 27032;
    Richmond, VA 23273; (804) 672-5100
J. Larkin Brown, Cultural Arts Coordinator

One-Act Playwriting Competition

Types of material: one-acts, one-act musicals. **Frequency:** annual. **Remuneration:** $250; production; $150 and possible production for runner-up. **Guidelines:** unproduced, unpublished work; no controversial themes; prefers small cast, simple set; write for guidelines. **Submission procedure:** 2 copies of script. **Deadline:** 15 Sep 1992. **Notification:** 1 Nov 1992.

Full-Length Play Competition

Types of material: full-length plays and plays with music. **Remuneration:** $200; production; videotape of production. **Guidelines:** full-length work relating to Christmas season (specific Christmas story or general seasonal theme); prefers small cast, simple set; write for guidelines. **Submission procedure:** 2 copies of script. **Deadline:** 15 Sep 1992. **Notification:** 1 Nov 1992.

INNER CITY CULTURAL CENTER COMPETITION
1308 South New Hampshire Ave; Los Angeles, CA 90006; (213) 387-1161
C. Bernard Jackson, *Executive Director*

Types of material: one-acts, translations, adaptations, plays for young audiences, musicals, operas. **Frequency:** annual. **Remuneration:** cash award ($1000 1st prize, $500 2nd prize, $250 3rd prize) or paid professional internship with film studio to winner (past winners awarded internships with Warner Brothers and Universal Studios); publication by Inner City Press. **Guidelines:** fully mounted productions compete in series of elimination rounds; running time of 20–45 minutes; small cast, minimal set; translations and adaptations must be of unpublished work; write for guidelines. **Submission procedure:** completed application with $35 fee. **Deadline:** TBA (26 Jun in 1992).

JAPAN–UNITED STATES FRIENDSHIP COMMISSION PRIZE
Donald Keene Center of Japanese Culture; 407 Kent Hall; Columbia University;
    New York, NY 10027; (212) 854-5036
Victoria Lyon-Bestor, *Prize Administrator*

Types of material: translations. **Frequency:** annual. **Remuneration:** 2 prizes of $2500, 1 for classical work, 1 for modern. **Guidelines:** U.S. citizen; book-length translation of Japanese work; translation unpublished, "in press," or published since 1 Jan 1990; write for information. **Submission procedure:** script only. **Deadline:** 31 Dec 1992.

JEWEL BOX THEATRE PLAYWRITING AWARD
3700 North Walker; Oklahoma City, OK 73118; (405) 521-1786
Charles Tweed, *Production Director*

Types of material: full-length plays. **Frequency:** annual. **Remuneration:** $500; reading; possible production. **Guidelines:** unproduced full-length play of strong ensemble nature with emphasis on character rather than spectacle; write for guidelines and forms. **Submission procedure:** 2 copies of script with completed entry form and playwright's agreement. **Deadline:** 15 Jan 1993. **Notification:** Apr 1993.

KENNEDY CENTER AMERICAN COLLEGE THEATER FESTIVAL
(formerly American College Theater Festival)
Michael Kanin Playwriting Awards Program; The John F. Kennedy Center for the
    Performing Arts; Washington, DC 20566-0001; (202) 416-8850
David Young, *Producing Director*

The ACTF Musical Theater Award

Types of material: musicals. **Frequency:** annual. **Remuneration:** $1000 for lyrics; $1000 for music; $1000 for book; $1000 to producing college or university. **Guidelines:** original and copyrighted work produced by ACTF-participating college or university; at least 50% of writing team must be enrolled as full-time student(s) at college or university during year of production or during either of the 2 years preceding the production; write for ACTF brochure. **Submission procedure:** completed application, fee, and videotape of production at discretion of regional chair submitted by college or university. **Deadline:** established by region. **Notification:** spring 1993.

Columbia Pictures Television Award for Comedy Playwriting

Types of material: full-length comedies. **Frequency:** annual. **Remuneration:** assignment to write a teleplay for a Columbia Pictures Television series; fee (Writers Guild scale); travel and living expenses for 2-week conference period in Los Angeles; eligibility for Writers Guild of America membership with initiation fee paid; all-expenses-paid fellowship to attend Shenandoah Playwrights Retreat (see Development). **Guidelines:** comedy produced by an ACTF-participating college or university and entered in the Student Playwriting Awards Program; writer enrolled as full-time student at college or university during year of production or during either of the 2 years preceding the production; write for ACTF brochure. **Submission procedure:** completed application, fee, and videotape of production at discretion of regional chair submitted by college or university. **Deadline:** established by region. **Notification:** spring 1993.

The Lorraine Hansberry Playwriting Award

Types of material: full-length plays. **Frequency:** annual. **Remuneration:** 1st prize: $2500 plus all-expenses-paid fellowship to attend Shenandoah Playwrights Retreat (see Development) to playwright; $750 to producing college or university; 2nd prize: $1000 to playwright; $500 to producing college or university. **Guidelines:** play dealing with the black experience in America produced by an ACTF-partic-ipating college or university and entered in the Student Playwriting Awards Program; writer enrolled as full-time student at college or university during year of production or during either of the 2 years preceding the production; write for ACTF brochure. **Submission procedure:** completed application, fee, and videotape of production at discretion of regional chair submitted by college or university. **Deadline:** established by region. **Notification:** spring 1993.

The National Student Playwriting Award

Types of material: full-length plays, musicals. **Frequency:** annual. **Remuneration:** $2500; production at Kennedy Center during festival; publication by Samuel French with royalties; offer of William Morris Agency management contract; fellowship to attend Mount Sequoyah New Play Retreat (see Development); Dramatists Guild membership. **Guidelines:** work must be produced by ACTF-parti-cipating college or university; writer enrolled as full-time student at college or university during year of production or during either of the 2 years preceding the production; write for ACTF brochure. **Submission procedure:** completed application, fee, and videotape of production at discretion of regional chair submitted by college or university. **Deadline:** established by region. **Notification:** spring 1993.

The Short Play Awards Program

Types of material: one-acts. **Frequency:** annual. **Remuneration:** up to 3 awards: $1000; publication by Samuel French; offer of William Morris Agency manage-ment contract; Dramatists Guild membership. **Guidelines:** one-act 20–40 minutes long by student playwright; simple production demands (10-minute setup and strike); write for ACTF brochure. **Submission procedure:** contact regional chair for information. **Deadline:** established by region. **Notification:** spring 1993.

GEORGE R. KERNODLE PLAYWRITING CONTEST

Department of Drama; 406 Kimpel Hall; University of Arkansas;
    Fayetteville, AR 72701; (501) 575-2953
Director

Types of material: one-acts. **Frequency:** annual. **Remuneration:** $300 1st prize, $200 2nd prize, $100 3rd prize; possible staged reading or production. **Guide-lines:** unproduced, unpublished play by U.S. or Canadian playwright; 1-hour limit; cast limit of 8; 3-submission limit; write for guidelines. **Submission procedure:** script; statement that play has not received full production; $3 fee per submission. **Deadline:** 1 Jun 1993; no submission before 1 Jan 1993. **Notification:** 1 Oct 1993.

THE MARC A. KLEIN PLAYWRITING AWARD
Department of Theater Arts; Case Western Reserve University; 10900 Euclid Ave;
Cleveland, OH 44106-7077; (216) 368-2858
John Orlock, *Chair, Reading Committee*

Types of material: full-length plays, bills of related one-acts. **Frequency:** annual.
Remuneration: $1000, including $500 to cover residency expenses; production.
Guidelines: student currently enrolled at U.S. college or university; work,
endorsed by faculty member of university theatre department, that has not
received professional full production or trade-book publication. **Submission
procedure:** completed application and script. **Deadline:** 15 May 1993. **Notification:** 1 Jul 1993.

THE GREGORY KOLOVAKOS AWARD
PEN American Center; 568 Broadway; New York, NY 10012; (212) 334-1660
John Morrone, *Awards Coordinator*
Joan Dalin, *Awards Assistant*

Biennial translation award; next deadline 1 Dec 1993.

THE LEE KORF PLAYWRITING AWARDS
The Original Theatre Works; Burnight Center; Cerritos College;
11110 Alondra Blvd; Norwalk, CA 90650-6298; (310) 924-2100
Gloria Manriquez, *Production Coordinator*

Types of material: full-length plays, musicals, theatre pieces, extravaganzas.
Frequency: annual. **Remuneration:** $750; production. **Submission procedure:** send
SASE for guidelines. **Deadline:** 1 Jan 1993. **Notification:** 1 Apr 1993.

KUMU KAHUA PLAYWRITING CONTEST
Department of Theatre and Dance; University of Hawaii at Manoa;
1770 East-West Rd; Honolulu, HI 96822; (808) 956-2588
Dennis Carroll

Types of material: full-length plays, one-acts. **Frequency:** annual. **Remuneration:**
first category: $500 for full-length play, $200 for one-act; *second category:* $250 for
full-length play, $100 for one-act; reading and/or production if playwright
present. **Guidelines:** unproduced play; previous entries ineligible; *first category:* play
set in HI and dealing with some aspect of HI experience; *second category:* play not
dealing with HI by HI resident only. **Submission procedure:** write for entry
brochure. **Deadline:** 1 Jan 1993. **Notification:** 1 May 1993.

LAMIA INK! INTERNATIONAL ONE-PAGE PLAY COMPETITION
Box 202, Prince St Station; New York, NY 10012
Cortland Jessup, *Editor*

Types of material: 1-page plays. **Frequency:** annual. **Remuneration:** $200; reading in New York City and publication in magazine (see entry in Publication) for winner and 9 other best plays. **Guidelines:** 3-submission limit; send SASE for guidelines after 15 Sep 1992. **Submission procedure:** completed application and script with SASE for response. **Deadline:** 1 Mar 1993. **Notification:** 1 May 1993.

LANDERS CHILDREN'S MUSICAL COMPETITION
Landers Theatre; 311 East Walnut St; Springfield, MO 65806; (417) 869-3869
Mick Denniston, *Executive Director*

Contest has no set frequency; next deadline Dec 1993, exact date TBA.

HAROLD MORTON LANDON TRANSLATION AWARD
The Academy of American Poets; 177 East 87th St; New York, NY 10128;
(212) 427-5665
Beth McCabe, *Program Director*

Types of material: translations. **Frequency:** annual. **Remuneration:** $1000. **Guidelines:** U.S. citizen; published translation of verse, including verse drama, from any language into English verse; book published in 1992; no anthologies or collaborations. **Submission procedure:** 2 copies of book (no manuscripts). **Deadline:** 31 Dec 1992.

LETRAS DE ORO SPANISH LITERARY PRIZE COMPETITION
University of Miami; 1531 Brescia Ave; Coral Gables, FL 33124-3010;
(305) 284-3266
Joaquin Roy, *Graduate School of International Studies*

Types of material: full-length plays, one-acts, adaptations, plays for young audiences. **Frequency:** annual. **Remuneration:** $2500; publication. **Guidelines:** U.S. resident; unpublished play written in Spanish that has not won a previous award; 1 submission; write for rules. **Submission procedure:** 3 copies of script. **Deadline:** 12 Oct 1992. **Notification:** Mar 1993.

THE LITTLE THEATRE OF ALEXANDRIA NATIONAL ONE-ACT PLAYWRITING COMPETITION
Little Theatre of Alexandria; 600 Wolfe St; Alexandria, VA 22314;
(703) 683-5778
Chairman, Playreading Committee

Types of material: one-acts. **Frequency:** annual. **Remuneration:** $350 1st prize, $250 2nd prize, $150 3rd prize; possible production. **Guidelines:** U.S. citizen; 1 submission, unpublished, unproduced, 20–60 minutes long. **Submission proce-**

dure: send SASE for guidelines. **Deadline:** 31 Mar 1993. **Notification:** Aug/Sep 1993.

LIVE OAK THEATRE NEW PLAY AWARDS
311 Nueces St; Austin, TX 78701; (512) 472-5143
Mari Marchbanks, *Executive Director, New Play Development*

Types of material: full-length plays, adaptations. **Frequency:** annual. **Remuneration:** $1000 for best play; $1000 for best TX playwright; workshop production, or full production with royalty plus travel, room and board to attend rehearsals; possible reading for runners-up. **Guidelines:** U.S. citizen; TX playwright must be able to show proof of current TX residency (1-year minimum) on notification of award; 1 unpublished full-length submission, not produced professionally; send SASE for guidelines. **Submission procedure:** script with cast of characters and brief synopsis; entry form. **Deadline:** 1 Nov 1992. **Notification:** spring 1993.

LOS ANGELES DESIGNERS' THEATRE COMMISSIONS
Box 1883; Studio City, CA 91614-0883; (213) 650-9600
Richard Niederberg, *Artistic Director*

Types of material: full-length plays, bills of related one-acts, translations, adaptations, plays for young audiences, musicals, operas. **Frequency:** ongoing. **Remuneration:** negotiable commissioning fee; possible travel to attend rehearsals if developmental work is needed. **Guidelines:** work with commercial potential which has not received professional full production, is not under option and is free of commitment to specific director, actors or other personnel; large casts and multiple sets welcome; prefers controversial material. **Application procedure:** script or synopsis; resume; cassette for musical. **Deadline:** ongoing. **Notification:** at least 4 months.

LOVE CREEK ONE-ACT FESTIVALS
42 Sunset Dr; Croton-on-Hudson, NY 10520
Cynthia Granville, *Festival Literary Manager/Chair, Reading Committee*

Annual Short Play Festival

Types of material: one-acts. **Frequency:** annual. **Remuneration:** approximately 40 finalists receive mini-showcase production in New York City during festival; each week's finalists compete in last week for cash award of $300. **Guidelines:** unpublished play, not produced in NYC area within past year; maximum length of 40 minutes; cast of 2 or more, simple sets and costumes; 2-submission limit; send SASE for guidelines. **Submission procedure:** script with letter giving theatre permission to produce play if chosen and specifying whether Equity showcase is acceptable. **Deadline:** 30 Sep 1992.

One-Act Mini-Festivals

Types of material: one-acts. **Frequency:** biannual. **Remuneration:** 12 or more finalists receive mini-showcase production in New York City during festival; critics' choice scripts compete in final evening for cash award of $200. **Guidelines:** unpublished play not produced in NYC area within past year; maximum length of 40 minutes; cast of 2 or more, simple sets and costumes; 2-submission limit; scripts must concern theme which varies with each mini-festival; send SASE for guidelines. **Submission procedure:** script with letter giving theatre permission to produce play if chosen and specifying whether Equity showcase acceptable. **Deadline:** 1 Mar 1993 for May festival (theme "Women in the 90's: Friends, Lovers, Companions"); 15 Jun 1993 for Sep festival (theme TBA).

MAXIM MAZUMDAR NEW PLAY COMPETITION
Alleyway Theatre; 1 Curtain Up Alley; Buffalo, NY 14202-1911; (716) 852-2266
Joyce Stilson, *Dramaturg*

Types of material: full-length plays, one-acts, musicals. **Frequency:** annual. **Remuneration:** $400, production with royalty, and travel and housing to attend rehearsals for full-length play or musical; $100 and production for one-act play or musical. **Guidelines:** unproduced full-length work not less than 90 minutes long with cast limit of 10 and unit set or simple set, or unproduced one-act work less than 60 minutes long with cast limit of 6 and simple set; prefers work with unconventional setting that explores the boundaries of theatricality; limit of 1 submission in each category; write for guidelines. **Submission procedure:** script and resume. **Deadline:** 1 Sep 1992. **Notification:** 1 Jan 1993 for finalists; 1 Feb 1993 for winners.

THE DENNIS McINTYRE PLAYWRITING AWARD
Philadelphia Festival Theatre for New Plays; 3900 Chestnut St;
    Philadelphia, PA 19104-3105; (215) 222-5000
Michael Hollinger, *Literary Manager*

Types of material: full-length plays. **Frequency:** annual. **Remuneration:** cash award; production with travel and 4 weeks' room and board to attend rehearsals, or staged reading with travel and housing to attend reading. **Guidelines:** unproduced play by emerging playwright of conscience examining society's problems with honest scrutiny. **Submission procedure:** submit synopsis, resume and letter of inquiry. **Deadline:** ongoing.

McLAREN MEMORIAL COMEDY PLAYWRITING COMPETITION
Midland Community Theatre; 2000 West Wadley Ave; Midland, TX 79705;
    (915) 682-2544
Mary Lou Cassidy, *Coordinator*

Types of material: full-length plays, one-acts, translations, adaptations, plays for young audiences, musicals. **Frequency:** annual. **Remuneration:** $400; staged reading; travel, room and board to attend rehearsals. **Guidelines:** comedy which has not received professional full production. **Submission procedure:** script with $5 processing fee. **Deadline:** 31 Jan 1993. **Notification:** 1 May 1993.

MIDSOUTH PLAYWRIGHTS' COMPETITION

Playhouse on the Square; 51 South Cooper St; Memphis, TN 38104;
    (901) 725-0776, 726-4498
Jackie Nichols, *Executive Director*

Types of material: full-length plays, musicals. **Frequency:** annual. **Remuneration:** $500; production. **Guidelines:** unproduced work; small cast; full arrangement for piano for musical; prefers southern playwrights. **Submission procedure:** script only. **Deadline:** 1 Apr 1993.

THE MILL MOUNTAIN THEATRE NEW PLAY COMPETITION: THE NORFOLK SOUTHERN FESTIVAL OF NEW WORKS

1 Market Square SE, Suite 6; Roanoke, VA 24011-1437; (703) 342-5730
Jo Weinstein, *Literary Manager*

Types of material: full-length plays, one-acts. **Frequency:** annual. **Remuneration:** $1000; staged reading with possibility of production; travel stipend and housing for limited residency. **Guidelines:** U.S. resident; unproduced, unpublished play; cast limit of 10; 1 submission; send SASE for guidelines. **Submission procedure:** script; brief synopsis of scenes, character descriptions, history of play; resume. **Deadline:** 1 Jan 1993; no submission before 1 Oct 1992. **Notification:** Aug 1993.

MIXED BLOOD VERSUS AMERICA

Mixed Blood Theatre Company; 1501 South 4th St; Minneapolis, MN 55454;
    (612) 338-0937
David Kunz, *Script Czar*

Types of material: full-length plays, musicals. **Frequency:** annual. **Remuneration:** $2000; production. **Guidelines:** unproduced, unpublished work by writer who has had at least 1 work produced or workshopped professionally or by educational institution; 2-submission limit; write for guidelines. **Submission procedure:** script; cassette of songs for musical; resume or other evidence of work produced or workshopped; mark all contest submissions "Mixed Blood Versus America." **Deadline:** 15 Mar 1993. **Notification:** fall 1993.

MRTW SCRIPT CONTEST

Midwest Radio Theatre Workshop; KOPN Radio; 915 East Broadway;
    Columbia, MO 65201; (314) 874-1139
Diane Huneke, *Director*

Types of material: short radio plays. **Frequency:** annual. **Remuneration:** $800 to be divided among approximately 3 winners; possible radio production for local broadcast and national distribution via satellite and tape sales; scholarship to attend fall 1994 Midwest Radio Theatre Workshop Conference (see Development); publication in MRTW Scriptbook. **Guidelines:** original radio play 15–52 minutes long (no adaptations) by established or emerging writer; special interest in plays by women and writers of color and in issue-oriented plays on contemporary themes; 2-submission limit; write for guidelines. **Submission procedure:** 3

copies of script in radio format with cover letter indicating if play has been produced. **Deadline:** 30 Jul 1993. **Notification:** 15 Dec 1993.

NATIONAL PLAY AWARD
National Repertory Theatre Foundation; 630 North Grand Ave, Suite 405;
  Los Angeles, CA 90012; (213) 626-5944
Lloyd Steele, *Literary Manager*

Biennial contest; next deadline TBA (30 Jun in 1992).

NATIONAL TEN-MINUTE PLAY CONTEST
Actors Theatre of Louisville; 316 West Main St; Louisville, KY 40202-4218;
  (502) 584-1265
Michael Bigelow Dixon, *Literary Manager*

Types of material: 10-minute plays. **Frequency:** annual. **Remuneration:** Heideman Award of $1000; possible production with royalties. **Guidelines:** U.S. citizen or resident; play 10 pages long or less which has not had Equity production; 2-submission limit; previous entries ineligible; write for guidelines. **Submission procedure:** script only. **Deadline:** 1 Dec 1992. **Notification:** fall 1993.

NEW AMERICAN COMEDY (NAC) FESTIVAL
Ukiah Players Theatre; 1041 Low Gap Rd; Ukiah, CA 95482; (707) 462-1210
Catherine Babcock Magruder, *Artistic Director*

Biennial contest; next deadline 31 Dec 1993.

NEW AMERICAN MUSICAL WRITERS COMPETITION
NEW STAGES Musical Arts; 118 East 4th St, #14; New York, NY 10003;
  (212) 505-1947
Joe Miloscia, *Artistic Director*

Types of material: music-theatre works, including musicals, operettas and revues. **Frequency:** annual. **Remuneration:** possible cash award; stage reading in NEW STAGES festival for up to 5 works; possible selection for additional development in NEW STAGES Musical Workshop Program (see Development). **Guidelines:** U.S. citizen or resident who has not received significant recognition in the musical theatre field; unpublished original work or adaptation (adapter must obtain rights for work not in public domain); unfinished work eligible if writer(s) can submit 50% of book and songs plus detailed outline of unwritten scenes; 2-submission limit; write for guidelines. **Submission procedure:** project synopsis; latest draft of libretto; cassette of songs (do not submit score); list of any previous productions of work; resumes of composer, librettist and lyricist. **Deadline:** 1 Mar 1993.

OFF-OFF BROADWAY ORIGINAL SHORT PLAY FESTIVAL
Samuel French; 45 West 25th St; New York, NY 10010; (212) 206-8990
Ken Hailey, *Festival Coordinator*

Types of material: one-acts, segments of full-length plays. **Frequency:** annual.
Remuneration: festival production hosted by Love Creek Productions; possible
publication contract from Samuel French. **Guidelines:** presentation less than 40
minutes long of work developed and produced by theatre, professional school or
college that has fostered playwriting for at least 2 years. **Submission procedure:**
no submission by playwright; submission by producing organization. **Deadline:**
Apr 1993 (30 Apr in 1992). **Notification:** within 2 weeks. **Dates:** Jun 1993.

OGLEBAY INSTITUTE TOWNGATE THEATRE PLAYWRITING CONTEST
Oglebay Institute; Oglebay Park; Wheeling, WV 26003; (304) 242-4200
Debbie Hynes, *Associate Director, Performing Arts*

Types of material: full-length plays. **Frequency:** annual. **Remuneration:** $300;
production; partial travel to attend rehearsals. **Guidelines:** unpublished,
unproduced play; simple set. **Submission procedure:** script with resume. **Deadline:**
1 Jan 1993. **Notification:** 1 May 1993.

PEN-BOOK-OF-THE-MONTH CLUB TRANSLATION PRIZE
PEN American Center; 568 Broadway; New York, NY 10012; (212) 334-1660
John Morrone, *Program Coordinator*

Types of material: translation. **Frequency:** annual. **Remuneration:** $3000.
Guidelines: book-length translation from any language into English published in
U.S. during current calendar year. **Submission procedure:** 3 copies of book.
Deadline: 31 Dec 1992. **Notification:** spring 1993.

JAMES D. PHELAN AWARD IN LITERATURE
The San Francisco Foundation; 685 Market St, Suite 910;
        San Francisco, CA 94105; (415) 495-3100
Liela Greiman, *Awards Program Coordinator*

Types of material: full-length plays, one-acts, plays for young audiences.
Frequency: annual. **Remuneration:** $2000. **Guidelines:** unpublished play-in-
progress; author CA born and aged 20–35 years as of 15 Jan 1993. **Submission
procedure:** completed application and script. **Deadline:** 15 Jan 1993; no submission before 15 Nov 1992. **Notification:** 15 Jun 1993.

ROBERT J. PICKERING AWARD FOR PLAYWRITING EXCELLENCE

Coldwater Community Theater; c/o 89 South Division; Coldwater, MI 49036;
(517) 279-7963
J. Richard Colbeck, *Chairman, Play Selection Committee*

Types of material: full-length plays. **Frequency:** annual. **Remuneration:** 1st prize $200, production and housing to attend performance; 2nd prize $50; 3rd prize $25. **Guidelines:** unproduced play suited to midwestern audience. **Submission procedure:** script only. **Deadline:** 31 Dec 1992. **Notification:** 1 Feb 1993.

PLAY WORKS NEW ONE-ACT PLAY AND THEATER COMPETITION

Play Works at Try Arts; 623 South St; Philadelphia, PA 19147; (215) 592-8393
Christopher J. Rushton, *Co-Artistic Director*

Types of material: one-acts. **Frequency:** annual. **Remuneration:** $250–450 to be divided between 1st- and 2nd-place winners. **Guidelines:** most entries submitted by producers on behalf of theatre companies but scripts submitted by individual playwrights will be considered for production by pool of individual Play Works directors and producers; unpublished one-acts that explore nontraditional content and forms; prefers small cast, simple technical demands; write for guidelines. **Submission procedure:** producer or playwright submits script, resume, completed application and $5 fee; producer pays additional $70 fee if production is selected for competition. **Deadline:** 1 May 1993 (early submission recommended for playwrights outside Delaware Valley area). **Notification:** approximately 1 month.

PLAYWRIGHTS' FORUM AWARDS

Theatreworks; University of Colorado; Box 7150;
Colorado Springs, CO 80933-7150; (719) 593-3232, -3275
Whit Andrews, *Producing Director*

Types of material: one-acts. **Frequency:** annual. **Remuneration:** 2 awards: $200; production; up to $350 travel to attend performance. **Guidelines:** 1 unproduced, unpublished submission not more than 1 hour long. **Submission procedure:** script only. **Deadline:** 1 Dec 1992. **Notification:** 1 Mar 1993.

PLAYWRIGHTS' THEATER OF DENTON ONE-ACT PLAY COMPETITION

Box 732; Denton, TX 76202-0732; (817) 387-4908
Mark Pearce, *Artistic Director*

Types of material: one-acts. **Frequency:** annual. **Remuneration:** $1000; possible production. **Guidelines:** 5–45 minutes long. **Submission procedure:** script and $15 fee (check payable to Sigma Corporation). **Deadline:** 15 Sep 1992. **Notification:** 15 Jan 1993.

PLEIADES PLAYWRIGHT GRANT

Box 4025; North Hollywood, CA 91617; (818) 761-6136
Elizabeth Hansen, *Secretary*

Types of material: full-length plays. **Frequency:** annual. **Remuneration:** $2000 (paid in 3 installments); series of 3 staged readings as part of year-long workshop program. **Guidelines:** unpublished, unproduced play at least 90 minutes long; playwright who has had no more than 2 plays produced by Equity theatres; 1 submission; write for guidelines and application. **Submission procedure:** completed application and script; synopsis; resume; $5 fee. **Deadline:** 28 Feb 1993. **Notification:** 30 Apr 1993.

RENATO POGGIOLI AWARD

PEN American Center; 568 Broadway; New York, NY 10012; (212) 334-1660
John Morrone, *Program Coordinator*

Types of material: translations. **Frequency:** annual. **Remuneration:** $3000. **Guidelines:** book-length translation from Italian into English by promising young translator; work-in-progress eligible. **Submission procedure:** curriculum vitae with sample of translation and original Italian text. **Deadline:** 15 Jan 1993. **Notification:** May 1993.

QRL POETRY SERIES AWARDS

Quarterly Review of Literature; Princeton University; 26 Haslet Ave;
     Princeton, NJ 08540
Renee Weiss, *Co-Editor*

Types of material: full-length plays, one-acts, translations. **Frequency:** annual. **Remuneration:** $1000; publication in QRL Poetry Series; 100 complimentary paperback copies. **Guidelines:** up to 5 awards a year for poetry and poetic drama only; play 50–100 pages in length; send SASE for guidelines. **Submission procedure:** submissions accepted in Nov and May only; must be accompanied by $20 subscription for books published in series.

RCI FESTIVAL OF EMERGING AMERICAN THEATRE

Phoenix Theatre; 749 North Park; Indianapolis, IN 46202; (317) 635-7529
Bryan Fonseca, *Artistic Director*

Types of material: full-length plays, one-acts, translations, adaptations. **Frequency:** annual. **Remuneration:** $750 for full-length play, $300 for one-act; 2 full-production slots will be filled, each with a full-length play or a bill of one-acts; housing to attend rehearsals. **Guidelines:** unpublished play, suitable for 150-seat house, that has not received more than 1 production; availability of playwright for rehearsals a consideration; 1 submission. **Submission procedure:** script with synopsis and bio; $5 entry fee. **Deadline:** 30 Mar 1993. **Notification:** 1 Jun 1993. **Dates:** summer 1993.

SUMMERFIELD G. ROBERTS AWARD

The Sons of the Republic of Texas; 5942 Abrams Rd, Suite 222;
Dallas, TX 75231; (214) 343-2145
Maydee J. Scurlock

Types of material: full-length plays. **Frequency:** annual. **Remuneration:** $2500.
Guidelines: play about living in the Republic of Texas, completed during calendar
year preceding deadline. **Submission procedure:** 5 copies of script; scripts will not
be returned. **Deadline:** 15 Jan 1993. **Notification:** early Apr 1993.

THE RICHARD RODGERS PRODUCTION AWARD

American Academy and Institute of Arts and Letters; 633 West 155th St;
New York, NY 10032-7599; (212) 368-5900
Domenica Brockman, *Programs Assistant*

Types of material: musicals, revues, operettas, plays with music, bills of related
shorter pieces. **Frequency:** annual. **Remuneration:** Production Award of up to
$80,000 and/or Development Grants of up to $15,000 for professional readings.
Guidelines: U.S. citizen or permanent resident; work not professionally produced
by writer/composer not already established in musical theatre field; innovative,
experimental work encouraged; 1 submission; previous entries ineligible; readings
and productions by New York City nonprofit theatres. **Submission procedure:**
send SASE for application form and information. **Deadline:** 2 Nov 1992.

LOIS AND RICHARD ROSENTHAL NEW PLAY PRIZE

Cincinnati Playhouse in the Park; Box 6537; Cincinnati, OH 45206;
(513) 345-2242
Susan Banks, *Literary Manager*

Types of material: full-length plays, musicals. **Frequency:** annual. **Remuneration:**
$2000 advance on royalties; production; $1500 stipend; travel, room and board
to attend rehearsals. **Guidelines:** 1 unpublished submission, not produced
professionally; write for guidelines. **Submission procedure:** script only; playwright
or playwright's agent may submit. **Deadline:** 15 Jan 1993; no submission before
15 Oct 1992.

SANTA BARBARA PLAYWRIGHTS FESTIVAL

Actors & Playwrights Theater; Box 361; Santa Barbara, CA 93120
Jim Cook, *Coordinator*

Types of material: full-length plays, one-acts. **Frequency:** annual. **Remuneration:**
1st prize $500, production, travel (from U.S. location) and housing during 2-week
festival; 2nd prize $200 and production; 3rd prize $100 and possible staged
reading. **Guidelines:** work not published or professionally produced; limit of 10
actors; multicultural theme. **Submission procedure:** script only. **Deadline:** 31 Oct
1992. **Notification:** 15 Feb 1993.

MORTON R. SARETT MEMORIAL AWARD

Department of Theatre Arts; University of Nevada, Las Vegas;
  4505 Maryland Pkwy; Las Vegas, NV 89154; (702) 739-3666
Robert Burgan, *Coordinator*

Biennial contest; details of 1993–94 contest TBA mid-Aug 1993.

SCHOLASTIC WRITING AWARDS

730 Broadway; New York, NY 10003; (212) 505-3404

Types of material: one-acts; radio, television and film scripts. **Frequency:** annual. **Remuneration:** award of $1000 toward college tuition, and staged reading to winning high school senior; 2 additional awards of $1000; top 15 of 40 other scripts selected for national honors receive cash awards of up to $125. **Guidelines:** writer must be student in grades 7–12; unpublished script not more than 30 minutes long. **Submission procedure:** completed application and script; write for information by 1 Jan 1993. **Deadline:** mid-Jan 1993; exact date TBA. **Notification:** May 1993.

SHIRAS INSTITUTE/MILDRED AND ALBERT PANOWSKI PLAYWRITING AWARD

Forest A. Roberts Theatre; Northern Michigan University; Marquette, MI 49855;
  (906) 227-2553
James A. Panowski, *Director*

Types of material: full-length plays, adaptations. **Frequency:** annual. **Remuneration:** $2000; production; travel, room and board for 1-week residency. **Guidelines:** 1 unpublished, unproduced submission; rewrites of previous entries ineligible. **Submission procedure:** completed application and script. **Deadline:** 20 Nov 1992. **Notification:** Apr 1993.

SIENA COLLEGE INTERNATIONAL PLAYWRIGHTS COMPETITION

Department of Fine Arts; Siena College; Loudonville, NY 12211; (518) 783-2381
Mark Heckler, *Director of Theatre*

Biennial contest; next deadline 30 Jun 1994.

DOROTHY SILVER PLAYWRITING COMPETITION

Jewish Community Center of Cleveland; 3505 Mayfield Rd;
  Cleveland Heights, OH 44118; (216) 382-4000, ext 275
Elaine Rembrandt, *Director of Visual and Performing Arts*

Types of material: full-length plays. **Frequency:** annual. **Remuneration:** $1000 (including $500 to cover residency expenses); staged reading; possible production. **Guidelines:** unproduced play that provides fresh and significant perspective on the range of Jewish experience. **Submission procedure:** script only. **Deadline:** 15 Dec 1992. **Notification:** 1 Jul 1993.

THE SOCIETY OF MIDLAND AUTHORS DRAMA AWARD

152 North Scoville; Oak Park, IL 60302; (312) 383-7568
Jim Bowman, *President*

Types of material: full-length plays, one-acts. **Frequency:** annual. **Remuneration:** $400; production by professional company. **Guidelines:** playwright currently living and working in IA, IL, IN, KS, MI, MN, MO, ND, NE, OH, SD or WI; new play given its first professional (not community theatre or college) production in 1992. **Submission procedure:** send SASE for guidelines and application form. **Deadline:** 15 Dec 1992. **Notification:** spring 1993.

SOURCE THEATRE COMPANY
NATIONAL PLAYWRITING COMPETITION

1835 14th St NW; Washington, DC 20009; (202) 462-1073
Keith Parker, *Literary Manager*

Types of material: full-length plays, one-acts, musicals. **Frequency:** annual. **Remuneration:** $250; possible production in festival (see below). **Guidelines:** work not produced professionally; each submission also considered for SourceWorks reading series and the annual Washington Theatre Festival (send SASE for details). **Submission procedure:** script with synopsis and resume. **Deadline:** 1 Feb 1993. **Notification:** 1 Jun 1993, if selected.

SOUTH CAROLINA PLAYWRIGHTS' FESTIVAL

Trustus Theatre; Box 11721; Columbia, SC 29211; (803) 254-9732
Jim Thigpen, *Artistic Director*

Types of material: full-length plays, one-acts, plays for young audiences. **Frequency:** annual. **Remuneration:** 1st prize of $500 and production with travel and housing to attend rehearsals and opening; 2nd prize of $250 and staged reading with travel and housing to attend reading. **Guidelines:** play not produced professionally; cast limit of 8; prefers 1 set. **Submission procedure:** script; 1-page synopsis with character descriptions; resume. **Deadline:** 1 Apr 1993; no submission before 1 Jan 1993. **Notification:** 1 Jul 1993.

SOUTHEASTERN THEATRE CONFERENCE NEW PLAY PROJECT

Department of Theatre and Dance; University of Alabama; Box 870239;
        Tuscaloosa, AL 35487; (205) 348-9032
Paul C. Castagno, *Chair*

Types of material: full-length plays, bills of 2 related one-acts. **Frequency:** annual. **Remuneration:** $1000; staged reading at SETC Annual Convention; travel, room and board to attend convention; submission of work by SETC to O'Neill Center for favored consideration for National Playwrights Conference (see Development). **Guidelines:** resident of state in SETC region (AL, FL, GA, KY, MS, NC, SC, TN, VA, WV); unproduced work; bills of one-acts bound in 1 cover; limit of 1 full-length submission or bill of 2 one-acts; write for guidelines. **Submission**

procedure: script only. **Deadline:** 1 Jun 1993; no submission before 15 Mar 1993. **Notification:** Nov 1993.

SOUTHEAST REGION CHILDREN'S THEATRE FESTIVAL
Theatre Winter Haven; Box 1230; Winter Haven, FL 33882; (813) 299-2672
Beth Smith, *Director of Theatre School*

Types of material: works for young audiences, including full-length plays, one-acts and musicals. **Frequency:** annual. **Remuneration:** $200; production in summer festival; up to $500 travel, and housing to attend final rehearsals and festival. **Guidelines:** original, unpublished work (no adaptations); send SASE for guidelines. **Submission procedure:** script with playwright's contact information on title page; $5 fee. **Deadline:**15 Jan 1993. **Notification:** 15 Mar 1993. **Dates:** 18–27 Jun 1993.

SOUTHERN PLAYWRIGHTS COMPETITION
Center for Southern Studies; Jacksonville State University; Jacksonville, AL 36265;
    (205) 782-5411
Steven J. Whitton, *Coordinator*

Types of material: full-length plays. **Frequency:** annual. **Remuneration:** $1000; production; housing to attend rehearsals. **Guidelines:** native or resident of AL, AR, FL, GA, KY, LA, MS, NC, SC, TN, TX, VA or WV; unproduced, unpublished original play dealing with the southern experience; 1 submission; write for guidelines. **Submission procedure:** script with synopsis and completed entry form. **Deadline:** 15 Feb 1993. **Notification:** 1 May 1993.

THE STANLEY DRAMA AWARD
Department of Humanities; Wagner College; Howard Ave and Campus Rd;
    Staten Island, NY 10301; (718) 390-3256
Bill Bly, *Director*

Types of material: full-length plays, bills of related one-acts, musicals. **Frequency:** annual. **Remuneration:** $2000; possible production. **Guidelines:** work not published or professionally produced and recommended by drama/creative writing teacher or theatre professional; previous winners ineligible. **Submission procedure:** completed application and script; letter recommending submitted work; cassette for musical. **Deadline:** 1 Sep 1992. **Notification:** Mar 1993.

TADA! SPRING STAGED READING SERIES
120 West 28th St; New York, NY 10001; (212) 627-1732
Janine Nina Trevens, *Artistic Director*

Types of material: plays and musicals for young audiences. **Frequency:** annual. **Remuneration:** 3 awards of $200; staged reading; possible production. **Guidelines:** unproduced play or musical written for child actors, who do not play adult characters. **Submission procedure:** script with character breakdown; cassette for musical. **Deadline:** 15 Jan 1993. **Notification:**15 Mar 1993.

MARVIN TAYLOR PLAYWRITING AWARD
Sierra Repertory Theatre; Box 3030; Sonora, CA 95370; (209) 532-3120
Dennis Jones, *Producing Director*

Types of material: full-length plays, adaptations, musicals. **Frequency:** annual. **Remuneration:** $500; production. **Guidelines:** 1 submission that has received no more than 2 productions or staged readings; cast limit of 15; prefers limit of 6; 2-set limit. **Submission procedure:** script only. **Deadline:** 31 Aug 1993. **Notification:** Mar 1994.

THEATRE IN PROCESS AT THE WHEELOCK FAMILY THEATRE PLAYWRITING AWARD
220 Marlborough St; Boston, MA 02116; (617) 267-1053
June Judson, *Artistic Director, Theatre in Process*

Types of material: full-length plays, adaptations. **Frequency:** annual. **Remunerations:** $200; workshop or full production. **Guidelines:** U.S. playwright; play suitable for multiracial casting that deals with social issues; no sitcoms or soap operas; adapter must have rights. **Submission procedure:** script only. **Deadline:** 15 Oct 1992. **Notification:** Jan 1993.

THEATRE MEMPHIS NEW PLAY COMPETITION
630 Perkins St Extended; Memphis, TN 38117-4799; (901) 682-8323
Kim Ford and Iris Dichtel, *Co-Chairs, New Play Competition*

Types of material: full-length plays. **Frequency:** triennial. **Remuneration:** $1500 (may be split between 2 winners); possible production with travel and housing to attend performance. **Guidelines:** original work not produced with royalty payment prior to deadline date; write for guidelines. **Submission procedure:** script submitted anonymously with detached title page giving playwright's name and address; resume. **Deadline:** 1 Jul 1993. **Notification:** Dec 1993.

THEATREWORKS/USA COMMISSIONING PROGRAM
Theatreworks/USA; 890 Broadway; New York, NY 10003; (212) 677-5959
Barbara Pasternack, *Literary Manager*

Types of material: plays with music and musicals for young and family audiences. **Frequency:** ongoing. **Remuneration:** step commissioning process; production. **Guidelines:** works dealing with issues relevant to target audiences; special interest in historical/biographical subject matter and musical adaptations of fairy tales and traditional or contemporary classics; 1 hour long; cast of 5 actors, set suitable for touring. **Submission procedure:** treatment with sample scenes; lyric sheets and cassette of music. **Deadline:** ongoing.

TOWSON STATE UNIVERSITY PRIZE FOR LITERATURE
Towson State University; Towson, MD 21204-7097; (301) 321-2128
Annette Chappell, *Dean, College of Liberal Arts*

Types of material: book or book-length manuscript. **Frequency:** annual.
Remuneration: $1200. **Guidelines:** work published within 3 years prior to
nomination or scheduled for publication within the year; author no more than
40 years of age, MD resident for 3 years and at time prize awarded. **Submission
procedure:** completed application, 4 copies of work; write for guidelines.
Deadline: 1 May 1993. **Notification:** 1 Sep 1993.

TRIBAD PRODUCTIONS LESBIAN PLAYWRITING COMPETITION
Box 1745; Guerneville, CA 95446; (707) 869-0155
Tiana Lee, *Artistic Director*

Types of material: full-length plays, one-acts, small musicals. **Frequency:** annual.
Remuneration: $200; production. **Guidelines:** play with lesbian theme, suitable for
all-woman cast, written by woman. **Submission procedure:** script and resume.
Deadline: 1 Nov 1992. **Notification:** 1 Jan 1993.

MARK TWAIN MASQUERS PLAYWRITING COMPETITION/FESTIVAL
170 Kingswood Rd, West Hartford, CT 06119; (203) 666-5763, 232-7808
Jerilyn Nagel, *Producer*

Types of material: one-acts. **Frequency:** annual. **Remuneration:** 6 finalists given
staged readings at festival; $200 in saving bonds awarded to best play; all entrants
receive complimentary tickets. **Guidelines:** original, unpublished play 35–45
minutes long; 1 submission; write for rules. **Submission procedure:** script with
synopsis and $10 fee. **Deadline:** 15 Oct 1992. **Notification:** 5 Jan 1993. **Dates:** 5–7
Feb 1993.

UNICORN THEATRE NATIONAL PLAYWRIGHTS' AWARD
3820 Main St; Kansas City, MO 64111; (816) 531-7529
Jan Kohl, *Literary Manager*

Types of material: full-length plays. **Frequency:** no set dates. **Remuneration:**
$1000; production; possible travel and residency. **Guidelines:** unpublished play
not produced professionally; special interest in social issues; contemporary (post-
1950) themes and settings only; cast limit of 10; 2-submission limit. **Submission
procedure:** no scripts; send synopsis, at least 10 pages of dialogue, resume and
letter of inquiry. **Deadline:** ongoing. **Notification:** 2 weeks; 2–4 months if script
is requested.

UNIVERSITY OF LOUISVILLE GRAWEMEYER AWARD FOR MUSIC COMPOSITION

Grawemeyer Music Award Committee; School of Music; University of Louisville;
   Louisville, KY 40292; (502) 588-6907
David R. Harman, *Executive Secretary*

Types of material: works in major musical genres, including music-theatre works and operas. **Frequency:** annual. **Remuneration:** $150,000 (paid in 5 annual installments of $30,000). **Guidelines:** work premiered during previous 5 years; entry must be sponsored by professional music organization or individual; write for guidelines. **Submission procedure:** completed application with score, cassette, supporting materials and $30 fee submitted jointly by composer and sponsoring organization. **Deadline:** 22 Jan 1993. **Notification:** late spring 1993.

VERMONT PLAYWRIGHTS AWARD

(formerly Northern New England Playwrights Award
The Valley Players; Box 441; Waitsfield, VT 05673
Howard Chapman, *Chairperson*

Types of material: full-length plays. **Frequency:** annual. **Remuneration:** $1000; possible production. **Guidelines:** NH, ME or VT resident; unproduced, unpublished play suitable for community group and for theatre's facilities; plays that have received readings or workshops encouraged; send SASE for guidelines. **Submission procedure:** completed application and script. **Deadline:** 1 Oct 1992.

VERY SPECIAL ARTS YOUNG PLAYWRIGHTS PROGRAM

Education Office; The John F. Kennedy Center for the Performing Arts;
   Washington, DC 20566; (202) 628-2800 (voice),
   737-0645 (Telecommunications Device for the Deaf)
Janet Rice Elmon, *Manager, National Programs*

Types of material: full-length plays, one-acts. **Frequency:** annual. **Remuneration:** professional production at Kennedy Center; travel, room and board to attend performance. **Guidelines:** play dealing with some aspect of disability by writer aged 12–18 years; write for guidelines. **Submission procedure:** 3 copies of script; short bio. **Deadline:** 13 Feb 1993.

THEODORE WARD PRIZE FOR PLAYWRITING

Columbia College Chicago Theater/Music Center; 72 East 11th St;
   Chicago, IL 60605; (312) 663-9462
Chuck Smith, *Facilitator*

Types of material: full-length plays, translations, adaptations. **Frequency:** annual. **Remuneration:** 1st prize $2000, production, travel and housing to attend rehearsals; 2nd prize $500, staged reading. **Guidelines:** U.S. resident of African-American descent; 1 full-length submission not professionally produced; translations and adaptations of material in public domain only. **Submission procedure:** script with short synopsis and production history; brief resume; write for guidelines. **Deadline:** 1 Aug 1993; no submission before 1 May 1993. **Notification:** Nov 1993.

WAREHOUSE THEATRE COMPANY ONE-ACT COMPETITION
Stephens College; Columbia, MO 65215; (314) 876-7194
Artistic Director

Types of material: one-acts. **Frequency:** annual. **Remuneration:** $200; possible production as part of company's Evening of One-Acts. **Guidelines:** unpublished, unproduced script by undergraduate or graduate student; special interest in scripts by, for or about women. **Submission procedure:** script with $7.50 fee. **Deadline:** 31 Dec 1992. **Notification:** 1 Feb 1993.

L. ARNOLD WEISSBERGER PLAYWRITING COMPETITION
New Dramatists; 424 West 44th St; New York, NY 10036; (212) 757-6960
Coordinator

Types of material: full-length plays. **Frequency:** annual. **Remuneration:** $5000. **Guidelines:** 1 unpublished submission, not produced professionally; write for guidelines. **Submission procedure:** script only. **Deadline:** 31 May 1993; no submission before 15 Sep 1992. **Notification:** May 1994.

WEST COAST ENSEMBLE CONTESTS
Box 38728; Los Angeles, CA 90038; (213) 871-8673
Les Hanson, *Artistic Director*

West Coast Ensemble Full-Length Play Competition

Types of material: full-length plays. **Frequency:** annual. **Remuneration:** $500; production; royalty on any performances beyond 6-week run. **Guidelines:** unproduced, unpublished play. **Submission procedure:** script with SASE or SASP for acknowledgment of receipt. **Deadline:** 31 Dec 1992. **Notification:** within 6 months of deadline.

West Coast Ensemble Musical Stairs

Types of material: musical theatre works. **Frequency:** annual. **Remuneration:** $500; production; royalty on any performances beyond 6-week run. **Guidelines:** unpublished musical work not produced in southern CA; all genres and styles eligible, including pop, rock, country and western, etc. **Submission procedure:** script with cassette of score (include lead sheets if available). **Deadline:** 30 Jun 1993. **Notification:** within 6 months.

WESTERN GREAT LAKES PLAYWRITING COMPETITION
South Bend Civic Theatre; 701 Portage Ave; South Bend, IN 46616;
(219) 234-1112

Types of material: full-length plays. **Frequency:** annual. **Remuneration:** $500; staged reading; possible production; travel, room and board to attend reading or production. **Guidelines:** resident of IL, IN, MI, MN, OH or WI; play unproduced professionally; send SASE for guidelines. **Submission procedure:** script with signed statement that play has not been professionally produced. **Deadline:** 1 May 1993. **Notification:** 1 Aug 1993.

WESTERN PUBLIC RADIO PLAYWRITING CONTEST
Western Public Radio; Fort Mason Center; San Francisco, CA 94123;
(415) 771-1160
Leo C. Lee, *Project Director*

Types of material: one-acts. **Frequency:** annual. **Remuneration:** $300 for each of 3 plays; production as part of WPR's *California Radio Theatre* series. **Guidelines:** original play no longer than 30 minutes and suitable for radio. **Submission procedure:** script only. **Deadline:** 15 Jun 1993.

WHITE BIRD ANNUAL PLAYWRITING CONTEST
White Bird Productions; Box 20233, Columbus Circle Station;
New York, NY 10023; (718) 788-5984
Kathryn Dickinson, *Artistic Director*

Types of material: full-length plays, one-acts. **Frequency:** annual. **Remuneration:** $200; staged reading; possible travel to attend rehearsals. **Guidelines:** play whose theme, plot and/or central idea deals in a general or specific way with the environment; 2-submission limit. **Submission procedure:** script with resume. **Deadline:** 15 Feb 1993. **Notification:** Apr 1993.

THE ANN WHITE NEW PLAYWRIGHTS CONTEST
The Ann White Theatre; 5266 Gate Lake Rd; Fort Lauderdale, FL 33319;
(305) 722-4371
Ann White, *Founder/Executive Director*

Types of material: full-length plays. **Frequency:** annual. **Remuneration:** $500; production. **Guidelines:** unpublished, unproduced play; small cast, simple set preferred; write for guidelines. **Submission procedure:** script only. **Deadline:** 15 Nov 1992. **Notification:** Mar 1993.

JACKIE WHITE MEMORIAL NATIONAL CHILDREN'S PLAYWRITING CONTEST

(formerly Columbia Entertainment Company
Children's Theatre Playwriting Contest)
309 Parkade Blvd; Columbia, MO 65202; (314) 874-5628
Betsy Phillips, *Chairperson*

Types of material: plays and musicals to be performed by young actors. **Frequency:** annual. **Remuneration:** $250; production by Columbia Entertainment Company Children's Theatre School; room, board and partial travel to attend rehearsals; entrants receive written evaluation. **Guidelines:** unpublished original work, 60–90 minutes in length, with speaking roles for 20–30 characters of all ages to be played by students aged 10–15; send SASE for guidelines. **Submission procedure:** script with character breakdown and act/scene synopsis; cassette for musical; resume; $10 fee. **Deadline:** 30 Jun 1993. **Notification:** 30 Aug 1993.

WICHITA STATE UNIVERSITY PLAYWRITING CONTEST

University Theatre; Wichita State University, Box 31; Wichita, KS 67208;
    (316) 689-3185
Bela Kiralyfalvi, *Contest Director*

Types of material: full-length plays, bills of related one-acts. **Frequency:** annual. **Remuneration:** production; expenses for playwright to attend production. **Guidelines:** unpublished, unproduced work at least 90 minutes long by student currently enrolled at U.S. college or university; write for guidelines. **Submission procedure:** script only. **Deadline:** 15 Feb 1993. **Notification:** 15 Apr 1993.

TENNESSEE WILLIAMS/NEW ORLEANS LITERARY FESTIVAL ONE-ACT PLAY CONTEST

Creative Writing Workshop; College of Liberal Arts; University of New Orleans;
    New Orleans, LA 70148
Fredrick Barton, *Coordinating Judge*

Types of material: one-acts. **Frequency:** annual. **Remuneration:** $1000; reading. **Guidelines:** unpublished play on an American subject not produced professionally. **Submission procedure:** script with $15 fee. **Deadline:** 1 Jan 1993. **Notification:** 1 Apr 1993.

WRITER'S DIGEST WRITING COMPETITION

1507 Dana Ave; Cincinnati, OH 45207-1005; (513) 531-2222
Script Judge

Types of materials: full-length plays, one-acts, screenplays, teleplays, radio plays. **Frequency:** annual. **Remuneration:** Grand Prize: expenses-paid trip to New York City to meet with 4 editors or agents; 1st prize: $250 plus 1992 *Writer's Market* (see Useful Publications); 2nd prize: set of 5 reference books; 3rd prize: 1-year subscription to *Publishers Weekly*; 4th prize: creative-writing computer tutorial program; scripts by winners of Grand Prize and 1st and 2nd prizes published in

Contest Booklet. **Guidelines:** unproduced, unpublished work, not accepted by publisher or producer at time of submission; previous entries ineligible; write for guidelines. **Submission procedure:** first 15 pages of script with 1-page synopsis and indication of projected market for work; completed entry form and $5 fee. **Deadline:** 31 May 1993. **Notification:** Oct 1993.

YEAR-END-SERIES (Y.E.S.) NEW PLAY FESTIVAL
Department of Theatre; Northern Kentucky University;
Highland Heights, KY 41099; (606) 572-5560
Joseph Conger, *Project Director*

Types of material: full-length plays, one-acts, musicals. **Frequency:** biennial. **Remuneration:** 3 prizes: $400; production; travel and expenses to attend late rehearsals and performance. **Guidelines:** unproduced work in which majority of roles can be handled by students; small orchestra for musicals; 1 submission (2 one-acts allowed); playwright available for visit 15–25 Apr 1993. **Submission procedure:** completed application and script. **Deadline:** 1 Dec 1992. **Notification:** Feb 1993.

YOUNG PLAYWRIGHTS FESTIVAL
The Foundation of the Dramatists Guild; 321 West 44th St, Suite 906;
New York, NY 10036; (212) 307-1140
Nancy Quinn, *Producing Director*

Types of material: full-length plays, one-acts. **Frequency:** annual. **Remuneration:** staged reading or production with royalty; travel and residency; 1-year Dramatists Guild membership. **Guidelines:** playwright under the age of 19 on 1 Jul 1992; write for guidelines. **Submission procedure:** script with playwright's name, date of birth, home address and phone number on title page. **Deadline:** 1 Oct 1992.

ANNA ZORNIO MEMORIAL CHILDREN'S THEATRE PLAYWRITING AWARD
Theater Resources for Youth; Department of Theater and Dance; Paul Creative
Arts Center; University of New Hampshire; Durham, NH 03824-3538;
(603) 862-2291, -2150
Carol Lucha-Burns, *Director of Youth Drama*

Types of material: plays and musicals for young audiences. **Frequency:** annual. **Remuneration:** up to $250; production. **Guidelines:** U.S. or Canadian resident; unpublished work not produced professionally; 1-hour limit; single or unit set preferred; 3-submission limit; write for rules. **Deadline:** 15 Apr 1993. **Notification:** 30 Jun 1993.

Publication

What is listed in this section?

Those who are primarily or exclusively play publishers and who consider work of unpublished writers. In addition, we list literary magazines and other small presses which have indicated they publish plays.

How can I determine the best places to submit my play?

Think of these publishers as highly individual people looking for very particular kinds of material, which means you should find out as much as possible about their operations before submitting scripts. One of the best ways to do research is by contacting the Council of Literary Magazines and Presses: 154 Christopher St, Suite 3C; New York, NY 10014-2839; (212) 741-9110. Ask for *The 1992-93 Directory of Literary Magazines* ($13.50), a descriptive listing of hundreds of magazines, including many which say they publish plays. You may be able to look at copies of some of these in a local library or bookstore. Other leads may be found in the *1992-93 International Directory of Little Magazines and Small Presses* (Dustbooks; Box 100; Paradise, CA 95967; (916) 877-6110; $26.95 paper, $42.95 cloth, plus $5.00 shipping and handling). You can also write to individual publishers listed here and ask for style sheets, catalogues, sample copies, etc. Don't forget that when publishers say they accept unsolicited scripts, they *always* require you to enclose an SASE for return of the manuscript.

ALABAMA LITERARY REVIEW
253 Smith Hall; Troy State University; Troy, AL 36082; (205) 670-3307
Theron Montgomery, *Chief Editor*

Types of material: full-length plays, one-acts, translations, adaptations, plays for young audiences, musicals. **Remuneration:** 2 complimentary copies (more on request). **Guidelines:** biannual literary journal publishing 1 play a year; plays under 50 pages long, under 30 pages preferred. **Submission procedure:** accepts unsolicited scripts. **Response time:** 2 months.

AMELIA MAGAZINE
329 "E" St; Bakersfield, CA 93304; (805) 323-4064
Frederick A. Raborg, Jr., *Editor*

Types of material: one-acts, including translations. **Remuneration:** $150 prize; 10 complimentary copies. **Guidelines:** winner of annual Frank McClure One-Act Play Award published in magazine Oct 1993; unpublished play not more than 45 minutes long. **Submission procedure:** submit script including note of any productions, and $15 fee (includes copy of magazine containing winning entry). **Deadline:** 15 May 1993. **Notification:** 15 Jul 1993.

AMERICAN THEATRE
Theatre Communications Group; 355 Lexington Ave; New York, NY 10017;
    (212) 697-5230
Jim O'Quinn, *Editor*
Gillian Richards, *Literary Coordinator*

Types of material: full-length plays, one-acts, translations, adaptations, plays for young audiences. **Remuneration:** negotiated fee; complimentary copies. **Guidelines:** significant works from the contemporary world theatre. **Submission procedure:** no unsolicited scripts; submissions at literary coordinator's request only.

AMERICAN WRITING: A MAGAZINE
4343 Manayunk Ave; Philadelphia, PA 19128; (215) 483-7051
Alexandra Grilikhes, *Editor*

Types of material: musicals, short experimental theatre pieces, performance pieces. **Remuneration:** 3 complimentary copies. **Guidelines:** biannual literary/arts journal publishing 1 or 2 theatrical works a year; seeks new writing that takes risks and explores new forms; interested in "the voice of the loner"; 10,000 words maximum. **Submission procedure:** accepts unsolicited scripts. **Response time:** 3–4 months.

THE AMERICAS REVIEW
Arte Público Press; University of Houston; Houston, TX 77204-2090;
(713) 749-4768
Nicolás Kanellos, *Publisher*
José Saldivar, Juan Olivares, *Editors*

Types of material: full-length plays, one-acts, adaptations, plays for young audiences, musicals. **Remuneration:** fee; 2 complimentary copies. **Guidelines:** unpublished works in English or Spanish by Hispanic writers only. **Submission procedure:** accepts unsolicited scripts. **Response time:** 3 months.

ANCHORAGE PRESS
Box 8067; New Orleans, LA 70182; (504) 283-8868
Orlin Corey, *Editor*

Types of material: works for young audiences, including full-length plays, one-acts, translations, adaptations and musicals. **Remuneration:** negotiated royalty. **Guidelines:** specialty house publishing quality works for young audiences only; works produced at least 3 times. **Submission procedure:** accepts unsolicited scripts with proof of production. **Response time:** 45–90 days.

ARAN PRESS
1320 South 3rd St; Louisville, KY 40208-2306; (502) 636-0115
Tom Eagan, *Editor and Publisher*

Types of material: full-length plays, one-acts, translations, adaptations. **Remuneration:** 10% book royalty, 50% production royalty; playwright contributes to publishing costs: $200 for full-length play, $100 for one-act. **Guidelines:** plays suitable for marketing to community, college and university, summer stock, dinner and professional theatres. **Submission procedure:** accepts unsolicited scripts; prefers letter of inquiry with SASE for response. **Response time:** 3 weeks.

ART CRAFT PLAY COMPANY
Box 1058; Cedar Rapids, IA 52406; (319) 364-6311
C. Emmet McMullen, *Editor and Publisher*

Types of material: full-length plays, one-acts, musicals. **Remuneration:** negotiated royalty or payment for amateur rights; complimentary copies. **Guidelines:** works suitable for junior and senior high school market. **Submission procedure:** accepts unsolicited scripts. **Response time:** 1–2 months.

ARTE PUBLICO PRESS
University of Houston; Houston, TX 77204-2090; (713) 749-4768
Nicolás Kanellos, *Publisher*

Types of material: full-length plays, one-acts, adaptations, plays for young audiences, musicals. **Remuneration:** negotiated royalty; complimentary copies. **Guidelines:** unpublished works in English or Spanish by Hispanic writers only;

usually writers whose work has previously been published in *The Americas Review* (see entry in this section). **Submission procedure:** accepts unsolicited scripts. **Response time:** 3 months.

ASYLUM
Box 6203; Santa Maria, CA 93456; (805) 928-8774
Greg Boyd, *Editor*

Types of material: full-length plays, one-acts. **Remuneration:** 3–5 complimentary copies. **Guidelines:** annual literary magazine publishing 1 play a year; special interest in contemporary experimental work and surrealism. **Submission procedure:** accepts unsolicited scripts. **Response time:** 3–6 months.

BAKER'S PLAYS
100 Chauncy St; Boston, MA 02111; (617) 482-1280
John B. Welch, *Editor*

Types of material: full-length plays, one-acts, plays for young audiences, musicals, chancel dramas. **Remuneration:** negotiated royalty. **Guidelines:** prefers produced plays suitable for high school, community and regional theatre; "Plays for Young Adults" division publishes plays with mature themes for teen audiences. **Submission procedure:** accepts unsolicited scripts. **Response time:** 3–4 months. **Special programs:** Baker's Plays High School Playwriting Contest (see Prizes).

THE BELLINGHAM REVIEW
The Signpost Press; 1007 Queen St; Bellingham, WA 98226
Susan Hilton, *Editor*

Types of material: one-acts. **Remuneration:** 1 complimentary copy; 1-year subscription. **Guidelines:** biannual small-press periodical featuring short plays, fiction and poetry; unpublished plays, preferably under 5000 words long. **Submission procedure:** accepts unsolicited scripts. **Response time:** 4 months.

BLUE CORNER DRAMA
(formerly listed under Sun & Moon Press)
Gertrude Stein Plaza; 6148 Wilshire Blvd; Los Angeles, CA 90048-9377;
   (213) 857-1115
Peter Fahrni, *Editor*

Types of material: full-length plays, translations. **Remuneration:** royalty; 10 complimentary copies. **Guidelines:** small press publishing average of 5 plays a year; unpublished plays. **Submission procedure:** accepts unsolicited scripts. **Response time:** 2–6 months.

BROADWAY PLAY PUBLISHING
357 West 20th St; New York, NY 10011; (212) 627-1055

Types of material: full-length plays. **Remuneration:** 10% book royalty, 80% amateur royalty, 90% stock royalty; 10 complimentary copies. **Guidelines:** major interest is in original, innovative work by American playwrights; no historical or autobiographical plays. **Submission procedure:** no unsolicited scripts; letter of inquiry. **Response time:** 3 months.

BROOKLYN REVIEW
Department of English; Brooklyn College; Brooklyn, NY 11210; (718) 780-5195
Playwriting Editor

Types of material: one-acts. **Remuneration:** 2 complimentary copies. **Guidelines:** annual journal of poetry, fiction and drama publishing an average of 2 plays a year; unpublished plays not more than 10 pages long. **Submission procedure:** accepts unsolicited scripts; submit Oct–Nov only. **Response time:** 6 weeks–6 months.

CALLALOO
Department of English; University of Virginia; Wilson Hall;
    Charlottesville, VA 22903; (804) 924-6637
Charles H. Rowell, *Editor*

Types of material: one-acts, including translations. **Remuneration:** complimentary copies and offprints; payment when grant money is available. **Guidelines:** journal of Afro-American and African arts and letters published by Johns Hopkins University Press. **Submission procedure:** accepts unsolicited scripts. **Response time:** 6 months.

CEILIDH
Box 6367; San Mateo, CA 94403; (415) 591-9902
Patrick Sullivan, *Editor/Publisher*

Types of material: short full-length plays, one-acts. **Remuneration:** 2 complimentary copies. **Guidelines:** literary journal publishing an average of 1 short play a year; modern writing with a strong voice. **Submission procedure:** accepts unsolicited scripts; send SASE for guidelines; if requesting sample copy, include $5 and ask for copy containing play. **Response time:** 8 weeks.

CHICAGO PLAYS
2632 North Lincoln; Chicago, IL 60614; (312) 348-4658
Bill Massolia

Types of material: full-length plays, one-acts, adaptations, plays for young audiences, musicals. **Remuneration:** book and performance royalties; complimentary copies negotiable (usually 10). **Guidelines:** plays produced professionally in Chicago area; prefers plays with Chicago or Midwest flavor, or by Chicago or

Midwest authors; write for guidelines. **Submission procedure:** accepts unsolicited scripts with proof of or notice of application for copyright, programs, reviews and publicity material. **Response time:** 3 months.

CHILD LIFE
1100 Waterway Blvd; Box 567; Indianapolis, IN 46206; (317) 636-8881
Steve Charles, *Editor*

Types of material: works for young audiences, including one-acts, adaptations and brief playlets. **Remuneration:** 10¢ a word; up to 10 complimentary copies. **Guidelines:** children's magazine with a special interest in health issues published 8 times a year; 800 words maximum. **Submission procedure:** accepts unsolicited scripts. **Deadline:** 8 months in advance for seasonal pieces. **Response time:** 8–10 weeks.

CHILDREN'S PLAYMATE MAGAZINE
1100 Waterway Blvd; Box 567; Indianapolis, IN 46206; (317) 636-8881, ext 249
Elizabeth Rinck, *Editor*

Types of material: plays for young audiences. **Remuneration:** approximately 10¢ a word. **Guidelines:** unpublished plays; 500–800 words; prefers health-related themes. **Submission procedure:** accepts unsolicited scripts. **Deadline:** submit seasonal material 8 months in advance. **Response time:** 8–10 weeks.

I. E. CLARK
Saint John's Rd; Box 246; Schulenburg, TX 78956; (409) 743-3232
Donna Cozzaglio, *Editorial Department*

Types of material: full-length plays, one-acts, translations, adaptations, plays for young audiences, musicals. **Remuneration:** book and performance royalties. **Guidelines:** publishes for worldwide professional, amateur and educational market; prefers produced works. **Submission procedure:** accepts unsolicited scripts; cassette or videotape must accompany musical; include proof of production with reviews and photos for produced works. **Response time:** 6–9 months.

COLLAGES AND BRICOLAGES
Box 86; Clarion, PA 16214; (814) 226-5799
Marie-José Fortis, *Editor*

Types of material: one-acts, minimalist plays. **Remuneration:** 2 complimentary copies. **Guidelines:** annual journal of international writing publishing poetry, fiction, drama and criticism, including 1–5 plays a year; avant-garde and feminist work; innovative plays under 30 pages long reflecting philosophical and social concerns. **Submission procedure:** accepts unsolicited scripts; submit 1 Aug–1 Nov only. **Response time:** 2 weeks–3 months.

CONFRONTATION
English Department; C.W. Post College of Long Island University;
Greenvale, NY 11548; (516) 299-2391
Martin Tucker, *Editor*

Types of material: one-acts. **Remuneration:** $15–75; 1 complimentary copy. **Guidelines:** general magazine for literate audience; unpublished plays. **Submission procedure:** accepts unsolicited scripts. **Response time:** 8–10 weeks.

CONTEMPORARY DRAMA SERVICE
Meriwether Publishing, Ltd; 885 Elkton Dr; Colorado Springs, CO 80907
Arthur Zapel, *Editor*

Types of material: full-length plays, one-acts, adaptations, plays for young audiences, musicals, readers' theatre, monologues. **Remuneration:** book and performance royalties or payment for amateur and publishing rights. **Guidelines:** works suitable for teenage, high school and college market; no works for preteen audience; prefers comedies; prefers produced works. **Submission procedure:** accepts unsolicited scripts; send $2 for sample catalogue and guidelines. **Response time:** 2 months.

CRAZY QUILT QUARTERLY
Box 632729; San Diego, CA 92163-2729; (619) 688-1023
Marsh Cassady, *Drama Editor*

Types of material: one-acts. **Remuneration:** 2 complimentary copies. **Guidelines:** quarterly literary journal publishing 3–4 plays a year. **Submission procedure:** accepts unsolicited scripts. **Response time:** 3 months.

THE CREAM CITY REVIEW
English Department; Box 413; University of Wisconsin–Milwaukee;
Milwaukee, WI 53201; (414) 229-4708
Sandra Nelson, *Editor-in-Chief*

Types of material: one-acts. **Remuneration:** payment varies; 2 complimentary copies. **Guidelines:** biannual literary magazine publishing mainstream and experimental work, including an average of 1 play a year; plays not more than 30 pages long. **Submission procedure:** accepts unsolicited scripts. **Response time:** 6–8 weeks.

DRAMA BOOK PUBLISHERS
260 Fifth Ave; New York, NY 10001; (212) 725-5377
Ralph Pine, *Editor-in-Chief*

Types of material: full-length plays, translations, musicals. **Remuneration:** advance against royalties. **Guidelines:** plays that have been professionally produced, preferably on Broadway. **Submission procedure:** accepts unsolicited scripts with proof of professional production. **Response time:** 2 weeks.

THE DRAMATIC PUBLISHING COMPANY
311 Washington St; Box 129; Woodstock, IL 60098; (815) 338-7170
Sara Clark, *Editor*

Types of material: full-length plays, one-acts, translations, adaptations, plays for young audiences, musicals. **Remuneration:** standard royalty; 10 complimentary copies (30% discount on additional copies). **Guidelines:** works for stock and amateur market; at least 30 minutes long; prefers produced plays. **Submission procedure:** accepts unsolicited scripts. **Response time:** 2–4 months.

DRAMATICS MAGAZINE
3368 Central Pkwy; Cincinnati, OH 45225; (513) 559-1996
Don Corathers, *Editor*

Types of material: full-length plays, one-acts. **Remuneration:** payment for one-time publication rights; complimentary copies. **Guidelines:** educational theatre magazine; plays suitable for high school production; prefers produced plays. **Submission procedure:** accepts unsolicited scripts. **Response time:** 2–3 months.

DRAMATIKA
429 Hope St; Tarpon Springs, FL 34689
John Pyros, *Editor*

Types of material: one-acts, 1-page plays, performance-art texts, "dramatic cartoons." **Remuneration:** complimentary copies. **Guidelines:** irregularly published small magazine; "we like to think of ourselves as a bit adventurous." **Submission procedure:** no unsolicited scripts; letter of inquiry. **Response time:** 1 month.

DRAMATISTS PLAY SERVICE
440 Park Ave South; New York, NY 10016; (212) 683-8960
Bradley G. Kalos, *President*

Types of material: full-length plays, one-acts, translations, adaptations, plays for young audiences, musicals. **Remuneration:** usually advance against royalties; 10% book royalty, 80% amateur royalty, 90% stock royalty; 10 complimentary copies. **Guidelines:** works for stock and amateur market; prefers work produced in New York City. **Submission procedure:** no unsolicited scripts; letter of inquiry. **Response time:** 2–4 months.

EARTH'S DAUGHTERS
Box 622, Station C; Buffalo, NY 14209; (716) 837-7778

Types of material: full-length plays, one-acts, translations, adaptations, plays for young audiences. **Remuneration:** 2 complimentary copies. **Guidelines:** triannual feminist literary and art periodical with focus on experience and creative expression of women; frequently publishes play excerpts with occasional issue devoted to complete text of play. **Submission procedure:** accepts unsolicited scripts. **Response time:** 2 months.

ELDRIDGE PUBLISHING COMPANY
Drawer 216; Franklin, OH 45005; (513) 746-6531
Nancy S. Vorhis, *Editor*

Types of material: full-length plays, one-acts, musicals. **Remuneration:** outright purchase, percent of royalties or percent of sales; complimentary copies (50% discount on additional copies). **Guidelines:** plays for school, church and community theatre; comedies, mysteries or serious drama; special interest in junior/senior high school full-length plays; seeks Christmas plays. **Submission procedure:** accepts unsolicited scripts; prefers tapes with musicals. **Response time:** 2 months.

ENCORE PERFORMANCE PUBLISHING
Box 692; Orem, UT 84057; (801) 225-0605
Michael C. Perry, *President*

Types of material: full-length plays, one-acts, translations, adaptations, plays for young audiences, musicals. **Remuneration:** 10% book royalty, 50% performance royalty; 10 complimentary copies (discount on additional copies). **Guidelines:** publishes 10–20 plays and musicals a year; works must have had at least 2 amateur or professional productions; special interest in works with strong family or Christian message and in Christmas, Halloween and other holiday plays. **Submission procedure:** synopsis, production information and letter of inquiry. **Response time:** 2–4 weeks.

EVENT: THE DOUGLAS COLLEGE REVIEW
Douglas College; Box 2503; New Westminster, BC; Canada V3L 5B2;
     (604) 520-5400
Dale Zieroth

Types of material: one-acts. **Remuneration:** honorarium. **Guidelines:** triannual journal published Mar, Jul and Nov and featuring both new and established writers; welcomes narrative work that invites involvement; unpublished plays. **Submission procedure:** accepts unsolicited scripts; write for guidelines. **Response time:** 2–3 months.

FREELANCE PRESS
Box 548; Dover, MA 02030; (508) 785-1260
Narcissa Campion, *Managing Editor*

Types of material: musicals for young audiences only. **Remuneration:** 10% book royalty, 70% performance royalty; 1 complimentary copy. **Guidelines:** unpublished issue-oriented musicals and musical adaptations of classics; approximately 1 hour long, suitable for performing by and for young people. **Submission procedure:** accepts unsolicited scripts. **Response time:** 3 months.

SAMUEL FRENCH
45 West 25th St; New York, NY 10010; (212) 206-8990
Lawrence Harbison, *Editor*

Types of material: full-length plays, one-acts, plays for young audiences, musicals. **Remuneration:** generally, advance against royalties; 10% book royalty, 80% amateur royalty, 90% stock royalty; 10 complimentary copies (40% discount on additional copies). **Guidelines:** "Many of our publications have never been produced in New York; these are generally comprised of light comedies, mysteries, mystery-comedies, a handful of one-acts and plays for young audiences, and plays with a preponderance of female roles; however, do not hesitate to send in your Future Pulitzer Prize Winner"; prefers script format presented in *Guidelines* booklet ($4 postpaid). **Submission procedure:** accepts unsolicited scripts. **Response time:** 2–12 months.

GREATWORKS PLAY SERVICE
Box 3148; Shell Beach, CA 93448; (805) 773-3419
Richard Sharp, *Editor*

Types of material: translations and adaptations, including full-length plays, one-acts and musicals. **Remuneration:** production royalty (75% professional, 50% amateur). **Guidelines:** playwright/translator cooperative marketing works and distributing them in manuscript form to potential producers; works of literary merit and/or known titles; produced works; write for guidelines. **Submission procedure:** accepts unsolicited scripts; prefers synopsis and letter of inquiry. **Response time:** 1–6 months.

HAWAI'I REVIEW
c/o UH Mānoa Department of English; 1733 Donaghho Rd; Honolulu, HI 96822; (808) 956-8548
Jeanne K. Tsutsui, *Editor-in-Chief*

Types of material: one-acts, translations, adaptations. **Remuneration:** $5 a page; 2 complimentary copies. **Guidelines:** triquarterly literary journal; submit up to 28 double-spaced pages. **Submission procedure:** accepts unsolicited scripts with SASE for reply. **Response time:** 3–4 months.

HEUER PUBLISHING COMPANY
Box 248; Cedar Rapids, IA 52406; (319) 364-6311
C. Emmet McMullen, *Editor and Publisher*

Types of material: full-length plays, one-acts, musicals. **Remuneration:** negotiated royalty or payment for amateur rights; complimentary copies. **Guidelines:** works suitable for junior and senior high school market. **Submission procedure:** accepts unsolicited scripts. **Response time:** 1–2 months.

KALLIOPE, A JOURNAL OF WOMEN'S ART
3939 Roosevelt Blvd; Jacksonville, FL 32205; (904) 387-8211
Mary Sue Koeppel, *Editor*

Types of material: one-acts. **Remuneration:** 3 complimentary copies or free 1-year subscription. **Guidelines:** triannual journal of women's art publishing short fiction, poetry, artwork, photography, interviews, reviews and an average of 1 play a year; unpublished plays, under 25 pages long, by women only; no trite themes or erotica. **Submission procedure:** accepts unsolicited scripts. **Response time:** 3–6 months.

THE KENYON REVIEW
Kenyon College; Gambier, OH 43022; (614) 427-3339
Marilyn Hacker, *Editor*

Types of material: one-acts; excerpts from full-length plays. **Remuneration:** cash payment; 2 complimentary copies. **Guidelines:** literary quarterly publishing an average of 2 plays a year. **Submission procedure:** accepts unsolicited scripts. **Response time:** 3 months.

LAMIA INK!
Box 202, Prince St Station; New York, NY 10012
Cortland Jessup, *Editor*

Types of material: very short monologues and performance pieces, 1-page plays. **Remuneration:** 4 complimentary copies. **Guidelines:** biannual "art rag" magazine; experimental theatre pieces not more than 10 pages long, prefers 2–3 pages; special interest in Native American writers, poets' theatre, performance poems, theatre manifestos and essays. **Submission procedure:** accepts unsolicited scripts. **Deadline:** 30 Nov for Feb issue; 30 Mar for May issue. **Response time:** 2–3 weeks after deadline. **Special programs:** Lamia Ink! International One-Page Play Competition (see Prizes).

LA NUEZ
Box 1655; New York, NY 10276; (212) 260-3130
Rafael Bordao, *Editor*

Types of material: one-acts, including translations. **Remuneration:** 2 complimentary copies. **Guidelines:** international quarterly of art and literature published in Spanish; unpublished plays in Spanish not more than 10 pages long; special interest in innovative work. **Submission procedure:** accepts unsolicited scripts with short bio. **Response time:** 2 months.

LATIN AMERICAN LITERARY REVIEW
2300 Palmer St; Pittsburgh, PA 15218; (412) 351-1477
Yvette Miller, *Editor*

Types of material: one-act translations. **Remuneration:** 2 complimentary copies. **Guidelines:** biannual journal in English devoted to Latin American literature; publishes articles, reviews, and creative work, including an average of 1 play a year; translations of one-act Latin American plays, especially contemporary plays; 20-page maximum length. **Submission procedure:** accepts unsolicited scripts. **Response time:** 6 months.

LILLENAS DRAMA RESOURCES
Lillenas Publishing Company; Box 419527; Kansas City, MO 64141;
   (816) 931-1900
Paul M. Miller, *Consultant/Editor*

Types of material: full-length plays, one-acts, musicals, collections of sketches, skits, playlets, recitations. **Remuneration:** purchase or royalty. **Guidelines:** unpublished "creatively conceived and practically producible scripts and outlines that provide church and school with an opportunity to glorify God and his creation in drama." **Submission procedure:** accepts unsolicited scripts; send SASE for contributor's guidelines and current need sheet. **Response time:** 3 months.

THE MASSACHUSETTS REVIEW
Memorial Hall; University of Massachusetts–Amherst; Amherst, MA 01003;
   (413) 545-2689
Drama Editors

Types of material: one-acts. **Remuneration:** $50; 2 complimentary copies. **Guidelines:** quarterly review of literature, arts and current affairs; play not more than 30 pages long. **Submission procedure:** accepts unsolicited scripts; submit 1 Oct–1 Jun only. **Response time:** 1–2 months.

MODERN INTERNATIONAL DRAMA
Theatre Department; State University of New York–Binghamton; Box 6000;
   Binghamton, NY 13902-6000; (607) 777-2704
George E. Wellwarth and Anthony M. Pasquariello, *Editors*

Types of material: translations. **Remuneration:** 3 complimentary copies. **Guidelines:** biannual journal; unpublished translations of plays not previously translated; style guide sent on request. **Submission procedure:** accepts unsolicited scripts. **Response time:** 1 month.

MODERN LITURGY
160 East Virginia St, Suite 290; San Jose, CA 95112; (408) 286-8505
Charlotte Pace, *Managing Editor*

Types of material: short plays and skits, preferably 7–15 minutes long. **Remuneration:** 5 complimentary copies; subscription. **Guidelines:** unpublished plays with few props, suitable for religious celebrations and classes. **Submission procedure:** accepts unsolicited scripts. **Response time:** 6–8 weeks.

NEW PLAYS
Box 5074; Charlottesville, VA 22905; (804) 979-2777
Patricia Whitton, *Publisher*

Types of material: plays for young audiences. **Remuneration:** 10% book royalty, 50% production royalty. **Guidelines:** innovative material not duplicated by other sources of plays for young audiences; produced plays, directed by someone other than author. **Submission procedure:** accepts unsolicited scripts. **Response time:** at least 1–2 months.

OBSIDIAN II: BLACK LITERATURE IN REVIEW
Box 8105; Department of English; North Carolina State University;
Raleigh, NC 27695-8105; (919) 515-3870
Gerald Barrax, *Editor*

Types of material: short full-length plays, one-acts. **Remuneration:** 2 complimentary copies. **Guidelines:** triannual literary journal publishing an average of 3 plays a year; plays by black writers only; unpublished plays not under consideration elsewhere, 25–30 pages long. **Submission procedure:** accepts unsolicited scripts; send 2 copies of script. **Response time:** 3 months.

OUT/LOOK NATIONAL LESBIAN AND GAY QUARTERLY
540 Castro St; San Francisco, CA 94114; (415) 626-7929
Robin Stevens, *Editor*

Types of material: one-acts. **Remuneration:** $50–125; 5 complimentary copies. **Guidelines:** quarterly journal publishing 1–2 plays a year; plays under 4000 words long with gay or lesbian content. **Submission procedure:** accepts unsolicited scripts. **Response time:** 3 months.

PACIFIC REVIEW
English Department; California State University;
San Bernardino, CA 92407-2397; (714) 880-5894
James Brown, *Faculty Editor*

Types of material: one-acts. **Remuneration:** 2 complimentary copies. **Guidelines:** annual literary journal; plays 25 pages long or less. **Submission procedure:** accepts unsolicited scripts; submit 1 Sep–1 Feb only. **Response time:** 6 weeks.

PAJ PUBLICATIONS
131 Varick St, Suite 902; New York, NY 10013; (212) 243-3885
Bonnie Marranca and Gautam Dasgupta, *Co-Publishers/Editors*

Types of material: full-length plays, one-acts, translations. **Remuneration:** royalty and/or fee. **Guidelines:** publishes plays and critical literature on the performing arts from the international repertoire; special interest in translations. **Submission procedure:** no unsolicited scripts; synopsis and letter of inquiry. **Response time:** 1–2 months.

PASSAIC REVIEW
Forstmann Library; 195 Gregory Ave; Passaic, NJ 07055; (201) 772-4268
Richard Quatrone, *Publisher and Editor*

Types of material: short one-acts, including plays for young audiences. **Remuneration:** 1 complimentary copy. **Guidelines:** biannual literary review publishing an average of 1 play a year; seeks work which is passionate, powerful, free, personal and alive and which deals with the human condition; plays under 5 pages long. **Submission procedure:** accepts unsolicited scripts. **Response time:** up to 12 months.

PERFORMING ARTS JOURNAL
131 Varick St, Suite 902; New York, NY 10013; (212) 243-3885
Bonnie Marranca and Gautam Dasgupta, *Co-Publishers/Editors*

Types of material: short full-length plays, one-acts, translations. **Remuneration:** fee. **Guidelines:** publishes plays and critical literature on the performing arts from the international repertoire; special interest in translations; plays less than 40 pages in length. **Submission procedure:** no unsolicited scripts; synopsis and letter of inquiry. **Response time:** 1–2 months.

PIONEER DRAMA SERVICE
Box 22555; Denver, CO 80222-0555; (303) 759-4297

Types of material: full-length plays, plays for young audiences, musicals, Christmas plays. **Remuneration:** outright purchase or royalty. **Guidelines:** produced work suitable for educational theatre. **Submission procedure:** accepts unsolicited scripts; prefers synopsis and letter of inquiry. **Response time:** 2–6 weeks.

PLAYERS PRESS
Box 1132; Studio City, CA 91614-0132; (818) 789-4980
Robert W. Gordon, *Senior Editor*

Types of material: full-length plays, one-acts, translations, adaptations, plays for young audiences, musicals, monologues, scenes, teleplays, screenplays. **Remuneration:** royalty, outright purchase and/or cash option; complimentary copies (additional copies at 20% discount). **Guidelines:** theatre press publishing technical and reference books and scripts; produced works for professional, amateur and educational market. **Submission procedure:** accepts unsolicited scripts with proof of production, resume and 2 business-size SASEs; prefers synopsis, proof of production, resume and letter of inquiry with SASE for response. **Response time:** 1–6 months.

PLAYS IN PROCESS
Theatre Communications Group; 355 Lexington Ave; New York, NY 10017;
    (212) 697-5230
Gillian Richards, *Literary Coordinator*

Types of material: full-length plays, one-acts, translations, adaptations, plays for young audiences, musicals. **Remuneration:** script circulation to international subscribership interested in learning about and producing new American works; 10 complimentary copies. **Guidelines:** U.S. writer or translator; work produced by a TCG theatre during current season and nominated by artistic director or literary manager. **Submission procedure:** individual may not apply; application completed by nominating theatre; 4 copies of script; 4 cassettes for musical. **Deadline:** 30 Jun 1993 for 1992–93 season. **Response time:** within 3 months.

PLAYS, THE DRAMA MAGAZINE FOR YOUNG PEOPLE
120 Boylston St; Boston, MA 02116-4615; (617) 423-3157
Elizabeth Preston, *Managing Editor*

Types of material: one-act plays for young audiences, including adaptations of material in the public domain. **Remuneration:** payment on acceptance. **Guidelines:** publishes about 70 plays and programs a year; prefers work 25–30 minutes long for junior and senior high, 15–20 minutes for middle grades, 8–15 minutes for lower grades. **Submission procedure:** accepts unsolicited original scripts; letter of inquiry for adaptations; prefers format used in magazine (write for style sheet). **Response time:** 2 weeks.

PRIMAL VOICES
Lambert/McIntosh Enterprises; Box 3179; Poughkeepsie, NY 12603;
    (914) 471-0226
Susan McIntosh and Carol Lambert, *Editors*

Types of material: one-acts. **Remuneration:** 1 complimentary copy. **Guidelines:** average total of 2 plays a year published in 3 quarterly publications; maximum 30-page length; 1–2 characters; simple settings; write for brochure. **Submission procedure:** accepts unsolicited scripts. **Response time:** 4–6 weeks.

PRISM INTERNATIONAL
Department of Creative Writing; University of British Columbia;
    Buch E462–1866 Main Mall; Vancouver, BC; Canada V6T 1Z1;
    (604) 822-2514
Murray Logan, *Editor*

Types of material: one-acts, translations, excerpts from full-length plays. **Remuneration:** $20 per printed page; 1-year subscription. **Guidelines:** quarterly literary magazine; unpublished plays; 40 pages or less; write for guidelines. **Submission procedure:** accepts unsolicited scripts. **Response time:** 2–4 months.

PROVINCETOWN ARTS
650 Commercial St; Provincetown, MA 02657; (508) 487-3167
Christopher Busa, *Editor and Publisher*

Types of material: one-acts, translations, musicals, performance-art texts. **Remuneration:** $100–300; 2–12 complimentary copies. **Guidelines:** July magazine that focuses broadly on artists and writers who inhabit or visit the tip of Cape Cod; especially interested in performance-art texts; unpublished plays; 30 pages long or less. **Submission procedure:** accepts unsolicited scripts; submissions read Aug–Feb. **Response time:** 2 months.

RAG MAG
Box 12; Goodhue, MN 55027; (612) 923-4590
Beverly Voldseth, *Editor/Publisher*

Types of material: full-length plays, one-acts. **Remuneration:** 1 complimentary copy. **Guidelines:** biannual small-press literary magazine publishing artwork, prose and poetry, and interested in receiving play submissions; innovative character plays; prefers short one-acts but will consider longer plays with a view to publishing extracts or scenes. **Submission procedure:** accepts unsolicited short one-acts; send maximum 10-page sample and letter of inquiry for longer plays. **Best submission time:** Jan and Sep only. **Response time:** 1–2 months.

RESOURCE PUBLICATIONS
160 East Virginia St, #290; San Jose, CA 95112-5848; (408) 286-8505
Ken Guentert, *Editorial Director*

Types of material: plays 7–15 minutes long. **Remuneration:** royalty. **Guidelines:** unpublished plays or collections of plays suitable for celebrations, religious education classes, youth ministry, counseling and therapy. **Submission procedure:** accepts unsolicited scripts. **Response time:** 2 months.

ROCKFORD REVIEW/TRIBUTARY
Box 858; Rockford, IL 61105; (815) 963-2098
David Ross, *Editor*

Rockford Review

Types of material: one-acts. **Remuneration:** one-acts selected for publication eligible for annual "Editor's Choice" prize of $50; 1 complimentary copy. **Guidelines:** annual journal publishing poetry, fiction, satire, artwork and an average of 4–5 plays a year; one-acts not more than 15 pages long, preferably of a satirical nature; interested in work that provides new insight into the human dilemma ("to cope or not to cope"). **Submission procedure:** accepts unsolicited scripts; sample copy $6. **Response time:** 4 weeks.

Tributary

Types of material: monologues and brief plays. **Remuneration:** pieces selected for publication eligible for quarterly "Readers' Poll" prize of $25; 1 complimentary copy. **Guidelines:** quarterly supplement to *Review,* same material but shorter (see above); pieces 3–4 pages long; publishes 4–5 plays a year. **Submission procedure:** accepts unsolicited scripts; sample copy $2.50. **Response time:** 4 weeks.

SALOME
5548 North Sawyer Ave; Chicago, IL 60625; (312) 539-5745
Effie Mihopoulos, *Editor*

Types of material: one-acts. **Remuneration:** 1 complimentary copy. **Guidelines:** performing arts journal; plays dealing with the arts or with artist characters only. **Submission procedure:** accepts unsolicited scripts. **Response time:** 2 weeks–2 months.

SANDHILLS REVIEW
(formerly Sandhills/St. Andrews Review)
Sandhills Community College; 2200 Airport Rd; Pinehurst, NC 28374;
    (919) 692-6185
Stephen Smith, *Editor*

Types of material: short full-length plays, one-acts, translations. **Remuneration:** 2 complimentary copies. **Guidelines:** biannual literary review featuring new and established writers and publishing 1–2 plays a year; special interest in Black Mountain playwrights and plays about the Orient; plays 20–30 pages long. **Submission procedure:** no unsolicited scripts; synopsis and letter of inquiry. **Response time:** 1 month.

SCRIPTS AND SCRIBBLES
141 Wooster St; New York, NY 10012-3163; (212) 473-6695
Daryl Chin, *Consulting Editor*

Types of material: full-length plays, one-acts, performance-art texts or scenarios. **Remuneration:** 25 complimentary copies. **Guidelines:** series initiated to publish texts for nontraditional theatre work and works produced outside New York City. **Submission procedure:** no unsolicited scripts; synopsis and letter of inquiry. **Response time:** 6 months.

SINISTER WISDOM
Box 3252; Berkeley, CA 94703
Elana Dykewomon, *Editor*

Types of material: one-acts, excerpts from full-length plays (3000 words maximum). **Remuneration:** 2 complimentary copies. **Guidelines:** lesbian/feminist quarterly of art and literature; work by lesbians reflecting the diversity of lesbians; no heterosexual themes; send SASE for current themes. **Submission procedure:** accepts unsolicited scripts. **Response time:** 2–9 months.

SWIFT KICK
1711 Amherst St; Buffalo, NY 14214; (716) 837-7778
Robin Kay Willoughby, *Editor*

Types of material: full-length plays, one-acts, translations, adaptations, plays for young audiences, musicals, performance-art texts. **Remuneration:** 3 complimentary copies. **Guidelines:** quarterly magazine specializing in unusual formats, genres and styles; unpublished, unconventional work; most likely to be interested in work generally considered "unproducible." **Submission procedure:** accepts unsolicited scripts; state if submitting material elsewhere. **Response time:** 6 months.

THEATER
222 York St; New Haven, CT 06520; (203) 432-1568
Joel Schechter, *Editor*

Types of material: full-length plays, one-acts, translations, adaptations. **Remuneration:** approximately $150 and/or complimentary copies. **Guidelines:** triannual theatre journal; 1 play that has received a major production published in each issue. **Submission procedure:** no unsolicited scripts; synopsis and letter of inquiry. **Response time:** 2 months.

THEATREFORUM
Theatre Department; University of California–San Diego;
    9500 Gilman Dr; La Jolla, CA 92093-0344; (619) 534-2062
Theodore Shank, *Editor*

Types of material: full-length plays, translations, adaptations. **Remuneration:** varies by length; 2 complimentary copies. **Guidelines:** biannual international journal focusing on innovative work. **Submission procedure:** no unsolicited scripts; professional recommendation. **Response time:** varies.

TYUONYI
c/o Recursos; 826 Camino de Monte Rey; Santa Fe, NM 87501
Phillip Foss, *Editor*

Types of material: one-acts, including translations. **Remuneration:** 2 complimentary copies. **Guidelines:** multiethnic, eclectically avant-garde biannual literary magazine publishing poetry, fiction, plays and essays; special interest in formally innovative work. **Submission procedure:** accepts unsolicited scripts. **Response time:** up to 3 months.

UBU REPERTORY THEATER PUBLICATIONS
See Membership and Service Organizations.

UNITED ARTS
141 Wooster St; New York, NY 10012-3163; (212) 473-6695
Daryl Chin, *Editor*

Types of material: one-acts, translations, performance texts, scenarios, manifestos. **Remuneration:** complimentary copies. **Guidelines:** journal of analysis and opinion covering visual arts, film, video, theatre and dance, published 3–4 times a year by University Arts Resources; nontraditional, avant-garde plays. **Submission procedure:** accepts unsolicited scripts; prefers synopsis and letter of inquiry. **Response time:** 6 months.

THE JAMES WHITE REVIEW
Box 3356, Traffic Station; Minneapolis, MN 55403; (612) 291-2913 or 339-8317
Phil Willkie, *Publisher*

Types of material: excerpts from full-length plays, one-acts. **Remuneration:** $25; 3 complimentary copies. **Guidelines:** gay men's literary quarterly publishing an average of 1 play a year; one-act or excerpt, not more than 25 pages long. **Submission procedure:** accepts unsolicited scripts. **Deadline:** 1 Nov; 1 Feb; 1 May; 1 Aug. **Response time:** 3 months.

WOMEN AND PERFORMANCE: A JOURNAL OF FEMINIST THEORY
New York University; Tisch School of the Arts; 721 Broadway, 6th Floor;
 New York, NY 10003; (212) 998-1625

Types of material: full-length plays, one-acts, translations. **Remuneration:** 1 complimentary copy. **Guidelines:** biannual journal, primarily devoted to critical writings, which also publishes 2 plays a year; previously unpublished or unproduced plays for, by and about women; interested in feminist performance theory. **Submission procedure:** accepts unsolicited scripts; prefers letter of inquiry; write for guidelines. **Response time:** 6 months.

Development

What's in this section?

Conferences, festivals, workshops and programs whose primary purpose is to develop plays and playwrights, including a substantial number devoted to music-theatre. Also listed are some playwright groups and membership organizations whose main activity is play development. Developmental organizations such as New Dramatists whose many programs cannot be adequately described in the brief format used in this section are listed in Membership and Service Organizations.

How can I get into these programs?

Keep applying to those for which you are convinced your work is suited. If you're turned down one year, you may be accepted the next on the strength of your latest piece. If you're required to submit a script with your application, don't forget your SASE!

THE ISIDORA AGUIRRE PLAYWRIGHTING LAB
El Teatro de la Esperanza; Box 40578; San Francisco, CA 94140-0578;
(415) 255-2320
Eve Donovan, *General Manager*

Open to: playwrights. **Description:** 1–3 plays developed through individual sessions and weekly seminars with professional dramaturg over 6-week period, culminating in public staged reading; possible future full production for 1 or more plays. **Financial arrangement:** $1500 stipend to cover travel, room and board. **Guidelines:** Chicano/Latino playwright; full-length play-in-progress reflective of or adaptable to the Chicano experience; prefers bilingual plays, but accepts monolingual plays in Spanish or English; prefers cast limit of 6 (doubling allowed), set suitable for touring; write for guidelines. **Application procedure:** 3 copies of script and resume (material will not be returned). **Deadline:** 15 Mar 1993. **Notification:** 1 May 1993. **Dates:** Jul–Aug 1993.

AMERICAN PLAYWRIGHT PROGRAM
Westbeth Theatre Center; 151 Bank St; New York, NY 10014; (212) 691-2272
Stephen Bloom, *Script Development*

Open to: playwrights. **Description:** program to develop full-length plays through critiques, story conferences and staged readings; possible production by Westbeth Theatre Center or through referral to other producing organizations. **Financial arrangement:** free. **Guidelines:** contemporary themes; cast limit of 8, minimal set; welcomes work by minority playwrights; write for guidelines. **Application procedure:** script with SASE or SASP for response submitted by agent only. **Deadline:** ongoing.

MAXWELL ANDERSON PLAYWRIGHTS SERIES (MAPS)
11 Esquire Rd; Norwalk, CT 06851; (203) 847-4124
Muriel Nussbaum, *Artistic Director*

Open to: playwrights. **Description:** 6–8 new plays a year given 3 staged readings with professional actors and director, followed by audience discussion. **Financial arrangement:** free. **Guidelines:** unproduced play; write for guidelines. **Application procedure:** script only. **Deadline:** ongoing.

ASCAP MUSICAL THEATRE WORKSHOP
1 Lincoln Plaza; New York, NY 10023; (212) 621-6234
Michael A. Kerker, *Director of Musical Theatre*

Open to: composers, lyricists. **Description:** 10-week workshop meeting once a week for 3 hours under the direction of Charles Strouse; works presented to panels of musical theatre professionals. **Financial arrangement:** free; $500 Bernice Cohen Musical Theatre Fund Award given to most promising participating individual or team. **Guidelines:** limited number of previous participants with new projects also eligible. **Application procedure:** resume and cassette of 4 theatrical songs (no pop songs). **Deadline:** 1 Aug 1993; submissions will probably be accepted from 1 Jul 1993; call for information. **Notification:** Sep 1993. **Dates:** workshop begins early Oct 1993.

BAY AREA PLAYWRIGHTS FESTIVAL
The Playwrights Foundation; Box 460357; San Francisco, CA 94114;
   (415) 777-2996
Norah Holmgren, *President*

Open to: playwrights. **Description:** 6–12 scripts each given 2 rehearsed readings, separated by 2 weeks for rewrites, during month-long festival at the Magic Theatre; prefestival weekend for initial discussion with directors and dramaturgs. **Financial arrangement:** small stipend. **Guidelines:** northern CA playwright; unproduced play. **Application procedure:** script with resume. **Deadline:** 1 Feb 1993. **Notification:** Apr 1993. **Dates:** prefestival weekend May 1993; festival late Jul–early Aug 1993.

BMI–LEHMAN ENGEL MUSICAL THEATRE WORKSHOP
Broadcast Music, Inc; 320 West 57th St; New York, NY 10019; (212) 830-2515
Norma Grossman, *Director, Musical Theatre*

Open to: composers, lyricists. **Description:** 2-year program of weekly workshop meetings; showcase presentation to invited members of entertainment industry each year. **Financial arrangement:** free. **Application procedure:** completed application and work samples. **Deadline:** 1 Aug 1993.

BORDER PLAYWRIGHTS PROJECT
Borderlands Theater; Box 2791; Tucson, AZ 85702; (602) 882-8607
Debra J. T. Padilla, *Managing Director*

Open to: playwrights. **Description:** 3 plays developed over 10-day residency with actors, director and dramaturg, culminating in staged reading. **Financial arrangement:** $250 stipend, travel, housing. **Guidelines:** work which reflects the culturally diverse realities of the border region, or uses the border as metaphor; unproduced full-length play by writer of color; English, Spanish and bilingual scripts accepted; write for information. **Application procedure:** script only. **Deadline:** Jan 1993 (15 Jan in 1992). **Notification:** Mar 1993. **Dates:** Jun 1993.

BROADWAY TOMORROW
191 Claremont Ave, Suite 53; New York, NY 10027; (212) 864-4736
Elyse Curtis, *Artistic Director*

Open to: composers, librettists, lyricists. **Description:** new musicals presented in concert with writers' involvement. **Financial arrangement:** free. **Application procedure:** submissions accepted with professional recommendation only; cassette of 3 songs with description of 3 scenes in which they occur, synopsis, resume, reviews if available, and SASE for response. **Deadline:** 2 Sep 1992.

CAC PLAYWRIGHT'S FORUM
Contemporary Arts Center; Box 30498; New Orleans, LA 70190; (504) 523-1216

Open to: playwrights, translators, librettists, lyricists. **Description:** year-round workshop for 8–10 local and visiting writers; staged readings or workshops. **Financial arrangement:** free. **Guidelines:** professional writer. **Application procedure:** script only. **Deadline:** ongoing.

THE CHESTERFIELD FILM COMPANY/WRITER'S FILM PROJECT
Universal Studios; 100 Universal City Plaza, Bungalow 131;
Universal City, CA 91608; (818) 777-0998

Open to: playwrights, screenwriters. **Description:** up to 10 writers annually chosen for year-long screenwriting workshop meeting 3–5 times a week; writer creates 2 feature-length screenplays; company intends to produce best of year's work. **Financial arrangement:** $20,000 stipend. **Guidelines:** university-trained writers preferred; current and former writing-program students encouraged to apply; write or call for information. **Application procedure:** 2 copies completed application; writing samples; $30 fee. **Deadline:** May 1993 (19 May in 1992). **Notification:** 31 Aug 1993. **Dates:** Sep 1993–Aug 1994.

DISCOVEREADS
The Cleveland Play House; Box 1989; Cleveland, OH 44106; (216) 795-7010
Roger T. Danforth, *Literary Manager*

Open to: playwrights. **Description:** 5–8 plays developed in collaboration with director, actors and dramaturg, culminating in public reading; some scripts given staged reading with 4–5 days of rehearsal, others sit-down reading with 6–8 hours of rehearsal. **Financial arrangement:** stipend, travel, housing and per diem. **Guidelines:** unproduced play. **Application procedure:** agent submission only. **Deadline:** ongoing. **Dates:** late spring.

DISCOVERY '93
Paul Mellon Arts Center; Choate Rosemary Hall, Box 788;
Wallingford, CT 06492-0788; (203) 269-1113
Terrence Ortwein, *Director*

Open to: playwrights. **Description:** maximum of 3 playwrights participate in 3-week developmental workshop leading to script-in-hand reading by high school students. **Financial arrangement:** $700 stipend, housing and board. **Guidelines:** unproduced play written specifically for high school production; content that will appeal directly to teenagers; prefers maximum length of 1 hour; write for further details. **Application procedure:** script only. **Deadline:** 1 Mar 1993. **Notification:** 1 May 1993. **Dates:** Jul 1993.

FREDERICK DOUGLASS CREATIVE ARTS CENTER WRITING WORKSHOPS
168 West 46th St; New York, NY 10036; (212) 944-9870
Fred Hudson, *Artistic Director*

Open to: playwrights. **Description:** 3 cycles a year of 8-week workshops; beginning and advanced playwriting; latter includes readings and possible productions; also film and television writing workshops; weekly meetings. **Financial arrangement:** $90 fee per workshop; author of play given staged reading receives $50; author of produced play receives $500. **Application procedure:** contact FDCAC for information. **Deadline:** early Sep 1992 for 1st cycle; early Jan 1993 for 2nd and 3rd cycles; exact dates TBA. **Dates:** Oct–Dec 1992; Jan–Mar 1993; Apr–Jun 1993.

DRAMARAMA
The Playwrights' Center of San Francisco; 2215-R Market St, #423;
    San Francisco, CA 94114; (415) 626-4603
Sabra Bachelor, *President*

Open to: playwrights. **Description:** up to 11 scripts given 4–5 rehearsals and staged readings at summer festival. **Financial arrangement:** free; best play receives $100 prize. **Guidelines:** full-length or one-act play not previously produced in Bay Area. **Application procedure:** script with 1-page synopsis and character descriptions. **Deadline:** 15 Jan 1993. **Dates:** Jun 1993.

DUO THEATRE DEVELOPMENTAL PROGRAMS
Box 1200, Cooper Station; New York, NY 10276; (212) 598-4320

Latino Playwrights Lab
Gabriella Roepke, *Project Coordinator*

Open to: playwrights. **Description:** 16-week developmental workshop culminating in staged readings. **Financial arrangement:** free. **Guidelines:** Latino playwright wishing to write in Spanish. **Application procedure:** work sample in Spanish. **Deadline:** 1 Dec 1992. **Notification:** 15 Feb 1993. **Dates:** Mar–Jun 1993.

Musical Theatre Commission Program
Michael Alasá, *Executive Director*

Open to: composers, librettists, lyricists. **Description:** 4 musicals developed a year with a view to full production. **Financial arrangement:** $1500 commission. **Guidelines:** unproduced musical theatre work by Latino artist(s) writing in English. **Application procedure:** book and lyrics with cassette of music (if available); or project proposal with sample of past work. **Deadline:** ongoing. **Notification:** 2 months.

THE LEHMAN ENGEL MUSICAL THEATRE WORKSHOP
1605 North Cahuenga Blvd, #212; Hollywood, CA 90028; (213) 465-9142
John Sparks, *Co-Director*

Open to: composers, librettists, lyricists. **Description:** Sep–Jun workshop; in-house staged readings; industry showcase. **Financial arrangement:** workshop members pay annual dues of $200; 1st year's dues include nonrefundable application fee (see below). **Application procedure:** completed application; 1-page resume; cassette of 6 songs or equivalent for composer; 6 lyrics for lyricist; short scene for librettist; nonrefundable $25 fee. **Deadline:** 1 Aug 1993. **Notification:** Sep 1993. **Dates:** Sep 1993–Jun 1994.

FAIRCHESTER PLAYWRIGHTS
13 Clearview Terr; Ridgefield, CT 06877; (203) 967-6738
Roger Grannis, *Director*

Open to: playwrights, screenwriters, television writers. **Description:** Sep–Jun workshop meets bimonthly for public staged readings of members' works by professional actors. **Financial arrangement:** writer receiving reading pays for refreshments for public and fellow writers. **Guidelines:** unproduced work; plays may be full-length or one-act; adaptations eligible. **Application procedure:** write or call for guidelines, or to arrange to attend a reading. **Deadline:** ongoing.

FIRST STAGE
6817 Franklin Ave; Los Angeles,. CA 90028; (213) 850-6271
Dennis Safren, *Literary Manager*

Open to: playwrights, screenwriters. **Description:** organization providing year-round developmental services using professional actors, directors and dramaturgs; weekly staged readings of plays and screenplays followed by discussions; bimonthly playwriting and screenwriting workshops; periodic dramaturgy workshops; annual short-play marathon. **Financial arrangement:** subscription of $100 a year or $30 a quarter for resident of L.A., Orange or Ventura counties; $50 annual subscription for nonresident; nonmember may submit script for reading. **Application procedure:** script only. **Deadline:** ongoing.

FULL MOON PLAYWRIGHT'S EXCHANGE
160 West 71st St, PHA; New York, NY 10023; (212) 541-7600
Stuart Warmflash, *Literary Manager*

Open to: playwrights. **Description:** members meet weekly to develop their scripts through supportive critical process; public readings of selected members' work once a year. **Financial arrangement:** free. **Application procedure:** script with resume; following favorable script review, playwright attends 2 trial meetings. **Deadline:** ongoing. **Notification:** 3 months.

HISPANIC PLAYWRIGHTS PROJECT
South Coast Repertory; Box 2197; Costa Mesa, CA 92628; (714) 957-2602
José Cruz González, *Project Director*

Open to: playwrights. **Description:** up to 3 scripts given 6-day workshop with director, dramaturg and professional cast, culminating in public reading and discussion; playwright meets with director and dramaturg prior to workshop. **Financial arrangement:** honorarium, travel, living expenses. **Guidelines:** Hispanic-American playwright; unproduced play preferred but produced play which would benefit from further development will be considered; play must not be written entirely in Spanish; no musicals. **Application procedure:** script with synopsis and bio. **Deadline:** 9 Apr 1993. **Notification:** 7 May 1993. **Dates:** preworkshop meeting week of 11 Jun 1993; workshop 27 Jul–8 Aug 1993.

L.A. BLACK PLAYWRIGHTS
Box 191535; Los Angeles, CA 90019; (213) 292-9438
James Graham Bronson, *President*

Open to: playwrights, librettists, lyricists. **Description:** group meets every second Sunday for guest speakers, private and public readings, showcases. **Financial arrangement:** free. **Guidelines:** resident of L.A. area; members mainly but not exclusively black; prefers produced playwright. **Application procedure:** submit full-length play. **Deadline:** ongoing. **Dates:** year-round.

MAGIC THEATRE DEVELOPMENTAL PROGRAMS
Fort Mason Center, Bldg D; San Francisco, CA 94123; (415) 441-8001

Latino Writers Project
(formerly Hispanic Writers Project)
Roberto Gutierrez Varea, *Project Coordinator/Dramaturg*

Open to: playwrights. **Description:** 3 works a year selected for development with dramaturg, director and actors culminating in staged reading, workshop production or full production. **Financial arrangement:** stipend, travel and housing. **Guidelines:** unproduced play by Latino/Latina writer. **Application procedure:** send letter of inquiry describing proposed project, with 10 pages sample dialogue, synopsis, resume or artistic bio; theatre will request work if interested. **Deadline:** ongoing.

Springfest
Mary DeDanan, *Literary Manager*

Open to: playwrights. **Description:** 3 plays given full (but scaled-down) productions with 4 weeks of rehearsal and 2½–week run. **Financial arrangement:** stipend, travel and housing. **Guidelines:** play not produced professionally; cast limit of 5, simple set. **Application procedure:** letter of inquiry mentioning interest in Springfest, first 10–20 pages of dialogue, synopsis and resume or artistic bio; plays accepted for consideration by theatre automatically considered for Springfest. **Deadline:** ongoing. **Dates:** 1 Apr–30 May.

MANHATTAN PLAYWRIGHTS UNIT

338 West 19th St, #6B; New York, NY 10011; (212) 989-0948
Saul Zachary, *Artistic Director*

Open to: playwrights, screenwriters. **Description:** developmental workshop meeting weekly for in-house readings and discussions of members' works-in-progress; end-of-season series of staged readings of new plays. **Financial arrangement:** free. **Guidelines:** produced or published writer. **Application procedure:** letter of inquiry with resume and SASE for response. **Deadline:** ongoing.

MERELY PLAYERS

Box 606; New York, NY 10108; (212) 799-2253
Monica M. Hayes, *Artistic Director*

Open to: playwrights. **Description:** nonprofit theatre organization with a membership of over 65 actors, directors and writers develops new scripts through Directors Lab, bimonthly readings and critiques, Second Step staged readings and full productions. **Financial arrangement:** members pay annual dues of $80; initial free participation for playwright not yet enrolled as member. **Guidelines:** playwrights willing to participate in development of their plays may submit scripts; playwright who has had at least 2 full-length scripts developed through the group's process may be invited to become a member. **Application procedure:** script only. **Deadline:** ongoing.

MIDWEST RADIO THEATRE WORKSHOP

KOPN Radio; 915 East Broadway; Columbia, MO 65201; (314) 874-1139
Diane Huneke, *Director*

Open to: playwrights, radio writers. **Description:** annual program of 5-day radio-theatre workshops for writers, actors, directors and sound designers; Live Performance Workshop: 55 participants of all disciplines take workshops in production, direction, acting, writing and engineering; commissioned plays or scripts selected through MRTW Script Contest (see Prizes) produced for radio broadcast and live performance with audience; biennial Writers' Workshop: for approximately 16 writers. **Financial arrangement:** $200–300 fee for each workshop; some partial and full scholarships available based on financial need and experience, with priority given to women and people of color; possibility of free housing in community. **Application procedure:** completed registration form with deposit; write for information. **Deadline:** 2 months before start of workshop for scholarship applications; most workshops filled at least 1 month before starting date. **Dates:** Live Performance Workshop 26–30 Oct 1992; next Writers' Workshop summer 1993.

MOUNT SEQUOYAH NEW PLAY RETREAT

Department of Drama; Kimpel Hall 406; The University of Arkansas;
  Fayetteville, AR 72701; (501) 575-2953
Roger Gross

Open to: playwrights. Description: 3-week summer workshop/retreat for 6
playwrights; personal writing time combined with workshop sessions in which
plays are developed with participating directors and resident acting company
under supervision of retreat's staff of directors and produced playwrights; each
play receives public staged reading. Financial arrangement: fee for housing and
meals ($600 in 1992); fellowships available. Guidelines: write for guidelines after
1 Oct 1992. Application procedure: first draft of project or outline detailing
character development and dramatic action; sample of previous work; resume.
Deadline: 1 Feb 1993. Notification: 1 Apr 1993. Dates: 16 May–6 Jun 1993.

MULTICULTURAL PLAYWRIGHTS' FESTIVAL

Seattle Group Theatre; 3940 Brooklyn Ave NE; Seattle, WA 98105;
  (206) 685-4969
Nancy Griffiths, Dramaturg/Literary Manager

Open to: playwrights. Description: 2 scripts given workshop production with
3-week residency for playwright; 4–6 scripts given readings. Financial arrangement:
2 produced playwrights receive $1000 honorarium, travel and housing. Guide-
lines: U.S. resident; African-American, Asian-American, Chicano/Hispanic-
American or Native American playwright only; full-length or one-act play not fully
produced by Equity company; no musicals or plays for young audiences.
Application procedure: script with resume and brief cover letter: "Attn. Festival."
Deadline: 15 Nov 1992. Notification: Apr 1993. Dates: Jul 1993.

MUSICAL THEATRE WORKS

440 Lafayette St; New York, NY 10003; (212) 677-0040
Anthony J. Stimac, Artistic Director
Mike Teele, Managing Director

Open to: composers, librettists, lyricists. Description: new composers, librettists
and lyricists work with established musical theatre professionals to develop
projects through meetings, informal readings, staged readings and full Off-
Broadway productions. Financial arrangement: free. Guidelines: completed
unproduced work. Application procedure: script, cassette of music. Deadline:
ongoing.

NATIONAL MUSIC THEATER CONFERENCE

O'Neill Theater Center; 234 West 44th St, Suite 901; New York, NY 10036;
(212) 382-2790
Paulette Haupt, *Artistic Director*
Suzanne Munkelt, *Administrator*

Open to: composers, librettists, lyricists. **Description:** development period of 2–4 weeks at O'Neill Center, Waterford, CT for new music-theatre works of all genres, traditional and nontraditional; some works developed privately, others presented as staged readings. **Financial arrangement:** stipend, round-trip travel from NYC, room and board. **Guidelines:** U.S. citizen; unproduced work; adaptations acceptable if rights have been obtained. **Application procedure:** send SASE for guidelines and application form. **Deadline:** 1 Feb 1993; no submission before 1 Nov 1992. **Dates:** preconference sessions Jun 1993; conference Aug 1993.

NATIONAL MUSIC THEATER NETWORK

1460 Broadway, 3rd Floor; New York, NY 10036; (212) 382-0984
Timothy Jerome, *President*

Open to: composers, librettists, lyricists. **Description:** national screening of submitted opera and musical theatre works; written evaluations sent to all writers; descriptive listings of recommended works published in catalogue distributed to producers/theatres and 6–7 of these given staged readings in annual "Broadway Dozen," a showcase for potential producers. **Financial arrangement:** NMTN underwrites up to $2500 of expenses for each staged reading. **Guidelines:** completed work with original music which has not received a major production. **Application procedure:** completed application and $30 fee; write for details. **Deadline:** ongoing.

NATIONAL PLAYWRIGHTS CONFERENCE

O'Neill Theater Center; 234 West 44th St, Suite 901; New York, NY 10036;
(212) 382-2790
Lloyd Richards, *Artistic Director*
Peggy Vernieu, *Administrator*

Open to: playwrights, screenwriters, television writers. **Description:** 4-week workshop at O'Neill Center, Waterford, CT; 9–12 plays developed and presented as staged readings; 1–3 screenplays/teleplays developed and read; preconference weekend for initial reading and planning. **Financial arrangement:** stipend, travel, room and board. **Guidelines:** U.S. citizen or resident; unoptioned and unproduced work; no adaptations or translations. **Application procedure:** send SASE for application information. **Deadline:** 1 Dec 1992. **Notification:** Apr 1993. **Dates:** preconference weekend May 1993; conference Jul 1993.

THE NEW HARMONY PROJECT CONFERENCE/LABORATORY
613 North East St; Indianapolis, IN 46202; (317) 464-9405
Jeffrey L. Sparks, *Executive Director*

Open to: playwrights, composers, librettists, lyricists, screenwriters, television writers. **Description:** 2–3 theatre works and 2–3 screenplays or teleplays given up to 2 weeks of intensive development with professional community of directors, actors, producers and cinematographers, culminating in staged reading or screening; noted resource people join community to critique scripts on final weekend. **Financial arrangement:** stipend of $100–200, depending on length of stay; travel, room and board. **Guidelines:** play, musical, screenplay or teleplay by student, unproduced writer or established writer; work that combines sensitivity and truthfulness in exploring values in family, faith and society with ability to compete in the marketplace; participating writers required to attend pre-conference weekend; write for guidelines. **Application procedure:** script with maximum 2-page synopsis; 1-page bio. **Deadline:** 1 Dec 1992. **Notification:** 15 Mar 1993. **Dates:** preconference weekend 1–4 Apr 1993; conference 14–30 May 1993.

NEW STAGES MUSICAL WORKSHOP PROGRAM
NEW STAGES Musical Arts; 118 East 4th ST, #14; New York, NY 10003;
    (212) 505-1947
Joe Miloscia, *Artistic Director*

Open to: composers, librettists, lyricists. **Description:** up to 5 musicals each developed with resident company in workshop of 6–8 weeks culminating in public reading or workshop production. **Financial arrangement:** varies with level of production. **Guidelines:** unpublished musical by emerging American writer(s). **Application procedure:** libretto and cassette of songs with synopsis, resume(s) and production history (if any). **Deadline:** ongoing.

NEW WORKS THEATRE
3926 Iowa St; San Diego, CA 92104; (619) 284-1105
Jack G. Barefield, *Executive Director*

Open to: playwrights. **Description:** ongoing playwrights' workshop; activities include bimonthly meetings, Play Readers Theatre presenting 12 staged readings a year, and occasional full productions. **Financial arrangement:** playwright receives royalty if play is read or produced. **Guidelines:** southern CA resident only; committed playwright with some previous experience. **Application procedure:** script only. **Deadline:** ongoing.

NEW YORK FOUNDATION FOR THE ARTS
ARTISTS' NEW WORKS

155 Ave of the Americas; New York, NY 10013;
  call information for new phone number
Lynda A. Hansen, *Director*
Julia Hammer, *Program Assistant*

Open to: playwrights, translators, composers, librettists, lyricists, screenwriters, radio and television writers. **Description:** program supports development, production and distribution of creative new projects by individual artists, both emerging talents and established professionals, with strong emphasis on independent film and video but also including radio, literature, performance art, theatre, music, dance and visual arts; as sponsoring organization for nonprofit status, NYFA provides fiscal management assistance and proposal reviews with focus on fundraising counsel. **Financial arrangement:** as a service fee, NYFA retains 8% of grants and contributions it receives on behalf of a project; $50 contract fee payable on signing. **Guidelines:** majority of sponsored artists located in NY metropolitan area; solid project proposal with realistic budget (most selected projects budgeted at not less than $25,000); selection based on artistic excellence, uniqueness and fundability of project, and on artist's previous work and proven ability to complete proposed work. **Application procedure:** write for application form and further information. **Deadline:** ongoing. **Notification:** 2 months.

PADUA HILLS PLAYWRIGHTS WORKSHOP/FESTIVAL

Box 461450; Los Angeles, CA 90046; (213) 913-2636
Cheryl Slean, *Managing Director*

Open to: playwrights. **Description:** 7-week program combines development of site-specific, environmental theatre works by professional playwrights with student workshop taught by invited playwrights and Padua Hills staff, and culminates in outdoor theatre festival open to the public. **Financial arrangement:** professional playwright receives $500 for production and/or $500 teaching honorarium, plus travel and housing; student playwright pays $1000 workshop fee. **Guidelines:** festival produces an eclectic range of work but looks for professional playwrights who can fit into a collegial creative atmosphere and are not exclusively focused on own work and career; student playwrights write for information. **Application procedure:** professional playwright send resume, letter of inquiry and letter of recommendation from theatre professional familiar with festival's work; student playwright send small representative work sample (monologue, scene, short story or poetry), letter of intention and SASE for response. **Deadline:** ongoing for professional playwrights; Apr 1993 for students (exact date TBA). **Dates:** 21 Jun–8 Aug 1993.

PKE THEATRE

Patchett Kaufman Entertainment; 8621 Hayden Pl; Culver City, CA 90232
Stuart Silver, *Artistic Director*

Open to: playwrights. **Description:** at least 1 play per month given staged reading for audience including theatre, film and TV professionals; possibility of Equity-waiver production. **Financial arrangement:** writer receives remuneration for full production. **Guidelines:** unproduced play. **Application procedure:** script only. **Deadline:** ongoing.

PLAYFORMERS

20 Waterside Plaza, #5A; New York, NY 10010; (212) 685-5394
Romola Robb Allrud, *Artistic Director*

Open to: playwrights. **Description:** group meets biweekly Sep–Jun for readings and critiques; selected plays receive staged readings; possibility of full production. **Financial arrangement:** $20 initiation fee on acceptance; $150 annual dues; writer receives remuneration if play is produced. **Guidelines:** as openings arise, committed playwrights considered for membership. **Application procedure:** letter of recommendation from theatre professional or person familiar with group; resume. **Deadline:** ongoing. **Dates:** Sep, Dec, Mar.

PLAYLABS

(formerly Midwest PlayLabs)
The Playwrights' Center; 2301 Franklin Ave East; Minneapolis, MN 55406;
   (612) 332-7481
David Moore, Jr., *Executive Director*

Open to: playwrights. **Description:** 2-week workshop; 4–8 new plays developed and presented as staged readings. **Financial arrangement:** stipend, travel, room and per diem. **Guidelines:** U.S. citizen; unproduced, unpublished play; full-length plays preferred; playwright must be available to attend entire conference and preconference weekend. **Application procedure:** completed application and script; write for application after 1 Oct 1992. **Deadline:** 1 Dec 1992. **Notification:** 15 Apr 1993. **Dates:** preconference weekend May 1993 (exact dates TBA); conference 1–15 Aug 1993.

PLAYS-IN-PROGRESS FESTIVALS OF NEW WORKS

1525 Marsh Rd; Eureka, CA 95501; (707) 445-3353
Susan Bigelow-Marsh, *Executive Director*

Open to: playwrights. **Description:** 8–10 scripts each given 3–4 weeks development with actors and directors, culminating in staged reading, followed by discussion, in spring or fall festival of new work; ongoing development and Monday night reading series for local writers. **Financial arrangement:** negotiable; travel and housing. **Guidelines:** primarily CA writers; 1 out of state writer selected for each festival; unproduced, unpublished play. **Application procedure:** script and resume. **Deadline:** 1 Mar 1993; 1 Aug 1993. **Dates:** May 1993; Oct 1993.

THE PLAYWRIGHTS' CENTER
1222 West Wilson; Chicago, IL 60640; (312) 334-9981
Timothy Mooney, *Literary Manager*

Open to: playwrights. **Description:** membership organization in which playwrights, directors, designers and actors develop their own crafts while supporting development of fellow artists; support services and developmental opportunities for playwrights aim to help writer make transition from student to produced playwright; selected scripts developed through progressive series of cold readings, exploratory workshop readings, staged readings and full productions; improvisational development process offered to selected local playwrights. **Financial arrangement:** playwright receives royalty of $10 a performance for full production. **Guidelines:** nonmembers may submit scripts; member directors select scripts they wish to direct. **Application procedure:** 2 copies of script with synopsis and resume. **Deadline:** ongoing.

PLAYWRIGHTS FORUM
Box 11488; Washington, DC 20008; (301) 816-0569
Ernest Joselovitz, *President*

Open to: playwrights. **Description:** ongoing developmental program including 3-tier range of membership options: Forum 2, professional playwriting groups meeting biweekly; the Forum, workshop program offering three 3-month sessions a year for apprentice playwrights; and Associate membership offering a lower level of participation; depending on type of membership, members variously eligible for in-house and public readings, intensive workshop readings, production observerships, free theatre tickets, organization's newsletter and handbook, and new published series of members' scripts. **Financial arrangement:** for Forum 2, $80 every 4 months; for Forum, $80 per 15-week session; Associate membership $25 a year. **Guidelines:** resident of DC area only; for Forum, prefers playwright who has completed an introductory playwriting class; send SASE for further information. **Application procedure:** for Forum 2, script and bio; for Forum, send SASE or call for information; for Associate membership, send annual fee. **Deadline:** for Forum 2, ongoing; for Forum, flexible deadlines in Sep, Jan and May. **Notification:** 6 weeks.

PLAYWRIGHTS' PLATFORM
164 Brayton Rd; Boston, MA 02135; (617) 254-4482
Beverly Creasey, *President*

Open to: playwrights. **Description:** ongoing developmental program including weekly workshop, staged readings, summer festival of full productions, dramaturgical and referral services. **Financial arrangement:** playwright receives percentage of gate for festival productions; participants encouraged to become members of organization ($15 annual dues). **Guidelines:** MA resident only; unpublished, unproduced play; write for membership information. **Application procedure:** query only. **Deadline:** ongoing.

PLAYWRIGHT'S PREVIEW PRODUCTIONS
1160 Fifth Ave, #304; New York, NY 10029; (212) 996-7287
Frances W. Hill, *Artistic Director*
Deborah Goodman, *Literary Manager*

Open to: playwrights. **Description:** new plays developed through weekly staged readings and workshops, in some cases leading to production; see also Emerging Playwright Awards in Prizes. **Financial arrangement:** free. **Guidelines:** play not produced in New York City area. **Application procedure:** script only. **Deadline:** ongoing. **Dates:** Sep–Jun.

THE PLAYWRIGHTS THEATRE OF LOS ANGELES
10886 Le Conte Ave; Los Angeles, CA 90024
Richard Polak, *Artistic Director*

Open to: playwrights, composers (only if involved in collaborating on musical-theatre work), librettists, lyricists. **Description:** ongoing membership-based developmental workshop; activities include bimonthly readings of members' works, showcase productions, and full productions of excerpts from members' works to raise money for charitable causes. **Financial arrangement:** free. **Guidelines:** serious theatre writer who has completed at least 2 full-length works; work must be suitable for commercial theatre; no experimental works or teleplays. **Application procedure:** script or letter of inquiry with synopsis. **Deadline:** ongoing.

PLAYWRIGHTS THEATRE OF NEW JERSEY
NEW PLAY DEVELOPMENT PROGRAM
33 Green Village Rd; Madison, NJ 07940; (201) 514-1787
Michele Ortlip, *Literary Manager*

Open to: playwrights. **Description:** new plays developed through sit-down readings, staged readings and productions; liaison with other producing theatres provided. **Financial arrangement:** playwright receives royalty. **Guidelines:** unproduced play by American playwright; write for brochure. **Application procedure:** script with 1-page synopsis and developmental history, if any; resume. **Deadline:** ongoing.

PORTLAND STATE UNIVERSITY NEW PLAYS CONFERENCE
Theater Arts Department; Box 751; Portland, OR 97207; (503) 725-4612
Jack Featheringill, *Chair and Project Director*

Open to: playwrights. **Description:** 2–4 plays developed in 3- or 4-week workshop and each given 4 staged readings; preconference weekend for reading and planning. **Financial arrangement:** $50 royalty per reading; travel and housing. **Guidelines:** northwest playwright (ID, MT, OR, WA or BC); unoptioned, unproduced one-act or full-length play; no adaptations, translations or musicals; 1 submission. **Application procedure:** script, resume. **Deadline:** 15 Nov 1992. **Notification:** Jan 1993. **Dates:** preconference weekend Feb 1993; conference Mar–Apr 1993.

PRIMARY STAGES COMPANY
584 Ninth Ave; New York, NY 10036; (212) 333-7471
Seth Gordon, *Literary Manager*

Open to: playwrights. **Description:** organization committed to developing new plays through readings, workshops and full productions. **Financial arrangement:** playwright receives stipend for full production. **Guidelines:** unproduced play by American playwright. **Application procedure:** script or synopsis with 10-page dialogue sample; include letter of inquiry with SASE for response. **Deadline:** ongoing.

PUERTO RICAN TRAVELING THEATRE PLAYWRIGHTS' WORKSHOP
141 West 94th St; New York, NY 10025; (212) 354-1293
Allen Davis III, *Director*

Open to: playwrights. **Description:** units for professional playwrights and beginners; readings; weekly meetings. **Financial arrangement:** free. **Guidelines:** New York area resident; prefers Hispanic playwrights but others may apply. **Application procedure:** for professional unit, submit full-length play; beginners contact director. **Deadline:** 30 Sep 1992. **Notification:** within 2 weeks. **Dates:** Oct 1992–Jul 1993.

RED OCTOPUS THEATRE COMPANY ORIGINAL SCRIPTS WORKSHOP
Box 1403; Newport, OR 97365; (503) 265-9057
Edward Van Aelstyn, *Managing Director*

Open to: playwrights. **Description:** short plays or excerpts from plays developed over period of 2–3 weeks in collaboration with director and actors, culminating in staged reading or full production. **Financial arrangement:** free housing. **Guidelines:** 1 unproduced submission; cast limit of 6. **Application procedure:** script only. **Deadline:** 31 Jan 1993. **Notification:** 31 Mar 1993. **Dates:** Apr 1993.

SHENANDOAH PLAYWRIGHTS RETREAT
ShenanArts; Rt 5, Box 167-F; Staunton, VA 24401; (703) 248-1868
Robert Graham Small, *Director of Playwriting and Screenwriting Programs*
Kathleen Tosco, *Managing Director*

Open to: playwrights, screenwriters. **Description:** 3-week retreat for 8–10 writers at 21-acre farm in Shenandoah Valley; program geared to facilitate major rewrite of existing draft of script; personal writing time plus creative workshops with directors, dramaturgs and core acting company; writers' circle; staged readings. **Financial arrangement:** fellowships cover costs. **Guidelines:** competitive admission based on submitted work. **Application procedure:** 2 copies of completed draft of script to be worked on at retreat; personal statement of background as a writer; write for guidelines. **Deadline:** 1 Mar 1993. **Notification:** after 10 Jun 1993. **Dates:** 1–21 Aug 1993.

THE FRANK SILVERA WRITERS' WORKSHOP
317 West 125th St, Top Floor; New York, NY 10027; (212) 662-8463
Garland Lee Thompson, *Founding Executive Director*

Open to: playwrights. **Description:** program includes Monday series of readings of new plays by new and established writers, followed by critiques; Saturday technical theatre training; Tuesday seminars conducted by master playwrights; 2–5 staged readings and 2–3 full productions a year. **Financial arrangement:** $35 annual fee plus $10 per Tuesday class; Monday-night readings and Saturday technical seminars free. **Guidelines:** interested in new plays depicting the "true colors" and lifestyles. **Application procedure:** Sep open house; attending a Monday-night session encouraged; call for information.

THE AUDREY SKIRBALL-KENIS THEATRE
9478 West Olympic Blvd, Suite 304; Beverly Hills, CA 90212; (310) 284-8965
Dennis Clontz, *Director of Programs*

Open to: playwrights. **Description:** approximately 30 staged readings and 3–4 workshop productions presented a year either to develop works-in-progress or to attract potential producers. **Financial arrangement:** playwright receives $100 for staged reading, $500 plus for workshop production; travel occasionally paid. **Guidelines:** full-length play that has not had L.A. production. **Application procedure:** letter of inquiry from playwright, professional recommendation or agent submission. **Deadline:** ongoing. **Notification:** 3–4 months.

SOUTHERN APPALACHIAN PLAYWRIGHTS' CONFERENCE
Southern Appalachian Repertory Theatre; Box 620; Mars Hill, NC 28754-0620;
(704) 689-1384
Jan W. Blalock, *Assistant Managing Director*

Open to: playwrights. **Description:** up to 5 writers selected to participate in annual 3-day conference at which 1 work by each writer is given informal reading and critiqued by panel of theatre professionals; 1 work selected for production as part of summer 1993 season. **Financial arrangement:** room and board; writer of work selected for production receives $500 honorarium. **Guidelines:** unproduced and unpublished play. **Application procedure:** script with cast list, synopsis, resume. **Deadline:** 1 Oct 1992. **Dates:** January 1993.

STAGE II WORKSHOPS
Long Wharf Theatre; 222 Sargent Dr; New Haven, CT 06511; (203) 787-4284
Sari Bodi, *Literary Analyst*

Open to: playwrights, translators, composers, librettists, lyricists. **Description:** 4 scripts given 3 weeks of rehearsal, 3 weeks of performance with playwright in residence; optional discussion after performance with audience, who complete comment sheets (no critics); unit set, costumes and props from stock. **Financial arrangement:** stipend. **Application procedure:** script with professional recommendation, or agent submission. **Deadline:** ongoing. **Notification:** 6 months. **Dates:** Nov–Mar.

THE SUNDANCE CHILDREN'S THEATRE
(formerly The Sundance Playwrights Laboratory)
RR3, Box 624-D; Sundance, UT 84604; (801) 225-4107
Managing Director

Open to: playwrights. **Description:** 10–14 days of intensive developmental workshops and readings of 4–8 scripts; each assigned cast, director and dramaturg. **Financial arrangement:** travel, room and board. **Guidelines:** unproduced play written specifically for children; up to 60 minutes long; playwright and script must be nominated by nonprofit theatre. **Application procedure:** letter of nomination from theatre, script and playwright's resume. **Deadline:** 15 Dec 1992. **Notification:** Apr 1993. **Dates:** Jul 1993.

THE SUNDANCE INSTITUTE
INDEPENDENT FEATURE FILM PROGRAM
c/o CPE; 10202 West Washington Blvd; Culver City, CA 90232; (310) 204-2091

Open to: playwrights, screenwriters, filmmaking teams (e.g. writer/director, writer /producer). **Description:** program includes week-long Screenwriters Laboratories each Jan and Jun offering participants one-on-one problem-solving sessions with professional screenwriters; 1-month June Laboratory workshop in which projects are explored through work with writers, directors, actors, cinematographers, producers, designers, editors and other resource personnel; Network/Advisory Support offering practical and creative assistance to selected projects. **Financial arrangement:** travel, room and board for Jan and Jun labs. **Guidelines:** "transitional artist" (e.g. theatre artist who wants to work in film, writer who wants to direct); program interested in supporting "compelling, original narrative stories (they can be based on a true story or be adaptations of plays, novels, short stories, etc.) which represent the unique vision of the writer and/or director"; send SASE for guidelines. **Application procedure:** completed application with cover letter, synopsis and bios of project participants; after review process selected applicants will be contacted for further information. **Deadline:** Secondary Selection for 1993 (for available spaces in Jun 1993 labs) 8 Dec 1992; Primary Selection for 1994 (for all 1994 programs) 15 Jul 1993.

MARK TAPER FORUM DEVELOPMENTAL PROGRAMS
135 North Grand Ave; Los Angeles, CA 90012; (213) 972-7353

Mentor Playwrights' Project
Oliver Mayer, *Literary Associate*

Open to: playwrights. **Description:** playwrights' lab for 10–15 playwrights of culturally diverse backgrounds meeting weekly under direction of nationally known senior playwrights, who provide guidance through teaching, discussion, exercises and critiques; initial 6-month membership may be extended to 1–2 years. **Financial arrangement:** stipend of $1000–1500 for 6 months. **Guidelines:** early-career L.A. playwright who shows strong potential; guidelines of recently initiated program are still evolving. **Application procedure:** script with resume. **Deadline:** call for information.

New Work Festival
Mara Isaacs, *Festival Coordinator*

Open to: playwrights. **Description:** 16–18 plays given workshops (2 weeks rehearsal, 2 public presentations) or rehearsed readings. **Financial arrangement:** remuneration varies. **Guidelines:** unproduced, unpublished play. **Application procedure:** script only. **Deadline:** 1 Sep 1992. **Dates:** Oct–Nov 1992.

THE TEN-MINUTE MUSICALS PROJECT
Box 461194; West Hollywood, CA 90046
Michael Koppy, *Producer*

Open to: composers, librettists, lyricists. **Description:** up to 10 brief pieces selected during annual cycle for possible inclusion in full-length anthology musicals subsequently produced at Equity theatres in U.S. and Canada; occasionally some pieces workshopped using professional actors and director. **Financial arrangement:** $250 royalty advance with equal share of licensing royalties when produced. **Guidelines:** complete work with a definite beginning, middle and end, 8–14 minutes long, in any musical style or genre; adaptations of strongly structured material in the public domain, or for which rights have been obtained, are encouraged; cast of 2–9, prefers 6–9; write for guidelines. **Application procedure:** script, lead sheets and tape of sung material. **Deadline:** 1 Oct 1992 for 1992–93 cycle; 31 Aug 1993 for 1993–94 cycle. **Notification:** 2 months.

TEXAS PLAYWRIGHTS FESTIVAL
Stages Repertory Theatre; 3201 Allen Pkwy, #101; Houston, TX 77019;
    (713) 527-0240
Peter Bennett, *Artistic Director*

Open to: playwrights. **Description:** up to 5 plays chosen for development with dramaturg, director and actors over period of approximately 30 days, culminating in full production for 1 script, staged reading for others. **Financial arrangement:** small stipend. **Guidelines:** TX native or resident or non-TX playwright writing on TX theme; play not produced professionally; prefers small cast. **Application procedure:** script only. **Deadline:** 1 Feb 1993. **Notification:** May 1993. **Dates:** TBA (Jun in 1992).

THEATRE ARTISTS WORKSHOP OF WESTPORT
17 Morningside Dr South; Westport, CT 06880; (203) 227-5836
Admissions Committee

Open to: playwrights, composers, librettists, lyricists. **Description:** laboratory where professional writers can exercise their craft and develop projects in collaboration with member directors, actors and allied theatre artists; ongoing workshop meetings; work presented for peer evaluation. **Financial arrangement:** annual membership dues and contributions of $200; $50 initiation fee. **Guidelines:** serious, theatre-oriented writer of professional caliber. **Application procedure:** completed application and 3 copies of script. **Deadline:** ongoing.

THEATER IN THE WORKS
FAC #112, Fine Arts Center; University of Massachusetts; Amherst, MA 01003;
(413) 545-3490, -0681
Virginia Scott, *Resident Dramaturg*

Open to: playwrights. **Description:** 4 full-length plays or bills of related one-acts chosen for development; playwright's 2-week residency culminates in public staged reading by professional actors. **Financial arrangement:** stipend of $325 a week, travel, housing. **Guidelines:** substantially unproduced script; practical considerations a factor; possible interest in small musicals. **Application procedure:** script only. **Deadline:** 15 Mar 1993. **Notification:** 15 May 1993. **Dates:** Jul 1993.

THE THIRD STEP THEATRE COMPANY
412 West 48th St; New York, NY 10036; (212) 633-9760
Beate Hein Bennett, *Literary Manager*

Open to: playwrights, translators. **Description:** theatre's program includes Spring Festival of Staged Readings: 10 scripts rehearsed with professional director and cast and given staged readings followed by discussion with audience; some plays selected for future full production; International Reading Festival: staged readings of plays by non-American playwrights. **Financial arrangement:** playwright whose work is selected for either festival receives stipend. **Guidelines:** Spring Festival: unproduced one-act or full-length play by American playwright; special interest in plays by ethnic, minority and woman playwrights; 2-submission limit; write for guidelines; International Festival: play by non-American playwright written in or translated into English. **Application procedure:** 1st 15 pages of script, or scene not more than 15 pages long, with 1-page synopsis, 1-page character breakdown and optional short bio. **Deadline:** 1 Mar 1993 for Spring Festival; ongoing for International Festival. **Notification:** 1 Apr 1993 for Spring Festival. **Dates:** Spring Festival May–Jun 1993; International Festival TBA.

UNIVERSITY OF ALABAMA NEW PLAYWRIGHTS' PROGRAM
Department of Theatre and Dance; University of Alabama; Box 870239;
Tuscaloosa, AL 35487; (205) 348-9032
Paul C. Castagno, *Director and Dramaturg*

Open to: playwrights, composers, librettists, lyricists. **Description:** opportunity for writer to develop unproduced script or to pursue further development of produced play, culminating in full production; writer may visit campus several times during rehearsal process and required to offer limited playwriting workshops during visit(s); recent MFA playwrights encouraged to apply; production considered for entry in the Kennedy Center American College Theatre Festival (see Prizes). **Financial arrangement:** substantial stipend, travel and expenses. **Guidelines:** writer with some previous experience and script that has had some development; can consider plays with large casts and complex production demands. **Application procedure:** script or synopsis and cover letter. **Deadline:** ongoing. **Notification:** 6 months. **Dates:** fall–spring. **Other programs:** department will also consider writers' proposals for workshops with its playwriting and acting students.

UPSTART STAGE PLAYREADING SERIES
Box 725; Berkeley, Ca 94701; (510) 527-3123
Carter W. Lewis, *Literary Manager*

Open to: playwrights. **Description:** up to 18 rehearsed readings a year; 1 workshop production, 1 full production of plays selected from reading series. **Financial arrangement:** $25 royalty and housing for reading. **Guidelines:** full-length or one-act plays; no musicals; prefers unproduced play, unless work still "in process." **Application procedure:** accepts unsolicited scripts from CA residents only; all others submit synopsis and letter of inquiry; include production history if any. **Deadline:** ongoing.

U S WEST THEATREFEST
Denver Center Theatre Company; 1050 13th St; Denver, CO 80204;
    (303) 893-4200
Tom Szentgyorgyi, *Associate Artistic Director/New Play Development*

Open to: playwrights. **Description:** up to 8 plays-in-progress given 1 week rehearsal with resident company of actors and directors, culminating in staged reading during theatre's New Plays Festival; up to 4 likely to be produced in following year's festival and published. **Financial arrangement:** stipend, travel and housing. **Guidelines:** 1 submission not produced professionally; full-length play only; no 1-character plays, translations, adaptations or plays for young audiences. **Application procedure:** write for guidelines. **Deadline:** 1 Dec 1992. **Notification:** Mar 1993. **Dates:** May 1993.

VOICE AND VISION
RETREAT FOR WOMEN THEATRE ARTISTS
80 Cranberry St, #3M; Brooklyn, NY 11201; (718) 643-8233
Jean Wagner, *Artistic Director*

Open to: playwrights, translators, composers, librettists, lyricists. **Description:** up to 5 works-in-progress given 1-week rehearsal and workshop performance or staged reading at Smith College in Northampton, MA; projects chosen to reflect broad range of aesthetics, ethnic backgrounds, artistic experiences and age groups. **Financial arrangement:** travel, room, some meals, possible small stipend. **Guidelines:** project initiator must be a woman; emerging or established artist. **Application procedure:** script or project description; resume. **Deadline:** TBA (1 Jun in 1992). **Dates:** summer 1993 (17–24 Aug in 1992).

WAYNE STATE PLAYWRIGHTS' WORKSHOP

Department of Theatre; Wayne State University; Detroit, MI 48202;
(313) 577-7907, -3508
Joe Calarco, *Artistic Director*

Open to: playwrights, translators. **Description:** up to 6 plays-in-progress given 15–20 hours of rehearsal with resident actors and directors culminating in staged reading; possibility of full production by Hilberry Repertory. **Financial arrangement:** possible travel; videotape of reading. **Guidelines:** play or translation/adaptation not produced professionally in U.S.; translator/adapter must have rights to material. **Application procedure:** script only. **Deadline:** 10 Nov 1992. **Notification:** 3–6 months.

WHETSTONE THEATRE COMPANY PLAYWRIGHTS PROGRAM

139 Main St, #616; Brattleboro, VT 05301; (802) 257-2600
Bill Hickok, *Artistic Director*

Open to: playwrights, translators. **Description:** selected plays, translations and adaptations enter program of public workshop sessions, staged readings and discussions aimed at assisting development of writer's work, providing new opportunities for the company and informing audience about the playwriting process; possibility of selection for full production (1 new play produced each season). **Financial arrangement:** stipend of $100–500, depending on project; possible travel and housing. **Guidelines:** play not produced professionally; prefers small cast and simple technical requirements. **Application procedure:** script with resume. **Deadline:** ongoing.

WOMEN'S WORKSHOP

c/o Michael Carson Productions; 250 West 54th St; New York, NY 10036;
(212) 765-2300
Deanna Duplechain, *Co-Artistic Director*

Open to: playwrights, translators. **Description:** 4–5 scripts developed with director and actors and given staged readings or workshop productions with invited audience. **Financial arrangement:** free. **Guidelines:** woman writer only; work not produced professionally in New York City. **Application procedure:** script with resume, reviews (if any) and cover letter. **Deadline:** ongoing. **Notification:** 6–8 weeks.

Career Opportunities

- Agents
- Fellowships and Grants
- Emergency Funds
- State Arts Agencies
- Colonies and Residencies
- Membership and Service Organizations

Agents

I'm wondering whether or not I should have an agent. Where can I get information to help me decide?

Write to the Association of Authors' Representatives (the newly merged Society of Authors' Representatives and Independent Literary Agents' Association) at 10 Astor Pl, 3rd Floor; New York, NY 10003. Send a check or money order for $5 and a 52¢ SASE to receive the AAR's brochure describing the role of the literary agent and how to find an agent, and its membership list and canon of ethics. See Useful Publications for books you can consult on the subject. Ask fellow playwrights what they think.

How do I select the names of appropriate agents to contact?

All of the agents listed here represent playwrights. (In some cases, the name of the agency contains the name of the agent.) The Dramatists Guild also has a list of agents available to its members, and provides advice on relationships with agents (see Membership and Service Organizations). You may come across names that appear on none of these lists, but be wary, especially if someone tries to charge you a fee to read your script. Again, talk to other playwrights about their experiences. Look at copies of scripts for the names of agents representing specific playwrights. See what kinds of plays various agents handle in order to make an intelligent guess as to whether they would be interested in representing you and your work.

How do I approach an agent?

Do not telephone, do not drop in, do not send manuscripts. Write a brief letter describing your work and asking if the agent would like to see a script. Enclose your professional resume; it should show that you have had work produced or published and make clear that you look at writing as an ongoing career, not an occasional hobby. If you're a beginning writer who's just finished your first play, you'd probably do better to work on getting a production rather than an agent.

BRET ADAMS LTD.
448 West 44th St; New York, NY 10036; (212) 765-5630
Bret Adams, Mary Harden, *Agents*

AGENCY FOR THE PERFORMING ARTS
888 Seventh Ave, Suite 602; New York, NY 10106; (212) 582-1500
Anna Maria Allessi, Richard Krawetz, Rick Leed, *Agents*

ARTISTS AGENCY
230 West 55th St, Suite 29D; New York, NY 10019; (212) 245-6960
David Herter, Jonathan Russo, Barry Weiner, *Agents*

LOIS BERMAN
240 West 44th St; New York, NY 10036; (212) 575-5114
Lois Berman, Judy Boals, *Agents*

CURTIS BROWN LTD.
606 North Larchmont Blvd, Suite 309; Los Angeles, CA 90004; (213) 461-0148
Jeannine Edmunds, *Agent*

DON BUCHWALD AND ASSOCIATES
10 East 44th St; New York, NY 10017; (212) 867-1070
Michael Traum, *Agent*

DORESE AGENCY LTD.
37965 Palo Verde Dr; Cathedral City, CA 92234; (619) 321-1115
Alyss Dorese, *Agent*

THE DRAMATIC PUBLISHING COMPANY
311 Washington St; Box 129; Woodstock, IL 60098; (815) 338-7170
Margie Murray, Susan Sergel, *Agents*

ANN ELMO AGENCY
60 East 42nd St; New York, NY 10165; (212) 661-2880
Letti Lee, *Agent*

MARJE FIELDS
165 West 46th St, Room 909; New York, NY 10036; (212) 764-5740
Ray Powers, *Agent*

ROBERT A. FREEDMAN DRAMATIC AGENCY
1501 Broadway, Suite 2310; New York, NY 10036; (212) 840-5760
Robert Freedman, Selma Luttinger, *Agents*

SAMUEL FRENCH
45 West 25th St; New York, NY 10010; (212) 206-8990
Lawrence Harbison, William Talbot, *Agents*

THE GERSH AGENCY
130 West 42nd St; New York, NY 10036; (212) 997-1818
Mary Meagher, Scott Yoselow, *Agents*

GRAHAM AGENCY
311 West 43rd St; New York, NY 10036; (212) 489-7730
Earl Graham, *Agent*

HELEN HARVEY ASSOCIATES
410 West 24th St; New York, NY 10011; (212) 675-7445
Helen Harvey, Marion Matera, *Agents*

HUTTO MANAGEMENT
405 West 23rd St; New York, NY 10011; (212) 807-1234
Jack Hutto, *Agent*

ELLEN HYMAN
422 East 81st St, #4C; New York, NY 10028; (212) 861-5373

MICHAEL IMISON PLAYWRIGHTS
28 Almeida St; London N1 1TD; England; (71) 354-3174

INTERNATIONAL CREATIVE MANAGEMENT
40 West 57th St; New York, NY 10019; (212) 556-5600
Bridget Aschenberg, Mitch Douglas, Wiley Hausam, *Agents*

THE JOYCE KETAY AGENCY
334 West 89th St, #4F; New York, NY 10024; (212) 799-2398
Joyce P. Ketay, Carl Mulert, *Agents*

BERTHA KLAUSNER INTERNATIONAL LITERARY AGENCY
71 Park Ave; New York, NY 10016; (212) 685-2642

LUCY KROLL AGENCY
390 West End Ave, Suite 9B; New York, NY 10024; (212) 877-0627, -0556
Barbara Hogenson, Lucy Kroll, Holly Lebed, *Agents*

THE ROBERT LANTZ–JOY HARRIS LITERARY AGENCY
888 Seventh Ave, Suite 2500; New York, NY 10106
Robert Lantz, (212) 586-0200
Joy Harris, (212) 262-8177
In association with: The Roberts Company; 10345 West Olympic Blvd,
Penthouse; Los Angeles, CA 90064; (213) 552-7800
Nancy Roberts, *Agent*

ELISABETH MARTON AGENCY
1 Union Square West, Room 612; New York, NY 10003-3303; (212) 255-1908
Tonda Marton, *Agent*

HAROLD MATSON COMPANY
276 Fifth Ave, Suite 713; New York, NY 10001; (212) 679-4490

HELEN MERRILL
435 West 23rd St, Suite 1A; New York, NY 10011; (212) 691-5326
Mary Lou Aleskie, Helen Merrill, *Agents*

WILLIAM MORRIS AGENCY
1350 Ave of the Americas; New York, NY 10019; (212) 586-5100
Leo Bookman, Peter Franklin, Peter Hagan, George Lane, Owen Laster, Biff Liff,
Gilbert Parker, Esther Sherman, *Agents*

ABE NEWBORN ASSOCIATES
1365 York Ave, #25G; New York, NY 10021; (212) 861-4635
Abe Newborn, Joyce Newborn, *Agents*

FIFI OSCARD ASSOCIATES
24 West 40th St, 17th Floor; New York, NY 10018; (212) 764-1100
Carmen LaVia, Fifi Oscard, *Agents*

PARAMUSE ARTISTS ASSOCIATES
1414 Ave of the Americas; New York, NY 10019; (212) 758-5055
Shirley Bernstein, *Agent*

EVELYN J. POWERS
2311 Windingbrook Ct; Bloomington, IN 47401; (812) 332-9203

FLORA ROBERTS
157 West 57th St; New York, NY 10019; (212) 355-4165
Sarah Douglas, Flora Roberts, *Agents*

ROSENSTONE/WENDER
3 East 48th St, 4th Floor; New York, NY 10017; (212) 832-8330
Renata Cobbs, Howard Rosenstone, *Agents*

SUSAN SCHULMAN LITERARY AGENCY
454 West 44th St; New York, NY 10036; (212) 713-1633

MARION SEARCHINGER
327 Central Park West; New York, NY 10025; (212) 865-5777

THE TANTLEFF OFFICE
375 Greenwich St, Suite 700; New York, NY 10013; (212) 941-3939
Jill Bock, John B. Santoianni, Jack Tantleff, *Agents*

PEREGRINE WHITTLESEY AGENCY
345 East 80th St, #31F; New York, NY 10021; (212) 737-0153

WRITERS & ARTISTS AGENCY
19 West 44th St, Suite 1000; New York, NY 10036; (212) 391-1112
William Craver, Scott Hudson, *Agents*

Fellowships and Grants

Can I apply directly to all the programs listed in this section?

No. You will see that a number of the grant programs we list must be applied to by a producing or presenting organization. However, you should be aware that these programs exist so that you can bring them to the attention of organizations with which you have a working relationship. All or most of the funds disbursed directly benefit the individual artist since they go to cover commissioning fees, residencies and other expenses related to the creation of new works.

How can I enhance my chances of winning an award?

Start early. This is so important that in this section we are giving full listings to the increasing number of awards offered in alternate years, even when the deadline falls outside the period this *Sourcebook* covers. Use the Submission Calendar in the back of this book to help you plan your campaign. In the case of all awards for which you can apply directly, write for guidelines and application forms months ahead. Study the guidelines carefully and follow them meticulously. Don't hesitate to ask for advice and assistance from the organization to which you are applying. Submit a well thought-out, excellently written, neatly typed application. Apply for as many awards as you qualify for; once you have written the first grant proposal, you can often, with little additional work, adapt it to fit others' guidelines.

ACTS INSTITUTE ARTISTS COLONY GRANTS

Through 31 Dec 1992: Box 278; Lake Ozark, MO 65049; (314) 365-4404
From 1 Jan 1993: Box 10153; Kansas City, MO 64111; (816) 753-0208
Charlotte Plotsky, *President*

Open to: playwrights, translators, composers, librettists, lyricists. **Frequency:** annual. **Remuneration:** grant of up to $1000 to cover cost of attending artists colony. **Guidelines:** writer who has been accepted by a recognized artists colony and needs assistance to cover residency costs; send SASE for guidelines. **Application procedure:** completed application with $10 fee; work sample (include score, lyrics and cassette for musical); cover letter describing project to be pursued at colony; copy of colony's acceptance letter; letter of recommendation from theatre professional; reviews. **Deadline:** 1 Dec 1992 for summer 1993; 1 Jun 1993 for winter 1993.

THE AMERICAN-SCANDINAVIAN FOUNDATION

725 Park Ave; New York, NY 10021; (212) 879-9779
Exchange Division

Open to: playwrights, translators, composers, librettists, lyricists. **Frequency:** annual. **Remuneration:** $2500–15,000. **Guidelines:** grants and fellowships for research and study in Scandinavian countries; U.S. citizen or permanent resident with undergraduate degree; Scandinavian language competence expected. **Application procedure:** completed application and supplementary materials; $10 fee. **Deadline:** 1 Nov 1992. **Notification:** mid-Apr 1993.

ARTISTS-IN-BERLIN PROGRAMME

German Academic Exchange Service (DAAD); 950 Third Ave, 19th Floor;
    New York, NY 10022; (212) 758-3223
Wedigo de Vivanco, *Director, DAAD–New York*

Open to: playwrights, composers. **Frequency:** annual. **Remuneration:** monthly grant to cover living costs and rent during 1-year residency in Berlin (6 months in exceptional cases); workspace provided or paid for; travel for writer and any members of immediate family who will be staying in Berlin for period of residency; initial additional allowance for settling-in costs; German language courses, if desired; in some cases specific projects such as readings or publications can be subsidized. **Guidelines:** to enable internationally known artists to pursue own work while participating in the cultural life of the city and making contact with local artists; must reside in Berlin for period of grant; German nationals and foreign writers who are resident in Germany ineligible; write for guidelines. **Application procedure:** completed application; preferably published work for playwrights; scores, records, tapes or published work for composers. **Deadline:** 31 Dec 1992. **Notification:** May 1993. **Dates:** residency begins between 1 Jan and 30 Jun 1994.

ARTIST TRUST
1402 Third Ave, Suite 415; Seattle, WA 98101; (206) 467-8734
Jo Ellen Pasman, *Director*

Fellowships

Open to: playwrights, composers, librettists, lyricists, screenwriters, radio and television writers. **Frequency:** awards rotate among disciplines. **Remuneration:** $5000 award. **Guidelines:** WA resident only; practicing professional artist of exceptional talent and demonstrated ability; award based on creative excellence and continuing dedication to an artistic discipline; write for guidelines. **Application procedure:** completed application with work sample. **Deadline:** late 1992 for music; probably late 1993 for theatre and media (write for information Aug 1993); lyricists and librettists call to ask when they should apply; exact dates TBA.

GAP (Grants for Artist Projects)

Open to: playwrights, composers, librettists, lyricists, screenwriters, radio and television writers. **Frequency:** biannual. **Remuneration:** grant of up to $1000. **Guidelines:** WA resident only; grant for the initiation, continuation or completion of specific creative project undertaken by individual artist; award based on quality of work as represented by supporting material and on creativity and feasibility of proposed project; write for guidelines. **Application procedure:** completed application with work sample. **Deadline:** winter 1992; summer 1993; exact dates TBA.

ASIAN CULTURAL COUNCIL
1290 Ave of the Americas; New York, NY 10104; (212) 373-4300

Open to: playwrights, composers, librettists, lyricists. **Frequency:** biannual. **Remuneration:** amount varies. **Guidelines:** to support residencies in Japan for American artists for a variety of purposes, including creative activities (other than performances), research projects, professional observation tours and specialized training. **Application procedure:** write for information 8 months before desired starting date. **Deadline:** 1 Feb 1993; 1 Aug 1993.

ATLANTA BUREAU OF CULTURAL AFFAIRS
236 Forsyth St SW, Suite 402; Atlanta, GA 30303; (404) 653-7160
Emily Allen, *Project Adminstrator*

Artists Project

Open to: playwrights, composers, librettists, lyricists. **Frequency:** annual. **Remuneration:** grant of up to $2750. **Guidelines:** Atlanta resident who has demonstrated evidence of artistic quality. **Application procedure:** write for guidelines and application. **Deadline:** Oct 1992 (15 Oct in 1991). **Notification:** 3 months.

Mayor's Fellowship in the Arts

Open to: playwrights, composers, librettists, lyricists. **Frequency:** award rotates among disciplines. **Remuneration:** $6600 award. **Guidelines:** Atlanta resident who has demonstrated evidence of artistic quality; playwright may apply under literary arts or theatre; composer, librettist, lyricist applies under music. **Application procedure:** write for guidelines and application. **Deadline:** Nov 1992 for literary arts (exact date TBA); subsequent rotation not yet set. **Notification:** 3 months.

GEORGE BENNETT FELLOWSHIP

Phillips Exeter Academy; Exeter, NH 03833-1104
Charles Pratt, *Coordinator, Selection Committee*

Open to: playwrights. **Frequency:** annual. **Remuneration:** academic-year stipend of $5000; free room and board for fellow and family. **Guidelines:** individual who is seriously contemplating or pursuing a career as a writer and who needs time and freedom from material considerations to complete a project in progress; fellow expected to make self and talents available in informal and unofficial way to students interested in writing; write for guidelines. **Application procedure:** completed application with work sample, statement concerning work-in-progress, names of references and $5 fee. **Deadline:** 1 Dec 1992. **Notification:** 15 Mar 1993. **Dates:** Sep 1993–Jun 1994.

BRODY ARTS FUND

California Community Foundation; 606 South Olive St, Suite 2400;
    Los Angeles, CA 90014-1526; (213) 413-4042
Program Officer, Arts

Open to: playwrights, composers, librettists, lyricists, screenwriters, radio and television writers. **Frequency:** awards rotate among disciplines. **Remuneration:** fellowship of up to $5000. **Guidelines:** L.A. county resident; emerging artist; prefers artist in "expansion arts" field (minority, inner-city, rural and tribal arts); write for guidelines. **Application procedure:** completed application and supporting materials. **Deadline:** Mar 1993 for composers, librettists and lyricists; Mar 1994 for playwrights, screenwriters, radio and television writers; exact dates TBA. **Notification:** Jun.

BUNTING FELLOWSHIP PROGRAM

The Mary Ingraham Bunting Institute of Radcliffe College; 34 Concord Ave;
    Cambridge, MA 02138; (617) 495-8212
Fellowships Coordinator

Open to: playwrights, composers, librettists. **Frequency:** annual. **Remuneration:** $28,500 1-year fellowship. **Guidelines:** to provide opportunity and support for a professional woman of demonstrated accomplishment and exceptional promise to complete a substantial project in her field; full-time appointment; fellow required to reside in Boston area and expected to present work-in-progress in public colloquia during year; office or studio space, auditing privileges and access to libraries and other resources of Radcliffe and Harvard provided. **Application**

procedure: completed application with $40 fee. **Deadline:** 15 Oct 1992. **Notification:** Mar 1993. **Dates:** 1 Sep 1993–31 Aug 1994.

BUSH ARTIST FELLOWSHIPS
The Bush Foundation; E-900 First National Bank Bldg; 332 Minnesota St;
   St. Paul, MN 55101; (612) 227-5222
Sally Dixon, *Program Director*

Open to: playwrights, composers, screenwriters. **Frequency:** awards rotate among disciplines. **Remuneration:** $26,000 stipend plus $7000 for production and travel. **Guidelines:** MN, ND, SD or western WI resident at least 25 years old; playwright must have had at least 1 play given full production or workshop production by professional (not necessarily Equity) theatre; screenwriter must have had 1 public staged reading, professional workshop production, or screenplay sale or option. **Application procedure:** write for guidelines and application. **Deadline:** late Oct 1992; exact date TBA. **Notification:** late Mar 1993.

CINTAS FELLOWSHIP PROGRAM
Arts International; Institute of International Education; 809 United Nations Plaza;
New York, NY 10017-3580; (212) 984-5370
Associate Program Officer

Open to: playwrights, composers. **Frequency:** annual. **Remuneration:** $10,000 fellowship. **Guidelines:** professional artist of Cuban citizenship or parentage (at least 1 parent must have been Cuban citizen) but not presently residing in Cuba; composer must be writing for the concert stage or opera, not in the popular idiom. **Application procedure:** completed application with work sample; letters of reference. **Deadline:** 1 Mar 1993. **Notification:** 1 Aug 1993.

DOBIE-PAISANO FELLOWSHIP
University of Texas at Austin; Main Bldg 101; Austin, TX 78712; (512) 471-7213
Audrey Slate, *Coordinator*

Open to: playwrights. **Frequency:** annual. **Remuneration:** $7200 stipend to cover 6-month residency at 265-acre ranch; free housing; families welcome. **Guidelines:** TX resident, native Texan or playwright writing about TX; playwright whose life or work has been substantially identified with state; ordinarily 2 writers selected each year. **Application procedure:** write for application after 1 Oct 1992. **Deadline:** 29 Jan 1993. **Notification:** Apr 1993.

THE DRAMA LEAGUE OF NEW YORK
165 West 46th St, Suite 601; New York, NY 10036; (212) 302-2100
Playwright Awards Committee

Open to: playwrights. **Frequency:** annual. **Remuneration:** $1000 grant. **Guidelines:** U.S. citizen or permanent resident; completed draft of unproduced full-length play-in-progress (full or workshop production subsequent to submission does not disqualify play); program may expand; write for guidelines. **Application pro-**

cedure: completed application and script. **Deadline:** 15 Oct 1992. **Notification:** 1 May 1993.

ELECTRONIC ARTS GRANT PROGRAM

Experimental Television Center; 180 Front St; Owego, NY 13827;
  (607) 687-4341
Sherry Miller Hocking, *Program Director*

Finishing Funds

Open to: artists, including writers and composers, involved in creation of audio, video or computer-generated time-based works. **Frequency:** annual. **Remuneration:** 20–25 grants of up to $500. **Guidelines:** resident of NY State; funds to be used to assist completion of work which is time-based in conception and execution and is to be presented as tape or installation; work must be completed before 30 Sep 1993; write for guidelines. **Application procedure:** 3 copies of completed application with project description and resume; work samples. **Deadline:** 15 Mar 1993. **Notification:** 6 weeks.

Presentation Funds

Open to: nonprofit organizations presenting audio, video or computer-generated time-based works. **Frequency:** ongoing. **Remuneration:** grant of approximately $150–300 to assist presentation of work and artist's involvement in activities related to presentation. **Guidelines:** New York State organization; event must be open to public and should emphasize work of NY State artist(s); write for guidelines. **Application procedure:** individual may not apply; completed application with supporting materials submitted by organization well in advance of event. **Notification:** 15th of month following month of submission.

FULBRIGHT SCHOLAR AWARDS

Council for International Exchange of Scholars (CIES); 3007 Tilden St NW,
  Suite 5M, Box FEL; Washington, DC 20008; (202) 686-7877
Program Officer (specify country of interest)

Open to: scholars and professionals in all areas of theatre and the arts, including playwrights, translators, composers, librettists, lyricists. **Frequency:** annual. **Remuneration:** grant for university lecturing or research in more than 135 countries for 2–9 months; amount varies with country of award; travel; maintenance allowance for living costs of grantee and possibly family. **Guidelines:** U.S. citizen; MFA, Ph.D. or comparable professional qualifications; university or college teaching experience for lecturing awards; for selected countries, proficiency in a foreign language. **Application procedure:** completed application. **Deadline:** 15 Jun 1993 for Australasia, South Asia; 1 Aug 1993 for Africa, Latin America, the former USSR, Northeast and Southeast Asia, Europe, Middle East, Canada. **Notification:** up to 9 months, depending on country; average 6 months.

FUND FOR NEW AMERICAN PLAYS
John F. Kennedy Center for the Performing Arts; 2700 F St NW;
    Washington, DC 20566; (202) 416-8024
Sophy Burnham, *Project Director*

Open to: nonprofit professional theatres. **Frequency:** annual. **Remuneration:** $10,000 grant to playwright whose work theatre is producing, plus grant (amount dependent on quality of proposal and need) to theatre (7 in 1991); $2,500 Roger L. Stevens award to playwright whose work shows "extraordinary promise" (7 in 1991). **Guidelines:** $10,000 playwright grant to cover living and travel expenses during minimum of 4 weeks of rehearsal and during any necessary additional rehearsals and rewrites in course of run; theatre grant to cover expenses exceeding theatre's budget allocation for hiring of director, designer and guest actors; limit of 3 proposals per theatre; musicals ineligible; write for guidelines. **Application procedure:** playwright may not apply; proposal and supporting materials submitted by theatre. **Deadline:** 2 Apr 1993.

JOHN SIMON GUGGENHEIM MEMORIAL FOUNDATION
90 Park Ave; New York, NY 10016; (212) 687-4470

Open to: playwrights, composers. **Frequency:** annual. **Remuneration:** fellowship. **Guidelines:** recipient must demonstrate exceptional creative ability. **Application procedure:** write for information. **Deadline:** 1 Oct 1992. **Notification:** Mar 1993.

THE ALFRED HODDER FELLOWSHIP
The Council of the Humanities; 122 East Pyne; Princeton University;
    Princeton, NJ 08544-5264

Open to: playwrights, translators, composers. **Frequency:** annual. **Remuneration:** $39,500 fellowship. **Guidelines:** for pursuit of independent work in the humanities by person with "much more than ordinary intellectual and literary gifts"; usually writer or scholar outside of academia in early stages of career; fellow spends academic year at Princeton; write for guidelines. **Application procedure:** resume, 10-page work sample, project proposal (2–3 pages). **Deadline:** 15 Nov 1992. **Notification:** Feb 1993.

INSTITUTE OF INTERNATIONAL EDUCATION
809 United Nations Plaza; New York, NY 10017-3580; (212) 984-5330
U.S. Student Programs Division

Open to: playwrights, translators, composers, librettists, lyricists. **Frequency:** annual. **Remuneration:** fellowship or grant; amount varies with country of award. **Guidelines:** specific opportunities for study abroad in the arts; write for brochure. **Application procedure:** completed application and supporting materials. **Deadline:** 31 Oct 1992. **Notification:** Jan 1993.

INTERMEDIA ARTS DIVERSE VISIONS REGIONAL GRANTS PROGRAM
425 Ontario St SE; Minneapolis, MN 55414; (612) 627-4444
Al Kosters, *Artist Programs Manager*

Open to: writers and composers working in interdisciplinary forms. **Frequency:** annual. **Remuneration:** grant of $500–5000 to be used to create new interdisciplinary work. **Guidelines:** resident of IA, KS, MN, ND, NE, SD or WI for at least 1 of 2 years prior to deadline; students ineligible; write for guidelines after 30 Nov 1992. **Application procedure:** completed application, work sample, project description, budget; letter of recommendation helpful. **Deadline:** Apr 1993 (6 Apr in 1992).

THE JAPAN FOUNDATION
142 West 57th St, 6th Floor; New York, NY 10019; (212) 949-6360
Artists Fellowship Program

Open to: specialists in the fields of fine arts, performing arts, music, journalism and creative writing, including playwrights, composers, librettists, lyricists and screenwriters. **Frequency:** annual. **Remuneration:** monthly stipend of ¥370,000 (about $2850) or ¥430,000 (about $3300), depending on grantee's professional career; travel; monthly housing allowance. **Guidelines:** U.S. citizen or permanent resident; fellowship of 1–6 months, not to be held concurrently with another major grant, to support project substantially related to Japan. **Application procedure:** write for guidelines and application, stating theme of project, present position and citizenship. **Deadline:** 1 Dec 1992. **Notification:** late Mar 1993. **Dates:** between 1 Apr 1993 and 31 Mar 1994.

THE KLEBAN AWARD
270 Madison Ave, Suite 1410; New York, NY 10016; (212) 683-5320
Barbara Boe, *Correspondence Secretary*

Open to: TBA (librettists or lyricists). **Frequency:** annual. **Remuneration:** TBA ($75,000 each to lyricist and librettist, payable in installments of $37,500 a year, in 1992). **Guidelines:** applicant whose work has received a full or workshop production, or who has been a member or associate of a professional musical workshop or theatre group (e.g. ASCAP or BMI workshop or Dramatists Guild Musical Theater Development Program); writer whose work has been performed on the Broadway stage for a cumulative period of 2 years ineligible; write for guidelines. **Application procedure:** completed application with work sample. **Deadline:** TBA (30 Jun in 1992).

D.H. LAWRENCE FELLOWSHIP

English Department; Humanities Bldg; University of New Mexico;
  Albuquerque, NM 87131; (505) 277-6347
Chair, D.H. Lawrence Fellowship Committee

Open to: playwrights. **Frequency:** annual. **Remuneration:** $1250 stipend; free
housing. **Guidelines:** award based on "promise of enhancing the life of
contemporary letters"; residency of at least 10 weeks at D.H. Lawrence Ranch, 20
miles north of Taos; resident may be asked to present reading, lecture and/or
consultation service under auspices of UNM; write for guidelines before applying.
Application procedure: letter outlining goals for residency with resume and work
sample; $10 application fee. **Deadline:** 31 Jan 1993. **Notification:** 15 Apr 1993.
Dates: Jun–Aug 1993.

MEET THE COMPOSER GRANT PROGRAMS

2112 Broadway, Suite 505; New York, NY 10023; (212) 787-3601

Meet the Composer/Reader's Digest Commissioning Program

Tracy Williams, *Program Manager*

Open to: opera, theatre and music-theatre companies and presenting organizations. **Frequency:** annual. **Remuneration:** commissioning grant of $5,000–20,000
per composer to cover composer and librettist fees and copying costs (amount
dependent on scope and length of work). **Guidelines:** consortium of no fewer
than 2 American producing or presenting organizations with annual budgets of
at least $100,000 commissioning opera or music-theatre work by American
composer; plans must involve full production of work and at least 6 performances
with no fewer than 2 performances to be presented by each consortium member
within 18 months of premiere; write for guidelines. **Application procedure:**
individual may not apply; completed application with supporting materials
submitted by 1 member of consortium. **Deadline:** 15 Apr 1993. **Notification:** Jul
1993.

Meet the Composer/Rockefeller Foundation/AT&T Jazz Program

Liz Berseth, *Program Manager*

Open to: opera, theatre and music-theatre companies and presenting organizations. **Frequency:** annual. **Remuneration:** grant of $15,000–100,000 to provide
fellowship for composer working in traditional forms of jazz or in its continuing
innovative developments and extensions (amount dependent on scope and length
of work). **Guidelines:** nonprofit organization commissioning opera or music-
theatre work from American composer; fellowship covers composer's commission
fee, expenses related to creation of score and expenses for residency of 3–12
months, which may be divided into several developmental components over
period of 1–3 years, concluding with at least 2 public performances of commissioned work. **Application procedure:** individual may not apply; completed
application with supporting materials submitted by organization. **Deadline:** 15 Oct
1992.

MONEY FOR WOMEN/ BARBARA DEMING MEMORIAL FUND
Box 40–1043; Brooklyn, NY 11240-1043
Pam McAllister, *Administrator*

Open to: playwrights, composers, librettists, lyricists. **Frequency:** biannual. **Remuneration:** grants of up to $1000. **Guidelines:** U.S. or Canadian citizen; feminist active in the arts whose work speaks for peace and social justice. **Application procedure:** send SASE for application. **Deadline:** 1 Feb 1993; 1 Jul 1993. **Notification:** May 1993; Oct 1993.

NATIONAL ENDOWMENT FOR THE ARTS INTERNATIONAL ACTIVITIES
1100 Pennsylvania Ave NW; Washington, DC 20506; (202) 682-5562
Merianne Glickman, *Director*

U.S./Japan Artist Exchange

Open to: playwrights, translators, composers, librettists, lyricists. **Frequency:** annual. **Remuneration:** monthly stipend of up to ¥600,000 (about $4600); roundtrip transportation for artist and family members; language training and travel in Japan. **Guidelines:** U.S. citizen or permanent resident; to enable established artist to pursue discipline in Japan for 6 months; artists who have spent more than 2 months in Japan ineligible. **Application procedure:** completed application with supporting materials submitted to NEA Music Program, Opera-Musical Theater Program or Theater Program (see entries in this section); contact appropriate program office for information and guidelines. **Deadline:** varies according to discipline.

Fund for U.S. Artists at International Festivals and Exhibitions
All applications and inquiries to: Vanessa Palmer, Associate Program Officer; Arts International; Institute of International Education; 809 United Nations Plaza; New York, NY 10017-3580; (212) 984-5564

Open to: performing artists and groups, including playwrights, composers, librettists and lyricists who perform their own work. **Frequency:** triannual. **Remuneration:** grant to cover foreign travel, housing, per diem and production costs. **Guidelines:** U.S. citizen or permanent resident. **Application procedure:** completed application; copy of invitation from festival; full budget showing all costs of participation in festival and festival's contribution to these costs. **Deadline:** 1 Sep 1992; 1 Feb 1993; 1 May 1993. **Notification:** 1 Nov 1992; 1 Apr 1993; 1 Jul 1993.

Travel Grants Pilot Program
All applications and inquiries to: Vanessa Palmer at Arts International (see above listing)

Open to: playwrights, translators, composers, librettists, lyricists. **Frequency:** biannual. **Remuneration:** grant (up to $5000 in 1992). **Guidelines:** for individuals or groups of up to 5; supports international activities that enhance professional and creative growth (i.e. short residencies, master classes or workshops, or participation in significant international conferences or performance series); details may change; write for guidelines. **Application procedure:** completed application and supporting materials. **Deadline:** TBA (18 Feb, 15 May in 1992). **Notification:** 8 weeks.

NATIONAL ENDOWMENT FOR THE ARTS MEDIA ARTS: FILM/RADIO/TELEVISION PROGRAM
1100 Pennsylvania Ave NW; Washington, DC 20506; (202) 682-5452
Brian O'Doherty, *Director*

Writers involved in media projects may benefit from grants to support film, video and radio production. Film and video makers should contact the Film/Video Section and radio producers the Radio Section for guidelines and application.

NATIONAL ENDOWMENT FOR THE ARTS MUSIC PROGRAM
1100 Pennsylvania Ave NW; Washington, DC 20506; (202) 682-5445
D. Antoinette Handy, *Director*

Composers Program

Fellowships

Open to: composers. **Frequency:** annual. **Remuneration:** up to $25,000. **Guidelines:** money to be used for creation or completion of musical works; may be used to pay for composer's time, copying and reproduction costs, studio expenses (use of established electronic or experimental facilities only) and other expenses directly related to composer's creative activity. **Application procedure:** completed application with supporting materials and work sample. **Deadline:** 8 Jan 1993. **Notification:** Sep 1993.

Collaborative Fellowships

Open to: composers (and their collaborators). **Frequency:** annual. **Remuneration:** up to $35,000. **Guidelines:** money to be used for the creation or completion of collaborative works; may be used to pay for individual's time, copying and reproduction costs, studio expenses (use of established electronic or experimental facilities only) and other expenses directly related to project; only composer applies, 1 or more partners may be in collaboration. **Application procedure:** completed application with supporting materials and work sample of each member of collaboration. **Deadline:** 8 Jan 1993. **Notification:** Sep 1993.

NATIONAL ENDOWMENT FOR THE ARTS
OPERA-MUSICAL THEATER PROGRAM
1100 Pennyslvania Ave NW; Washington, DC 20506; (202) 682-5447
Tomás C. Hernández, *Director*

New American Works

Open to: individuals including composers, librettists, lyricists; not-for-profit professional producing organizations. **Frequency:** annual. **Remuneration:** matching grant to organization or individual (grants to individuals under creation phase nonmatching). **Guidelines:** individual must be U.S. citizen or permanent resident; money to be used for creation, development or production of new American opera-musical theatre works; seldom-produced American works of major significance also considered. **Application procedure:** completed application with supporting materials. **Deadline:** 4 Sep 1992. **Notification:** 1 Mar 1993.

Artist Fellowships

Open to: individuals who can demonstrate a commitment to opera-musical theatre, including composers, librettists, lyricists. **Frequency:** annual. **Remuneration:** fellowship. **Guidelines:** U.S. citizen or permanent resident; "to support individuals of significant artistic achievement and professional stature, for imaginative projects—involving a unique interaction with artist(s) or organization(s)—that would hope to: stretch the traditional boundaries of music theatre; extend the parameters of the individual's or organization's artistic vision and endeavors; create an extraordinary impact on the individual's artistic growth as a result of her/his interaction with other artist(s) or organization(s)." **Application procedure:** completed application with supporting materials. **Deadline:** 4 Sep 1992. **Notification:** 1 Mar 1993.

Special Projects

Open to: individuals and not-for-profit organizations. **Frequency:** annual. **Remuneration:** matching grant (grants to individuals may be nonmatching). **Guidelines:** individual must be U.S. citizen or permanent resident; for "innovative and exemplary projects that advance the art form or increase audience understanding and appreciation of opera-musical theatre"; contact program before applying. **Application procedure:** completed application with supporting materials. **Deadline:** 4 Sep 1992. **Notification:** 1 Mar 1993.

NATIONAL ENDOWMENT FOR THE ARTS PRESENTING AND COMMISSIONING PROGRAM

1100 Pennsylvania Ave NW; Washington, DC 20506; (202) 682-5444
Lenwood O. Sloan, *Director*

Artists' Projects
Carol Warrell, *Program Specialist*

Open to: producing and presenting organizations. **Frequency:** annual. **Remuneration:** matching grant of $5000–35,000. **Guidelines:** funds to be used by organization to support the creation and production of original interdisciplinary or collaborative works that extend or explore artistic form(s); works may be by individual artists, groups of collaborating artists and/or ongoing ensembles; only projects that cannot be appropriately submitted to NEA single-discipline program (Music Program, Theater Program, etc.); individual artists may also apply directly for support in this category to local regranting agencies through Artists' Projects Regional Initiative (contact Presenting and Commissioning Program for information) but may not accept grants for the same project from both sources; organizations call or write for Artists' Projects guidelines. **Application procedure:** individual may not apply; completed application with supporting materials submitted by organization. **Deadline:** 1 Oct 1992. **Notification:** Jun 1993.

NATIONAL ENDOWMENT FOR THE ARTS THEATER PROGRAM

1100 Pennsylvania Ave NW; Washington, DC 20506; (202) 682-5425
Ben Cameron, *Director*

Fellowships for Playwrights

Open to: playwrights. **Frequency:** annual (contingent on funding). **Remuneration:** 2-year fellowship (amount TBA); grantee may also receive additional sum of $2500 to defray costs of residency at a theatre of playwright's choice. **Guidelines:** U.S. citizen or permanent resident; must have had play produced within last 5 years by professional theatre under any AEA contract or by theatre that was NEA Theater Program grantee at time of production. **Application procedure:** completed application with supporting materials; write for guidelines after 30 Sep 1992. **Deadline:** 30 Jun 1993.

Special Projects

Open to: professional theatre companies (in rare cases, grants awarded to other types of organizations with appropriate projects). **Remuneration:** varies. **Guidelines:** innovative and exemplary project outside the organization's normal scope of activities and financial capabilities; includes playwright commissions. **Application procedure:** individual may not apply; organization submits letter of inquiry before making formal application; write for guidelines after 30 Sep 1992. **Deadline:** 24 Jan 1993 for letter of inquiry; 30 Mar 1993 for formal application.

NATIONAL ENDOWMENT FOR THE HUMANITIES GENERAL PROGRAMS
1100 Pennsylvania Ave NW; Washington, DC 20506; (202) 786-0267
Donald Gibson, *Director*

Humanities Projects in Media
James J. Dougherty, *Assistant Director* (202) 786-0278

Open to: independent producers, radio and television writers. **Frequency:** biannual. **Remuneration:** varies. **Guidelines:** support for planning, writing and/or production of television and radio projects focused on subjects and issues central to the humanities, and aimed at an adult national or broad regional audience. **Application procedure:** call, write or submit draft proposal. **Deadline:** 11 Sep 1992 for projects beginning on or after 1 Apr 1993; 12 Mar 1993 for projects beginning on or after 1 Oct 1993.

NATIONAL ENDOWMENT FOR THE HUMANITIES RESEARCH PROGRAMS
1100 Pennsylvania Ave NW; Washington, DC 20506; (202) 786-0200
Guinevere Griest, *Director*

Translations Program
Martha Chomiak (202) 786-0207

Open to: translators. **Frequency:** annual. **Remuneration:** grant; amount varies according to project. **Guidelines:** U.S. citizen or resident for 3 years; money to support individual or collaborative projects to translate into English works that provide insight into the history, literature, philosophy and artistic achievements of other cultures and that make available to scholars, students, teachers and the public the thought and learning of those civilizations. **Application procedure:** completed application; write for guidelines. **Deadline:** 1 Jun 1993.

NATIONAL THEATER TRANSLATION FUND
c/o Literary Managers and Dramaturgs of the Americas; Box 355–CASTA;
    CUNY Graduate Center; 33 West 42nd St; New York, NY 10036;
    (212) 642-2657

Open to: translators. **Frequency:** annual. **Remuneration:** $4000 commission (5 in 1992). **Guidelines:** for "translations playable on the American stage today"; write for guidelines. **Application procedure:** submit 1 previously translated play and proposal for translation to be undertaken; see guidelines. **Deadline:** 15 Oct 1992. **Notification:** 1 Jan 1993.

NEW YORK FOUNDATION FOR THE ARTS FELLOWSHIPS
155 Ave of the Americas; New York, NY 10013;
    call information for new phone number
Theodore S. Berger, *Executive Director*
Penelope Dannenberg, *Director, Artists' Fellowships*

Open to: playwrights, composers, screenwriters. **Frequency:** awards rotate among disciplines. **Remuneration:** $7000 fellowship; Geri Ashur Screenwriting Award of approximately $1000. **Guidelines:** NY State resident for 2 years prior to deadline; students ineligible; no direct application for Ashur award, which is given to 1 fellowship applicant in screenwriting field. **Application procedure:** completed application with supporting materials; application seminars held May–Jun each year. **Deadline:** next deadline for playwrights, composers and screenwriters fall 1993; exact date TBA.

THE DON AND GEE NICHOLL FELLOWSHIPS IN SCREENWRITING
Academy of Motion Picture Arts and Sciences; 8949 Wilshire Blvd;
    Beverly Hills, CA 90211-1972; (310) 247-3059
Greg Beal, *Program Coordinator*

Open to: playwrights, screenwriters. **Frequency:** annual. **Remuneration:** up to 5 fellowships of $20,000. **Guidelines:** writer who has not worked as a professional screenwriter for theatrical films or television or sold screen or television rights to any original story, treatment, stage play, screenplay or teleplay; 1st-round selection based on submission of original screenplay or screen adaptation of writer's own original work, 100–130 pages, written in standard screenplay format; send SASE for guidelines after 1 Jan 1993. **Application procedure:** completed application with screenplay and $25 application fee. **Deadline:** 1 May 1993. **Notification:** 1st-round selection 15 Aug 1993; winners 15 Oct 1993.

NLAPW SCHOLARSHIPS FOR MATURE WOMEN
National League of American Pen Women; 1300 17th St NW;
    Washington, DC 20036-1973; (202) 785-1997
Shirley Holden Helberg, *National Scholarship Chairman*

Biennial program; next deadline 15 Jan 1994.

PILGRIM PROJECT
156 Fifth Ave, Suite 400; New York, NY 10010; (212) 627-2288
Davida Goldman, *Secretary*

Open to: individual producers, including playwrights producing their own work, and theatre companies. **Frequency:** ongoing. **Remuneration:** grant of $1000–7000. **Guidelines:** grant towards cost of reading, workshop production or full production of new play that deals with questions of moral significance; write for further information. **Application procedure:** script only. **Deadline:** ongoing.

THE PLAYWRIGHTS' CENTER GRANT PROGRAMS
2301 Franklin Ave East; Minneapolis, MN 55406; (612) 332-7481
David Moore, Jr., *Executive Director*

Jerome Playwright-in-Residence Fellowships

Open to: playwrights. **Frequency:** annual. **Remuneration:** 6 1-year fellowships of $5000. **Guidelines:** U.S. citizen or permanent resident; emerging playwright whose work has not received more than 2 professional full productions; fellow must spend year in residence at center; send SASE for guidelines after 16 Nov 1992. **Application procedure:** completed application and script. **Deadline:** 15 Jan 1993. **Notification:** 8 Apr 1993. **Dates:** 1 Jul 1993–30 Jun 1994.

McKnight Fellowships

Open to: playwrights. **Frequency:** annual. **Remuneration:** 2 fellowships of $10,000; up to $2000 program allocation to cover reading/workshop expenses; possible partial travel and housing for fellows living outside 150-mile radius of Twin Cities. **Guidelines:** U.S. citizen whose work has made significant impact on contemporary theatre and who has had at least 2 plays fully produced by professional theatres; fellow must spend 1 month in residence at center; send SASE for guidelines after 15 Oct 1992. **Application procedure:** completed application with supporting materials. **Deadline:** 15 Dec 1992. **Notification:** 15 Apr 1993. **Dates:** 1 Jul 1993–30 Jun 1994.

McKnight Advancement Grants

Open to: playwrights. **Frequency:** annual. **Remuneration:** 4 grants of $8500; up to $1500 per fellow for workshops and staged readings using center's developmental program or for allocation to partner organization for joint development and/or production. **Guidelines:** U.S. citizen and legal MN resident since 1 May 1992; playwright of exceptional merit and potential who has had at least 2 plays fully produced by professional theatres; funds intended to significantly advance fellow's art and/or career and may be used to cover a variety of expenses, including writing time, residency at theatre or other arts organization, travel/study, production or presentation; fellow must attend or participate in at least 1 reading or workshop of a center member's work each week during 2 months of grant year; send SASE for guidelines after 2 Nov 1992. **Application procedure:** completed application with supporting materials. **Deadline:** 6 Jan 1993. **Notification:** 1 Apr 1993. **Dates:** 1 Jul 1993–30 Jun 1994.

THE MARY ROBERTS RINEHART FUND
English Department; George Mason University; 4400 University Dr;
     Fairfax, VA 22030-4444; (703) 323-2221
Roger Lathbury

Open to: playwrights. **Frequency:** biennial. **Remuneration:** grant; amount varies with fund's income (currently around $950). **Guidelines:** playwright who lacks financial means to complete a definitely projected work; playwrights who have had a play professionally produced or published, or who have previously received a Rinehart Fund Grant, are ineligible. **Application procedure:** playwright may not apply; nominations are accepted from established authors or editors. **Deadline:** 30 Nov 1992. **Notification:** Mar 1993.

TCG GRANT PROGRAMS

Theatre Communications Group; 355 Lexington Ave; New York, NY 10017;
   (212) 697-5230
Fran Kumin, *Director of Artistic Programs*

Extended Collaboration Grants

Open to: nonprofit theatres, in collaboration with playwrights. **Frequency:** annual, contingent on funding. **Remuneration:** grant of $3000–6000 (5 awarded in 1991–92). **Guidelines:** playwright and collaborating director, designer, choreographer, composer and/or artist from another discipline, sponsored by TCG Constituent theatre, who wish to work collaboratively for an extended period within the 1993 calendar year; collaborators must reside in geographically distant locations and period of collaboration must exceed that which theatre would normally support; funds cover inter-city transportation within the U.S. and Canada and other expenses related to research and meetings among the collaborators. **Application procedure:** playwright may not apply; completed application submitted by artistic director of theatre. **Deadline:** 30 Sep 1992.

National Theatre Artist Residency Program

Category I: Residency Grants

Open to: nonprofit professional theatres, in collaboration with playwrights, translators, composers, librettists, lyricists and other theatre artists. **Frequency:** 2nd year of 3-year pilot program. **Remuneration:** up to 10 grants of $100,000. **Guidelines:** experienced theatre artists who have created significant body of work and theatres with high artistic standards and organizational capacity to provide substantial support services to artists; funds cover compensation and project expenses of 1 or more resident artists, working singly or in collaboration, during discrete periods used exclusively for residency-related activities that total at least 6 full months over a 2-year period; proposals may be initiated by artists or institutions; write for guidelines. **Application procedure:** 10 copies of completed application and supporting materials; all aspects of application developed and endorsed by participating artists and theatre's artistic director. **Deadline:** TBA.

Category II: Program Development Grants

Open to: playwrights, translators, composers, librettists, lyricists and other theatre artists. **Frequency:** 2nd year of 3-year pilot program. **Remuneration:** grant of $1000–3000. **Guidelines:** experienced theatre artists who have created significant body of work may apply individually or with collaborators; funds cover transportation and out-of-town living expenses for artists to explore possibility of initiating National Theatre Artist Residency proposal. **Application procedure:** 2 copies of completed application and supporting materials. **Deadline:** TBA.

TRANSLATION CENTER AWARDS

412 Dodge Hall; Columbia University; New York, NY 10027; (212) 854-4500
Awards Secretary

Open to: translators. **Frequency:** annual. **Remuneration:** grant of $1000–2000. **Guidelines:** work published within past 3 years, or work in which publisher is seriously interested; write for guidelines. **Application procedure:** completed application and supporting materials. **Deadline:** 15 Jan 1993. **Notification:** spring–early summer.

TRAVEL AND STUDY GRANT PROGRAM

c/o Jerome Foundation; West 1050, First National Bank Bldg; 332 Minnesota St;
St. Paul, MN 55101; (612) 224-9431
Cynthia Gehrig, *President*

Open to: theatre artists and administrators, including playwrights, composers, librettists and lyricists. **Frequency:** annual. **Remuneration:** grant of up to $4000 for travel in the U.S., up to $5000 for foreign travel. **Guidelines:** resident of Twin Cities metropolitan area; program funded by Dayton-Hudson, General Mills and Jerome Foundation to support short-term travel, or period of significant professional development through travel and study, for independent professional artist or staff member of nonprofit organization; write for guidelines. **Application procedure:** completed application with work sample and resume. **Deadline:** 1 Oct 1992. **Notification:** 6 weeks.

VAN LIER PLAYWRITING FELLOWSHIPS

Manhattan Theatre Club; 453 West 16th St; New York, NY 10011;
(212) 645-5590
Bruce E. Whitacre, *Associate Director, Script Department*

Open to: playwrights. **Frequency:** biannual. **Remuneration:** $10,000 fellowship. **Guidelines:** NY resident age 30 or younger who has completed formal education; prefers disadvantaged and minority playwrights; includes commission for new play, production assistantship, 1-year residency at MTC; send SASE for information. **Application procedure:** sample script, resume, statement of purpose and letter of recommendation from theatre professional or professor. **Deadline:** fall and spring (1 Dec and 1 May in 1991–92).

WOMEN IN THEATRE NEW PLAY GRANT

Box 3718; Hollywood, CA 90078; (213) 465-5567
Sally Shore, *Coordinator*

Open to: theatres and independent producers. **Frequency:** annual. **Remuneration:** $1000 grant to assist production of play by woman playwright. **Guidelines:** play must be presented in theatre located in Los Angeles county that has at least 50 seats; independent producer must be experienced in play production; funds to be used to assist professional full production of new full-length play by emerging woman playwright within 1 year of receipt of grant; write for guidelines. **Application procedure:** playwright may not apply; 6 copies of script and supporting materials submitted by producer. **Deadline:** Nov 1992; exact date TBA.

Emergency Funds

How do emergency funds differ from other sources of financial aid?

Emergency funds are for writers in severe *temporary* financial difficulties. Some funds give outright grants, others make interest-free loans. For support for anything other than a genuine emergency, turn to Fellowships and Grants.

THE AUTHORS LEAGUE FUND AND
THE DRAMATISTS GUILD FUND
234 West 44th St, 11th Floor; New York, NY 10036; (212) 398-0842
Susan Drury, *Administrator*

Open to: playwrights, composers, librettists, lyricists. **Financial arrangement:** interest-free loan; no restriction on amount but request should be limited to immediate needs. **Guidelines:** published or produced working professional; must demonstrate real need. **Application procedure:** completed application with supporting materials. **Notification:** 2–4 weeks.

CARNEGIE FUND FOR AUTHORS
1 Old Country Rd, Suite 113; Carle Place, NY 11514

Open to: playwrights. **Financial arrangement:** grant. **Guidelines:** playwright who has had at least 1 play or collection of plays published commercially in book form (anthologies excluded); emergency which has placed applicant in substantial verifiable financial need. **Application procedure:** write for application form.

CHANGE
Box 705, Cooper Station; New York, NY 10276; (212) 473-3742

Open to: playwrights, composers, librettists, lyricists. **Financial arrangement:** grant of up to $1000. **Guidelines:** to assist in emergency financial situation such as overdue medical bills, utility turnoffs, eviction and fire damage; applicant must verify professional status and financial need. **Application procedure:** apply by letter only.

LOTTA THEATRICAL FUND
294 Washington St, Room 636; Boston, MA 02108; (617) 451-0698
Anna M. Acone, *Trust Manager*

Open to: playwrights, composers, librettists, lyricists. **Financial arrangement:** grant of $100–1000. **Guidelines:** fund provides scholarship assistance to talented young women training for theatrical profession (currently to students enrolled at Trinity Repertory Company Conservatory) but when funds are available will also assist deserving theatre professionals in financial need due to illness or other misfortune. **Application procedure:** letter and resume. **Notification:** within 1 month.

PEN WRITERS' FUND
PEN American Center; 568 Broadway; New York, NY 10012; (212) 334-1660
Joan Dalin, *Program Coordinator*

Open to: playwrights, translators. **Financial arrangement:** grant or interest-free loan of up to $1000. **Guidelines:** emergency assistance for published or produced writer in financial difficulties; PEN Fund for Writers and Editors with AIDS administered under similar guidelines. **Application procedure:** completed application with work sample and supporting material. **Notification:** within 6 weeks.

State Arts Agencies

What can my state arts agency do for me?

Possibly quite a bit—the only way to find out is to ask your agency for guidelines and study them carefully. State programs vary greatly and change frequently. Most have some sort of residency requirement, but eligibility is not always restricted to current residents, and may include people who were born in, raised in, attended school in or had some other association with the state in question.

What if my state doesn't give grants to individual artists?

A number of state arts agencies are restricted in this way. However, those with such restrictions, by and large, are eager to help artists locate nonprofit organizations that channel funds to individuals; you should ask specifically about this.

The New York State Council on the Arts, for example, is prohibited from funding individuals directly, and must contract with a sponsoring nonprofit organization when it awards grants to individual artists. Yet NYSCA has a number of ways of supporting the work of theatre writers. The Literature Program funds, in alternate years, translations, and writers' residencies in communities. The Individual Artists Program assists nonprofit organizations in commissioning works, including plays, music-theatre pieces and operas; theatre and composers' commissions are also granted in alternate years. Moreover, NYSCA subgrants funds to the New York Foundation for the Arts, which in turn provides project development assistance for individual artists and creative teams (see NYFA Artists' New Works in Development) and funds fellowships (see Fellowships and Grants). NYFA also assists residencies (see Artists-in-Residence...in Schools and Communities in Colonies and Residencies).

At the least, every state has some kind of Artist-in-Education program; if you are able and willing to function in an educational setting you should certainly investigate this possibility.

ALABAMA STATE COUNCIL ON THE ARTS
1 Dexter Ave; Montgomery, AL 36130-5401; (205) 242-4076
Al Head, *Executive Director*

ALASKA STATE COUNCIL ON THE ARTS
411 West 4th Ave, Suite 1E; Anchorage, AK 99501-2343; (907) 279-1558
Christine D'Arcy, *Executive Director*

AMERICAN SAMOA COUNCIL ON CULTURE, ART AND HUMANITIES
Box 1540, Office of the Governor; Pago Pago, AS 96799; (011) (684) 633-4347
Matilda Lolotai, *Executive Director*

ARIZONA COMMISSION ON THE ARTS
417 West Roosevelt Ave; Phoenix, AZ 85003; (602) 255-5882
Shelley Cohn, *Executive Director*

ARKANSAS ARTS COUNCIL
Heritage Center, Suite 200; 225 East Markham; Little Rock, AR 72201;
(501) 324-9337
Bill Puppione, *Executive Director*

CALIFORNIA ARTS COUNCIL
2411 Alhambra Blvd; Sacramento, CA 95817; (916) 739-3186
Joanne Kozberg, *Executive Director*

COLORADO COUNCIL ON THE ARTS
750 Pennsylvania St; Denver, CO 80203; (303) 894-2617
Barbara Neal, *Executive Director*

CONNECTICUT COMMISSION ON THE ARTS
227 Lawrence St; Hartford, CT 06106; (203) 566-4770
John Ostrout, *Executive Director*

DELAWARE DIVISION OF THE ARTS
820 North French St; Wilmington, DE 19801; (302) 577-3540
Cecelia Fitzgibbon, *Director*

DISTRICT OF COLUMBIA (DC) COMMISSION ON THE ARTS AND HUMANITIES
410 8th St NW, 5th Floor; Washington, DC 20004; (202) 724-5613
Pamela Holt, *Executive Director*

FLORIDA ARTS COUNCIL
Department of State; The Capitol; Tallahassee, FL 32399-0250; (904) 487-2980
Peyton C. Fearington, *Executive Director*

GEORGIA COUNCIL FOR THE ARTS
530 Means St NW, Suite 115; Atlanta, GA 30318; (404) 651-7920
Betsey Weltner, *Executive Director*

GUAM COUNCIL ON THE ARTS & HUMANITIES AGENCY
Office of the Governor; Box 2950; Agana, GU 96910; (011) (671) 477-7413
Alberto A. Lamorena, V, *Executive Director*

STATE FOUNDATION ON CULTURE AND THE ARTS (HAWAII)
335 Merchant St, Suite 202; Honolulu, HI 96813; (808) 586-0300
Wendell Silva, *Executive Director*

IDAHO COMMISSION ON THE ARTS
304 West State St; Boise, ID 83720; (208) 334-2119
Margot H. Knight, *Executive Director*

ILLINOIS ARTS COUNCIL
State of Illinois Center; 100 West Randolph St, Suite 10-500; Chicago, IL 60601; (312) 814-6750
Richard Huff, *Executive Director*

INDIANA ARTS COMMISSION
402 West Washington St, Room 072; Indianapolis, IN 46204; (317) 232-1268
Thomas Schorgl, *Executive Director*

IOWA ARTS COUNCIL
State Capitol Complex; 1223 East Court Ave; Des Moines, IA 50319;
(515) 281-4451
Natalie A. Hala, *Executive Director*

KANSAS ARTS COMMISSION
Jayhawk Tower; 700 Jackson, Suite 1004; Topeka, KS 66603; (913) 296-3335
Dorothy Ilgen, *Executive Director*

KENTUCKY ARTS COUNCIL
31 Fountain Pl; Frankfort, KY 40601; (502) 564-3757
Charles Newell, *Executive Director*

LOUISIANA STATE ARTS COUNCIL
900 Riverside North; Box 44247; Baton Rouge, LA 70804; (504) 342-8180
Emma Burnett, *Executive Director*

MAINE ARTS COMMISSION
55 Capitol St; State House Station 25; Augusta, ME 04333; (207) 289-2724
Alden C. Wilson, *Executive Director*

MARYLAND STATE ARTS COUNCIL
15 West Mulberry St; Baltimore, MD 21201; (301) 333-8232
Jim Backas, *Executive Director*

MASSACHUSETTS CULTURAL COUNCIL
80 Boylston St, 10th Floor; Boston, MA 02116; (617) 727-3668
Rose Austin, *Executive Director*

MICHIGAN COUNCIL FOR THE ARTS
1200 6th Ave, Executive Plaza; Detroit, MI 48226-2461; (313) 256-3735
Betty Boone, *Interim Director*

MINNESOTA STATE ARTS BOARD
432 Summit Ave; St. Paul, MN 55102; (612) 297-2603
Sam Grabarski, *Executive Director*

MISSISSIPPI ARTS COMMISSION
239 North Lamar St, 2nd Floor; Jackson, MS 39201; (601) 359-6030, -6040
Jane Hiatt, *Executive Director*

MISSOURI ARTS COUNCIL
111 North 7th St, Suite 105; St. Louis, MO 63101; (314) 340-6845
Anthony Radich, *Executive Director*

MONTANA ARTS COUNCIL
48 North Last Chance Gulch; Helena, MT 59620; (406) 443-4338
David Nelson, *Executive Director*

NEBRASKA ARTS COUNCIL
1313 Farnam-on-the-Mall; Omaha, NE 68102-1873; (402) 595-2122
Jennifer Clark, *Executive Director*

NEVADA STATE COUNCIL ON THE ARTS
329 Flint St; Reno, NV 89501; (702) 688-1225
Bill Fox, *Executive Director*

NEW HAMPSHIRE STATE COUNCIL ON THE ARTS
Phenix Hall; 40 North Main St; Concord, NH 03301; (603) 271-2789
Sue Bonaiuto, *Executive Director*

NEW JERSEY STATE COUNCIL ON THE ARTS
4 North Broad St, CN 306; Trenton, NJ 08625-0306; (609) 292-6130
Barbara Russo, *Executive Director*

NEW MEXICO ARTS DIVISION
228 East Palace Ave; Santa Fe, NM 87501; (505) 827-6490
Lara Morrow, *Executive Director*

NEW YORK STATE COUNCIL ON THE ARTS
915 Broadway; New York, NY 10010; (212) 387-7000
Mary Hays, *Executive Director*

NORTH CAROLINA ARTS COUNCIL
Department of Cultural Resources; Raleigh, NC 27611; (919) 733-2821
Mary Regan, *Executive Director*

NORTH DAKOTA COUNCIL ON THE ARTS
Black Bldg, Suite 606; Fargo, ND 58102; (701) 239-7150
Vern Goodin, *Executive Director*

COMMONWEALTH COUNCIL FOR ARTS AND CULTURE (NORTHERN MARIANAS ISLANDS)
Box 553, CHRB; Saipan, MP 96950; (011) (670) 322-9982, -9983
Sandra J. McKenzie, *Acting Director*

OHIO ARTS COUNCIL
727 East Main St; Columbus, OH 43205; (614) 466-2613
Wayne Lawson, *Executive Director*

STATE ARTS COUNCIL OF OKLAHOMA
Jim Thorpe Bldg, #640; Oklahoma City, OK 73105; (405) 521-2931
Betty Price, *Executive Director*

OREGON ARTS COMMISSION
550 Airport Rd, SE; Salem, OR 97301; (503) 378-3625
Leslie Tuomi, *Executive Director*

PENNSYLVANIA COUNCIL ON THE ARTS
216 Finance Bldg; Harrisburg, PA 17120; (717) 787-6883
Derek Gordon, *Executive Director*

INSTITUTE OF PUERTO RICAN CULTURE
Box 4184; San Juan, PR 00905; (809) 723-2115
Augustin Echevarria, *Executive Director*

RHODE ISLAND STATE COUNCIL ON THE ARTS
95 Cedar St, Suite 103; Providence, RI 02903-1034; (401) 277-3880
Iona Dobbins, *Executive Director*

SOUTH CAROLINA ARTS COMMISSION
1800 Gervais St; Columbia, SC 29201; (803) 734-8696
Scott Sanders, *Executive Director*

SOUTH DAKOTA ARTS COUNCIL
108 West 11th St; Sioux Falls, SD 57102; (605) 339-6646
Dennis Holub, *Executive Director*

TENNESSEE ARTS COMMISSION
320 6th Ave N, Suite 100; Nashville, TN 37243-0780; (615) 741-1701
Bennett Tarleton, *Executive Director*

TEXAS COMMISSION ON THE ARTS
Box 13406, Capitol Station; Austin, TX 78711; (512) 463-5535
John Paul Batiste, *Executive Director*

UTAH ARTS COUNCIL
617 East South Temple St; Salt Lake City, UT 84102; (801) 533-5895
Bonnie Stephens, *Executive Director*

VERMONT COUNCIL ON THE ARTS
136 State St; Montpelier, VT 05633-6001; (802) 828-3291
Nicolette Clarke, *Executive Director*

VIRGINIA COMMISSION FOR THE ARTS
223 Governor St; Richmond VA 23219; (804) 225-3132
Peggy Baggett, *Executive Director*

VIRGIN ISLANDS COUNCIL ON THE ARTS
41-42 Norre Gode; Box 103; St. Thomas, VI 00804; (809) 774-5984
John Jowers, *Executive Director*

WASHINGTON STATE ARTS COMMISSION
110 9th and Columbia Bldg; Mail Stop GH-11; Olympia, WA 98504-4111;
(206) 753-3860
John Firman, *Executive Director*

WEST VIRGINIA DEPARTMENT OF EDUCATION & THE ARTS
Arts & Humanities Section; Department of Culture and History; Capitol Complex;
Charleston, WV 25305; (304) 348-0240
Lakin Ray Cook, *Executive Director*

WISCONSIN ARTS BOARD
131 West Wilson St, Suite 301; Madison, WI 53703; (608) 266-0190
Dean Amhaus, *Executive Director*

WYOMING COUNCIL ON THE ARTS
2320 Capitol Ave; Cheyenne, WY 82002; (307) 777-7742
Rita Moxley, *Acting Director*

Colonies and Residencies

What entries make up this section?

Though artist colonies that admit theatre writers constitute the majority of the listings, there are other kinds of residencies, such as artist-in-residence positions at universities, listed here as well. You can also find listings in the Development and Fellowships and Grants sections that could be considered residencies. Finally, we have included several "writers' rooms" where playwrights in need of a quiet place for uninterrupted work are welcome.

THE ADAMANT PROGRAM
Box 73; Adamant, VT 05640-0073; (802) 223-2324
Winter address: 7055 Northeast Crawford Dr; Kingston, WA 98346;
    (206) 297-7220

Open to: playwrights, composers. **Description:** residencies of 4–8 weeks for artists, including writers, composers, visual artists and film/video artists, at retreat in small VT village of Adamant, near Montpelier; small individual studio in woods and private bedroom in one of 2 main houses; computer station provided in writers' studios, experimental theatre for the use of playwrights, grand pianos available for composers; lunch and dinner provided, residents make own breakfast and share light housekeeping chores. **Financial arrangement:** resident pays $25 a day towards cost of room, board and studio; very limited number of fellowships available for those who show genuine need. **Guidelines:** creative artist with professional standing in field; less established artists of recognized ability also considered; write to WA address for guidelines. **Application procedure:** completed application with work sample, 3 references and $10 fee. **Deadline:** TBA (30 Apr in 1992). **Dates:** Sep–Oct.

ALTOS DE CHAVON

c/o Parsons School of Design; 66 Fifth Ave; New York, NY 10011;
(212) 229-5370
Stephen Kaplan, *Arts/Education Director*

Open to: playwrights, composers. **Description:** residencies of 3½ months for 12 artists a year, 1–2 of whom are writers or composers, at nonprofit arts center located in tropical Caribbean surroundings 8 miles from town of La Romana in the Dominican Republic; shared housing in large self-contained apartments with kitchen and bathroom; small library; no typewriters for writers. **Financial arrangement:** $50 registration fee; free housing; residents provide own meals (estimated cost $20 a day). **Guidelines:** prefers Spanish-speaking artists who can use talents to benefit community, and whose work relates to Dominican or Latin American context; residents teach workshop and contribute to group exhibition/performance at end of stay; families welcome. **Application procedure:** letter of intent describing how writer plans to benefit from residency and contribute to community; work sample; resume and reviews; write for further information. **Deadline:** 15 Jul 1993. **Notification:** 15 Aug 1993. **Dates:** residencies start 1 Sep, 1 Feb, 1 Jun.

MARY ANDERSON CENTER FOR THE ARTS

101 St. Francis Dr; Mount St. Francis, IN 47146; (812) 923-8602
P. W. Aberli, *Executive Director*
Terri J. Williams, *Information Assistant*

Open to: playwrights, translators, composers, librettists, lyricists. **Description:** residencies of 1 week–3 months for 4 writers and visual artists concurrently at center on beautiful 400-acre wooded site with lake, 15 minutes from Louisville, KY; private studio/bedroom, communal kitchen and dining room. **Financial arrangement:** residents pay what they can afford; suggested minimum fee of $100 for 1 week, $175 for 2 weeks, $300 for 1 month; breakfast, lunch and dinner available for additional fee or residents may cook their own; possibility of funded residencies; write for information. **Guidelines:** formal education and production credits are not requirements but will be taken into consideration when applications are reviewed. **Application procedure:** completed application with project description, work sample, resume and 3 references. **Deadline:** 1 month before residency. **Dates:** Feb–Nov.

ARTISTS-IN-RESIDENCE...IN SCHOOLS AND COMMUNITIES
155 Ave of the Americas; New York, NY 10013;
  call information for new phone number
Greg McCaslin, *Director*

Open to: schools and cultural organizations. **Description:** matching grants to assist schools and organizations in bringing in artists, including playwrights, composers, librettists and lyricists, for residencies of 10–90 days; residency activities include artist-conducted student or teacher workshops, lecture-demonstrations, readings and performances. **Financial arrangement:** artist is paid by school or organization; recommended minimum fee of $250 a day. **Guidelines:** artist must be NY State resident. **Application procedure:** completed application from school or organization; individual artists may not apply but are encouraged to write for guidelines and to collaborate with eligible sponsors to set up residencies; artists may also contact program for information and for help in finding sponsors. **Deadline:** 2 Apr 1993; subsidiary deadlines for smaller grants in Oct, Nov, Feb and Jun each year. **Dates:** Sep 1993–Jun 1994.

ATLANTIC CENTER FOR THE ARTS
1414 Art Center Ave; New Smyrna Beach, FL 32168; (904) 427-6975
James J. Murphy, *Program Director*

Open to: playwrights, composers, librettists, lyricists. **Description:** 6 3-week workshops each year offering writers and visual and performing artists opportunity of concentrated study with internationally known master Artists-in-Residence. **Financial arrangement:** $200 tuition or $600 resident fee covering tuition plus private room with bath. **Application procedure:** master artist specifies submission materials and selects participants; write for brochure. **Deadline:** 4 months before residency. **Notification:** 3 months before residency. **Dates:** 4–30 Jan 1993; additional workshops TBA.

SAMUEL BECKETT PLAYWRITING INTERNSHIP
Gloucester Stage Company; 267 East Main St; Gloucester, MA 01930;
  (508) 281-4099
Israel Horovitz, *Artistic Director*

Open to: playwrights. **Description:** 10-week residency for 1–2 playwrights at Gloucester Stage Company (see entry in Production), a nonprofit professional theatre located in small working-class seaport on the Atlantic coast; intern, who is expected to start and complete new play under artistic director's guidance during residency, works on own writing each morning (word processor not provided), assists artistic director in afternoon and works as crew member on theatre's current production at night. **Financial arrangement:** $1000 stipend; free housing. **Guidelines:** early-career playwright. **Application procedure:** 20-page writing sample; detailed cover letter describing playwright's goals; resume; references; program dependent upon funding (call before submitting). **Deadline:** 1 Mar 1993. **Notification:** May 1993. **Dates:** summer 1993.

BELLAGIO STUDY AND CONFERENCE CENTER
The Rockefeller Foundation; 1133 Ave of the Americas; New York, NY 10036;
 (212) 869-8500
Susan E. Garfield, *Manager, Bellagio Center Office*

Open to: playwrights, composers, librettists, lyricists. **Description:** residency of 4–5 weeks at international conference center in the Italian Alps. **Financial arrangement:** free room and board for artist and spouse/spouse equivalent. **Guidelines:** prefers candidate who expects to publish work. **Application procedure:** completed application with sample of published work, project description and resume. **Deadline:** 1 year before residency. **Notification:** 9–10 months before residency. **Dates:** 20 Jan–20 Dec.

BLUE MOUNTAIN CENTER
Blue Mountain Lake, NY 12812; (518) 352-7391
Harriet Barlow, *Director*

Open to: playwrights, composers, librettists, lyricists. **Description:** 4-week residency at center in Adirondack Mountains; artist may offer reading to local community. **Financial arrangement:** free room and board; voluntary contribution requested. **Guidelines:** artist whose work is aimed at a general audience and reflects social concerns. **Application procedure:** plan for work at center with preference for early or late summer residency; bio, work sample and reviews; $20 fee. **Deadline:** 1 Feb 1993. **Notification:** early Apr 1993. **Dates:** 15 Jun–15 Oct 1993.

CAMARGO FOUNDATION
B.P. 75; 13260 Cassis; France; 42-01-1157, -1311
Michael Pretina, *Director*
U.S. Office:
64 Main St; Box 32; East Haddam, CT 06423

Open to: playwrights, translators, composers. **Description:** 11 concurrent residencies, most for scholars and teachers pursuing projects relative to France, but also including 1 for writer, 1 for composer and 1 for visual artist, at estate in ancient Mediterranean fishing port 30 minutes from Marseilles; furnished apartments; music studio available for composer. **Financial arrangement:** free housing; residents provide own meals. **Guidelines:** resident outlines project to fellow colony members during stay and writes final report; families welcome when space available. **Application procedure:** write to U.S. office for form and guidelines. **Deadline:** 1 Mar 1993. **Notification:** 15 Apr 1993. **Dates:** Sep–Dec; Jan–May.

CENTRUM ARTISTS IN RESIDENCE
Box 1158; Port Townsend, WA 98368; (206) 385-3102
Sarah Muirhead, *Program Coordinator*

Open to: playwrights, translators, composers, librettists, lyricists. **Description:** 1-month residencies for writers, composers, choreographers and visual artists at center near Victorian seaport in 440-acre Fort Worden State Park; small private cottage/studio with 2–3 bedrooms and kitchen; piano for composers. **Financial arrangement:** stipend of $75 a week. **Guidelines:** artist must present clear idea of how residency time will be used; admission based on merit of proposal, quality of work submitted and evidence of past achievement or extraordinary promise. **Application procedure:** completed application with project description, work sample and resume. **Deadline:** 1 Oct for Feb–May; 1 Apr for Sep–Jan. **Notification:** 2 months. **Dates:** Sep–May.

CHATEAU DE LESVAULT

Onlay; 58370 Villapourçon; France; 86-84-32-91
Bibbi Lee, *Director*

Open to: playwrights, translators, librettists, lyricists. **Description:** winter residency of 1–5 months at 19th-century French chateau located in "Le Morvan," a national park in western Burgundy 3½ hours from Paris; 5 large rooms with double bed and private bath available for writers and artists; use of salon, library, TV room and bar. **Financial arrangement:** special reduced rate of Fr. 4000 (about $735) a month per person for room and board. **Application procedure:** write or call for reservation; 50% deposit required 30 days before start of residency. **Deadline:** 2 months before proposed residency. **Dates:** Nov–Mar.

COLD HOLLOW CROSS DISCIPLINE PROJECT

RD 2, Box 3480; Enosburg Falls, VT 05450; (802) 933-2518
David and Sarah Stromeyer, *Organizers*

Open to: playwrights, composers, librettists, lyricists. **Description:** 6–8 concurrent 2-week residencies at 200-acre farm in northern VT for artists of all disciplines who are interested in exploring collective and collaborative questions and pursuits, as well as doing their own work; rustic living quarters and extensive studio facilities; meals provided. **Financial arrangement:** resident pays fee for housing and meals ($100 a week in 1991). **Guidelines:** artist with strong desire to communicate and confer with fellow residents. **Application procedure:** project suspended in 1992 but may be revived in 1993; write for information after 1 Dec 1992. **Deadline:** spring 1993; exact date TBA. **Dates:** summer 1993.

COTTAGES AT HEDGEBROOK

2197 East Millman Rd; Langley, WA 98260; (206) 321-4786
Linda Haverfield, *Director*

Open to: playwrights, librettists. **Description:** residencies of 1 week–3 months for 6 women writers of diverse cultural backgrounds concurrently in individual cottages at 33-acre farm on Whidbey Island, near Seattle; writer furnishes own typewriter; meals provided. **Financial arrangement:** free room and board. **Guidelines:** women writers only; women of color encouraged to apply. **Application procedure:** completed application with project description and work sample. **Deadline:** 1 Oct 1992 for spring 1993; 1 Apr 1993 for fall 1993. **Notification:** 30 Nov 1992; 30 May 1993.

CUMMINGTON COMMUNITY OF THE ARTS

RR1, Box 145; Cummington, MA 01026; (413) 634-2172
Kirk Stephens, *Director*

Open to: playwrights, translators, composers, librettists, lyricists. **Description:** residencies of 2 weeks–3 months for artists of all disciplines at 110-acre community in Berkshires; studio/living space in individual cottages or 2 main houses; children aged 5 and up welcome Jul–Aug. **Financial arrangement:** fee of $500–600, depending on season; limited number of scholarships available. **Application procedure:** write or call for information. **Deadline:** 1 Apr for Jun–Aug; 2 months prior to residency (flexible) for rest of year. **Dates:** year-round.

DJERASSI FOUNDATION RESIDENT ARTISTS PROGRAM

2325 Bear Gulch Rd; Woodside, CA 94062; (415) 851-8395
Charles Boone, *Executive Director*

Open to: playwrights, translators, composers, librettists, lyricists. **Description:** residencies of 2–6 months for 8 writers, choreographers, visual artists and performers concurrently at 1400-acre ranch in Santa Cruz mountains 1 hour south of San Francisco; interdisciplinary projects encouraged; weekday dinners served, residents prepare other meals. **Financial arrangement:** free room and board. **Guidelines:** artist who has clear direction and substantial accomplishment in field. **Application procedure:** write for brochure and application; sample of published work required. **Deadline:** 31 Mar 1993. **Notification:** 3 months. **Dates:** Apr–Sep.

DORLAND MOUNTAIN COLONY

Box 6; Temecula, CA 92593; (714) 676-5039
Admissions

Open to: playwrights, translators, composers, librettists, lyricists. **Description:** residencies of 2 weeks–3 months for 6 artists concurrently in individual studios on 300-acre nature preserve 50 miles northeast of San Diego; no electricity. **Financial arrangement:** $50 registration fee (payable on acceptance); $5 a day. **Guidelines:** artist must demonstrate clear direction and accomplishment in field. **Application procedure:** write for application and information. **Deadline:** 1 Sep 1992; 1 Mar 1993. **Notification:** 2 months.

DORSET COLONY FOR WRITERS

Box 519; Dorset, VT 05251; (802) 867-2223
John Nassivera, *Director*

Open to: playwrights, composers, librettists, lyricists and collaborative teams. **Description:** residency of 1 week–2 months at house in southern VT; project of American Theatre Works (see Production). **Financial arrangement:** housing cost according to writer's means; payment of $75 a week suggested; meals not provided; large, fully equipped kitchen. **Guidelines:** artist must demonstrate seriousness of purpose and have record of professional achievement (readings or productions of works); work sample may be requested from less established artist. **Application procedure:** letter of inquiry with description of proposed project and desired length and dates of stay; resume. **Deadline:** open. **Dates:** Sep–Nov 1992; Mar–May 1993.

ALDEN B. DOW CREATIVITY CENTER
Northwood Institute; Midland, MI 48640-2398; (517) 837-4478
Carol B. Coppage, *Executive Director*

Open to: playwrights, translators, composers, librettists, lyricists. **Description:** 4 "Creativity Fellowships" each year for individuals working in any field, including the arts; summer residency at Northwood Institute which provides environment for intense independent study; program includes interaction among fellows, consultation with local experts in fellows' fields as requested; formal presentation of work in Aug. **Financial arrangement:** travel, room, board, $250 for personal expenses; funds available for limited project budgets. **Guidelines:** projects that are creative, original and have potential for impact on applicant's field; prefers 1 applicant per project; no accommodation for spouses or children. **Application procedure:** completed application with budget, resume and work sample. **Deadline:** 31 Dec 1992. **Notification:** 1 Apr 1993. **Dates:** Jun–Aug 1993.

WILLIAM FLANAGAN MEMORIAL CREATIVE PERSONS CENTER
Edward F. Albee Foundation; 14 Harrison St; New York, NY 10013;
    (212) 226-2020

Open to: playwrights, translators, librettists, screenwriters. **Description:** 1-month residency at "The Barn" in Montauk, Long Island. **Financial arrangement:** free housing. **Guidelines:** admission based on talent and need. **Application procedure:** completed application with script and supporting materials; write for information. **Deadline:** 1 Apr 1993; no applications before 1 Jan 1993. **Notification:** May 1993. **Dates:** Jun–Sep 1993.

THE TYRONE GUTHRIE CENTRE
Annaghmakerrig; Newbliss; County Monaghan; Ireland; phone 47-54003
Bernard Loughlin, *Resident Director*

Open to: playwrights, composers, librettists, lyricists. **Description:** residency at former country home of Tyrone Guthrie; private apartments for artists of all disciplines from Ireland and abroad; library. **Financial arrangement:** non-Irish artists pay about Irish £1200 ($1990) a month. **Guidelines:** artist must show evidence of sustained dedication and a significant level of achievement; prefers artists with clearly defined projects; artist teams (e.g. writer/director, composer/librettist) welcome; several weeks reserved each year for development of projects. **Application procedure:** write for application and further information.

THE HAMBIDGE CENTER FOR CREATIVE ARTS AND SCIENCES
Box 339; Rabun Gap, GA 30568; (404) 746-5718
Judy Barber, *Executive Director*

Open to: playwrights, translators, composers, librettists, lyricists. **Description:** residencies of 2 weeks–2 months for professionals in all areas of arts and humanities on 600 acres in northeast GA mountains; private cottages with bedroom, kitchen and bathing facilities, and studio/work area; evening meal provided Mon–Fri. **Financial arrangement:** resident pays $100–125 a week toward total cost. **Application procedure:** send SASE (52¢) for application and guidelines. **Deadline:** 28 Feb 1993. **Notification:** 2–3 months. **Dates:** May–Oct.

HAWTHORNDEN CASTLE INTERNATIONAL RETREAT FOR WRITERS
Lasswade, Midlothian; Scotland EH18 1EG; (31) 440-2180
Pendleton Campbell, *Administrator*

Open to: playwrights. **Description:** spring, summer and fall residencies of 4 weeks at medieval castle on secluded crag overlooking valley of the River Esk 8 miles south of Edinburgh; 5 writers in residence at any one time; fully furnished study-bedroom; communal breakfast and dinner, lunch brought to writer's room; typewriter rental and use of excellent libraries in Edinburgh can be arranged. **Financial arrangement:** free room and board. **Guidelines:** author of at least 1 published work. **Application procedure:** write for application and further information. **Deadline:** 15 Sep 1992. **Notification:** Dec 1992. **Dates:** Feb–Dec 1993.

HEADLANDS CENTER FOR THE ARTS
944 Fort Barry; Sausalito, CA 94965; (415) 331-2787
Jennifer Dowley, *Director*

Open to: playwrights, translators, composers, librettists, lyricists, screenwriters (TV and film). **Description:** residencies of 1–6 months for artists in all disciplines from U.S. and abroad at center in national park on 13,000 acres of coastal wilderness across the bay from San Francisco; accomodation in 5-bedroom house with communal kitchen and dining room; part-time 9-month residencies for Bay Area artists only, providing studio space and access to Capital Center's facilities but no living accommodation; residents encouraged to interact with fellow artists in other media and with the environment; all residents have access to facilities of 6 other national park organizations, including the Presidio Museum. **Financial arrangement:** stipend of $200 a week and free housing for U.S./international artist; $2500 stipend and studio space for Bay Area artist. **Guidelines:** professional artist with established record but not yet at peak of career achievement. **Application procedure:** U.S./international artists by invitation only; completed application from Bay Area artists; applications available May 1993. **Deadline:** Aug 1993 for Bay Area artists (14 Aug in 1992). **Dates:** Feb–Dec 1994.

LEIGHTON ARTIST COLONY

The Banff Centre; Box 1020; Banff, Alberta; Canada TOL 0C0; (403) 762-6185
Registrar

Open to: playwrights, composers. **Description:** residencies of 1 week–3 months for up to 9 writers, composers and visual artists concurrently at colony situated in secluded pine grove on the side of Tunnel Mountain; 8 specially designed studios (3 for writers, 3 for composers, 2 for visual artists), each with washroom and kitchenette; living accommodation (single room with bath) in nearby Lloyd Hall; access to all amenities of Banff Center, including communal cafeteria, library, theatres, recital halls, art galleries and recreation complex. **Financial arrangement:** resident pays $62.22–82.23 a day; financial subsidy available for those who demonstrate need (maximum of $36 a day for Canadian citizen or resident, maximum of $25 a day for others). **Guidelines:** artist who can demonstrate sustained contribution to own field and show evidence of significant achievement. **Application procedure:** completed application with project description, work sample, resume and references. **Deadline:** open; submit application at least 4 months before desired residency. **Dates:** year-round.

THE MacDOWELL COLONY

100 High St; Peterborough, NH 03458; (603) 924-3886 or (212) 966-4860
Mary Carswell, *Executive Director*

Open to: playwrights, composers. **Description:** residencies of up to 2 months for writers, visual artists, video/filmmakers, architects and interdisciplinary artists at 450-acre estate; studios and common areas accessible for those with mobility impairments. **Financial arrangement:** voluntary contributions appreciated; fellowships and travel grants available. **Guidelines:** admission based on talent. **Application procedure:** completed application with work samples and names of 2 professional references; $20 application fee; collaborating artists must apply separately. **Deadline:** 15 Sep 1992 for Jan–May 1993; 15 Jan 1993 for May–Aug 1993; 15 Apr 1993 for Sep–Dec 1993. **Notification:** 2 months.

THE MILLAY COLONY FOR THE ARTS

Steepletop; Box 3; Austerlitz, NY 12017-0003; (518) 392-3103
Gail Giles, *Assistant Director*

Open to: playwrights, composers. **Description:** 1-month residencies for 5 artists concurrently at 600-acre estate in upstate NY; studio space and separate bedroom. **Financial arrangement:** free room, board and studio space. **Application procedure:** completed application with supporting materials. **Deadline:** 1 Sep for Feb–May; 1 Feb for Jun–Sep; 1 May for Oct–Jan. **Notification:** 10–12 weeks after deadline.

JENNY McKEAN MOORE VISITING WRITER IN WASHINGTON
Department of English; The George Washington University;
Washington, DC 20052; (202) 994-6180
Judith A. Plotz, *English Department*

Open to: writers, including playwrights. **Description:** 1-year fellowship/teaching position; writer gives public reading of own work in fall and teaches a community writing workshop and 1 class for GWU students each semester. **Financial arrangement:** minimum salary of $36,500, benefits, moving allowance. **Guidelines:** practicing writer with experience of and commitment to teaching; conventional academic credentials not necessary; must reside in Washington area Sep 1993–Apr 1994. **Application procedure:** resume, work sample, letters of recommendation; write for details. **Deadline:** 15 Nov 1992. **Notification:** Mar 1993.

NAPANOCH INTER-ARTS COLONY
Box 308, Napanoch, NY 12458; (914) 647-3608
Stephanie Caruana, *Director*

Open to: playwrights, translators, composers, librettists, lyricists, screenwriters. **Description:** residencies of 2 weeks–4 months for up to 20 creative people in 3 buildings on 11 mountain acres; single or double rooms; shared bath and kitchen facilities; studio space and workshop/performance space available. **Financial arrangement:** resident pays $125 a week Oct–May, $100 a week Jun–Sep; a few reduced-fee work scholarships available. **Guidelines:** new, developing arts center open to creative individuals or groups who seek a peaceful place to work, plus an opportunity to interact with others if desired. **Application procedure:** send SASE for information. **Deadline:** open. **Dates:** year-round.

PALENVILLE INTERARTS COLONY
2 Bond St; New York, NY 10012; (212) 254-4614
Jun–Sep: Box 59, Palenville, NY 12463; (518) 678-3332
Joanna M. Sherman and Patrick L. Sciarratta, *Colony Directors*

Open to: playwrights, translators, composers, librettists and their collaborators. **Description:** residency of 1–12 weeks at 110-acre estate in upstate NY; writers, performers and visual artists pursue individual or collaborative projects. **Financial arrangement:** participants pay what they can afford (in 1992, suggested fee of up to $260 a week for housing, studio space where applicable, and meals); a few free residencies available. **Guidelines:** minimum of 3 years' professional experience with high level of artistic ability. **Application procedure:** completed application; write for guidelines. **Deadline:** 1 Apr 1993; individual writers may inquire about remaining unassigned space after deadline. **Notification:** May 1993. **Dates:** 1 Jun–30 Sep 1993.

RAGDALE FOUNDATION
1260 North Green Bay Rd; Lake Forest, IL 60045; (708) 234-1063
Michael Wilkerson, *Director*

Open to: playwrights, translators, composers, librettists, lyricists. **Description:** residencies of 2 weeks–2 months at rural estate for writers and visual artists from all over the U.S. and abroad. **Financial arrangement:** resident pays $70 a week for room and board; partial or full scholarships available. **Guidelines:** admission based on quality of work submitted; applicant must show proof of commitment to serious project. **Application procedure:** completed application; resume; description of work-in-progress; work sample; 3 references; $20 fee. **Deadline:** 15 Sep for Jan–Apr; 15 Jan for May–Aug; 15 Apr for Sep–Dec. **Dates:** year-round except last 2 weeks of Jun and Dec.

ROCKY MOUNTAIN WOMEN'S INSTITUTE ASSOCIATESHIP
7150 Montview Blvd; Foote Hall, 317; Denver, CO 80220; (303) 871-6923
Cheryl Bezio-Gorham, *Executive Director*

Open to: playwrights, translators, composers, librettists, lyricists. **Description:** 1-year associateship for writer, visual artist or scholar with nonprofit institute located on the College of Law campus at the University of Denver; office/studio space, supporting and promotional services (but not housing) provided. **Financial arrangement:** small stipend. **Guidelines:** selection based on prior excellence, promise of growth, need, and ability to contribute to group dynamics; write for guidelines. **Application procedure:** completed application with information on project to be pursued at institute; to obtain application, send $5 processing fee after 1 Jan 1993. **Deadline:** 15 Mar 1993. **Notification:** 1 Jun 1993. **Dates:** Sep 1993–Aug 1994.

SASKATCHEWAN WRITERS/ARTISTS COLONIES
Box 3986; Regina, Saskatchewan; Canada S4P 3R9; (306) 757-6310
Paul Wilson, *Program Director*

Open to: playwrights. **Description:** residencies for writers and visual artists at 2 different sites in Saskatchewan. St. Peter's College: private rooms, some with bathrooms, in Guest Wing of Benedictine Abbey and former boys' school just outside Muenster; 2-week Feb residency; extended summer colony Jul–Aug; 2-week Playwrights Colony in Aug with actors and director available at end of each week for collaboration and readings; individual retreats for up to 3 artists concurrently in fall–winter. Emma Lake: 2-week summer colony at facility 25 miles north of Prince Albert; separate cabins or single rooms. **Financial arrangement:** resident pays $75 (Canadian) a week for housing and meals. **Guidelines:** preference given to Saskatchewan resident but any playwright may apply; write for brochure. **Application procedure:** description of work to be pursued at colony; 10-page writing sample; resume; names of 2 references; state length of stay and (for individual retreats) preferred dates. **Deadline:** 1 Dec 1992 for Feb residency; 1 Apr 1993 for summer colonies at St. Peter's and Emma Lake; at least 4 weeks in advance of preferred dates for individual retreats at St. Peter's; 3 weeks prior to starting date for all colonies at which space is still available. **Dates:** St. Peter's:

Feb residency 13–27 Feb 1993; extended summer colony Jul–Aug 1993; Playwrights Colony last 2 weeks of Aug 1993. Emma Lake: late Aug 1993.

SNUG HARBOR CULTURAL CENTER
1000 Richmond Terr; Staten Island, NY 10301; (718) 448-2500
Director of Visual and Performing Arts

Open to: playwrights, composers. **Description:** studio workspace in performing and visual arts center with theatre, art galleries, shops, museum, meeting rooms and banquet hall, located in 80-acre historic park. **Financial arrangement:** current monthly rental approximately $8.72 per sq. ft.; renewable 1-year lease; tenant must carry own insurance. **Guidelines:** professional artist; space assigned on basis of quality of work and immediacy of need. **Application procedure:** work sample with resume.

THE JOHN STEINBECK WRITER'S ROOM
Long Island University–Southampton Campus Library; Southampton, NY 11968; (516) 283-4000, ext 379
Robert Gerbereux, *Library Director*

Open to: playwrights. **Description:** small room, space for 4 writers; carrel, storage space, access to reference material in room and to library. **Financial arrangement:** free. **Guidelines:** writer working under contract or with specific commitment. **Application procedure:** completed application.

SYVENNA FOUNDATION
Rt 1, Box 193; Linden, TX 75563; (903) 835-8252
Barbara Carroll, *Associate Director*

Open to: playwrights. **Description:** 4 residencies a year of 1–3 months for women playwrights, fiction writers and poets at secluded 200-acre retreat in East Texas pinewoods; 2 writers concurrently each housed in private cottage with workroom, bedroom, kitchen, bathroom and open-air deck. **Financial arrangement:** stipend of $300 a month. **Guidelines:** beginning or emerging woman playwright. **Application procedure:** completed application and work sample; write for information. **Deadline:** 1 Oct for Apr–May; 1 Dec for Jun–Aug; 1 Apr for Sep–Nov; 1 Aug for Jan–Mar. **Dates:** year-round except Dec.

THE JAMES THURBER PLAYWRIGHT-IN-RESIDENCE
c/o The Thurber House; 77 Jefferson Ave; Columbus, OH 43215; (614) 464-1032
Michael J. Rosen, *Literary Director*

Open to: playwrights. **Description:** residency of 1 quarter during which writer teaches course in playwriting or works with a local theatre organization; half time devoted to own work. **Financial arrangement:** $5000 stipend; 2-bedroom apartment provided. **Guidelines:** writer who has had at least 1 play produced by a major theatre; teaching experience helpful. **Application procedure:** completed

204 / COLONIES AND RESIDENCIES

application; 2 work samples; send SASE for further information. **Deadline:** 1 Jan 1993. **Notification:** 15 Mar 1993. **Dates:** between Sep 1993 and Aug 1994.

UCROSS FOUNDATION RESIDENCY PROGRAM
2836 U.S. Hwy 1416 East; Clearmont, WY 82835; (307) 737-2291
Elizabeth Guheen, *Executive Director*

Open to: playwrights, translators, composers, librettists, lyricists. **Description:** residency of 2 weeks–4 months at "Big Red," restored historic headquarters for the Powder River Ranches in the foothills of the Big Horn Mountains; 8 concurrent residents who may be scholars, scientists or artists; opportunity to concentrate on own work without distraction and to present work to local communities, if desired. **Financial arrangement:** free room, board and studio space. **Guidelines:** criteria are quality of work and commitment. **Admission procedure:** completed application; work sample; project description; send SASE for further information. **Deadline:** 1 Oct for Jan–May; 1 Mar for Aug–Dec. **Notification:** 6–8 weeks.

VERMONT STUDIO CENTER
Box 613; Johnson, VT 05656; (802) 635-2727
Roger Kowalsky, *Administrative Director*

Open to: playwrights, translators, screenwriters. **Description:** residencies of 4 or 8 weeks for up to 25 writers and visual artists "who, together with the year-round VSC staff artists, form a dynamic working community" in Green Mountains of northern VT; opportunity for as much solitude or interchange and support as each resident wishes; private work space and housing for writers in village residencies within walking distance of Red Mill complex containing dining room, lounge, offices and galleries; Johnson State College also within walking distance. **Financial arrangement:** fellowships available, based on financial need; write for information. **Guidelines:** established writer or one who shows promise. **Application procedure:** completed application with project description and 3 copies of script; resume, names of 3 references and $25 fee. **Deadline:** open. **Notification:** 2–3 weeks. **Dates:** Jan–Apr.

VILLA MONTALVO CENTER FOR THE ARTS
Box 158; Saratoga, CA 95071-0158; (408) 741-3421
Programming Director

Open to: playwrights, composers. **Description:** residencies of 1–3 months for 5 writers, musicians and visual artists at Mediterranean-style villa on 175 acres; rural setting close to major urban center. **Financial arrangement:** free housing; resident provides own meals, transportation; 4 fellowships available. **Guidelines:** spouse welcome; no children or pets. **Application procedure:** send SASE for application and guidelines. **Deadline:** 1 Sep; 1 Mar.

VIRGINIA CENTER FOR THE CREATIVE ARTS

Box VCCA, Mt. San Angelo; Sweet Briar, VA 24595; (804) 946-7236
William Smart, *Director*

Open to: playwrights, translators, composers, librettists, lyricists. **Description:** residency of 1–3 months at 445-acre estate; separate studios and bedrooms; all meals provided. **Financial arrangement:** resident pays a minimum of $20 a day for room and board as means allow; financial status not a factor in selection process. **Guidelines:** admission based on achievement or promise of achievement. **Application procedure:** completed application; resume; work sample; 2 recommendations. **Deadline:** 25 Sep for Jan–May; 25 Jan for May–Sep; 25 May for Sep–Jan. **Notification:** 2 months.

WALDEN RESIDENCY PROGRAM

Northwest Writing Institute; Box 100, Lewis and Clark College;
     Portland, OR 97219; (503) 768-7745
Kim Stafford, *Director*

Open to: playwrights. **Description:** 2 6-week residencies and 1 12-week residency for writers of drama, fiction, poetry and creative nonfiction at farm near Ashland, OR; 1 writer at a time housed in cabin with kitchen facilities which opens onto meadow surrounded by forest. **Financial arrangement:** free; no meals provided. **Guidelines:** OR writer only; write for brochure in fall. **Application procedure:** completed application with project description, work sample and list of publications or productions. **Deadline:** 30 Nov 1992. **Notification:** 16 Dec 1992. **Dates:** Jan–Sep 1993.

THE WRITERS ROOM

153 Waverly Pl, 5th Floor; New York, NY 10014; (212) 807-9519
Renata Rizzo-Harvi, *Executive Director*

Open to: playwrights, translators, composers, librettists, lyricists. **Description:** large room with 30 desks separated by partitions, space for 150 writers; also private offices; open 24 hours a day year-round; kitchen, lounge and bathrooms, storage for files and typewriters, small reference library; monthly readings. **Financial arrangement:** $50 initiation fee; fee for 3-month period: $200 for permanent desk, $150 for "floater" desk; approximately $250 a month for private office. **Guidelines:** writer with specific project for 3-month period, renewal possible for up to 2 years or for duration of project. **Application procedure:** completed application with references; all inquiries by mail or phone (no visits without appointment).

THE WRITERS' STUDIO
The Mercantile Library Association; 17 East 47th St; New York, NY 10017;
   (212) 755-6710
Harold Augenbraum, *Director*

Open to: playwrights, composers. **Description:** carrel space for 17 writers (3 reserved for writers of children's literature) in nonprofit, private lending library of 175,000 volumes; storage for personal computers or typewriters, library membership, access to special reference collection and rare collection of 19th-century American and British literature. **Financial arrangement:** $200 fee for 3 months, renewal possible for up to 1 year. **Guidelines:** open to all writers; unpublished writer must submit evidence of serious intent. **Application procedure:** completed application with work sample or project outline.

HELENE WURLITZER FOUNDATION OF NEW MEXICO
Box 545; Taos, NM 87571; (505) 758-2413
Henry A. Sauerwein, Jr., *Executive Director*

Open to: playwrights, composers, librettists, lyricists. **Description:** 12 studio/apartments available to creative artists working in all media (performing artists ineligible); length of residency flexible, usually 3 months. **Financial arrangement:** free housing; resident provides own meals; no financial aid. **Application procedure:** completed application; project description; resume; work sample. **Deadline:** open. **Dates:** 1 Apr–30 Sep.

YADDO
Box 395; Saratoga Springs, NY 12866-0395; (518) 584-0746
Michael Sundell, *President*

Open to: playwrights, composers. **Description:** residencies of 2 weeks–2 months for writers and visual artists at 19th-century estate on 400 acres; approximate total of 200 residents a year (14 concurrently Sep–May, 32 concurrently May–Labor Day). **Financial arrangement:** free room, board and studio space; contribution suggested to help underwrite cost of program. **Guidelines:** admission based on review by judging panels composed of artists in each genre; quality of work submitted is major criterion. **Application procedure:** completed application; work sample. **Deadline:** 15 Jan 1993 for May 1993–May 1994; 1 Aug 1993 for Oct 1993–May 1994. **Notification:** 1 Apr 1993 for Jan deadline; 30 Sep 1993 for Aug deadline.

Membership and
Service Organizations

What's included here?

A number of organizations that exist to serve either the American playwright or a wider constituency of writers, composers and arts professionals. Some have a particular regional or special-interest orientation; some provide links to theatres in other countries. Taken together, these organizations represent an enormous range of services available to those who write for the theatre, and it is worth getting to know them.

THE ALLIANCE OF RESIDENT THEATRES/NEW YORK

131 Varick St, Room 904; New York, NY 10013; (212) 989-5257
Virginia P. Louloudes, *Executive Director*
Stephen Butler, *Director of Membership Services*

A.R.T./New York is the trade and service organization for the New York City nonprofit professional theatre, serving more than 130 New York theatre companies and Professional Affiliates (theatres outside NY, colleges and universities, and organizations providing services to the theatre field). Activities and services of interest to playwrights include referrals; *Theatre Member Directory* ($10), which provides constantly updated information on member theatres' performance spaces, staff, and script acceptance policies, together with the theatres' mission statements; and NYC Rehearsal and Performance Space Lists ($7 each) which provide information on spaces currently available for rent.

ALTERNATE ROOTS

1083 Austin Ave; Atlanta, GA 30307; (404) 577-1079
Kathie deNobriga, *Executive Director*

Alternate ROOTS is a service organization run by and for southeastern artists. Its mission is to support the creation and presentation of original performing art that is rooted in a particular community of place, tradition or spirit. It is committed to social and economic justice and the protection of the natural world and addresses these concerns through its programs and services. Founded in 1976, ROOTS now has more than 260 individual members across the 13 states of the Southeast, including playwrights, directors, choreographers, musicians, storytellers, clowns and new vaudevillians—both solo artists and representatives of 60 performing and presenting organizations. ROOTS aims to make artistic resources available to its members through workshops; to create appropriate distribution networks for the new work being generated in the region via touring, publications and liaison activity; and to provide opportunities for enhanced visibility and financial stability via publication and periodic performance festivals. Opportunities for member playwrights include readings and peer critiques of works-in-progress at the organization's annual meeting. Artists who are residents of the Southeast and whose work is consistent with the goals of ROOTS are accepted as new members after a year's provisional status. Annual membership dues are $50. The organization's meetings and workshops are open to the public and its quarterly newsletter is available free to the public.

THE AMERICAN ALLIANCE FOR THEATRE & EDUCATION (AATE)

c/o Department of Theatre; Arizona State University; Tempe, AZ 85287-3411;
(602) 965-6064 (Mon–Fri, 8:30–12:30)
Roger L. Bedard, *Executive Secretary*

AATE is a membership organization created in 1987 with the merger of the American Association of Theatre for Youth and the American Association for Theatre in Secondary Education. AATE provides a variety of services to support the work of theatre artists and educators who work with young people and to promote theatre and drama/theatre education in elementary and secondary schools. To encourage the development and production of plays for young audiences the AATE Unpublished Play Reading Project annually selects and publicizes promising new plays in this field. AATE also sponsors annual awards for the best play for young people and the outstanding book relating to any aspect of the field published in the past calendar year; those interested in nominating candidates for these awards (only the play's publisher may nominate for the play award) should contact Louisa Beilan, AATE Awards Co-Chair, 315 North Indiana, #2, Kansas City, MO 64123-1121. AATE's publications, which are free to members, include a quarterly newsletter; the quarterly *Youth Theatre Journal*; and the triannual *Drama/Theatre Teacher*. Membership is open to all and costs $95 for organizations, $68 for individuals, $48 for retirees, $38 for students and $75 for foreign members (outside Canada).

THE AMERICAN FILM INSTITUTE

2021 North Western Ave; Box 27999; Los Angeles, CA 90027; (213) 856-7600
Jean Picker Firstenberg, *Director*
James Hindman, *Deputy Director*

East Coast Offices:
John F. Kennedy Center for the Performing Arts; Washington, DC 20566;
    (202) 828-4000
1180 Ave of the Americas, 10th Floor; New York, NY 10036; (212) 398-6890

The American Film Institute is an independent nonprofit organization established by the National Endowment for the Arts in 1967 to advance and preserve the arts of film and television and to encourage and develop new talent in the field. In pursuit of these goals, the AFI awards grants to independent filmmakers, runs the Center for Advanced Film and Television Studies at its L.A. campus, coordinates the preservation of the nation's moving-image heritage through its National Center for Film and Video Preservation, and maintains the American Film Institute Theater at the Kennedy Center. AFI also sponsors festivals and touring programs and conducts workshops such as the Directing Workshop for Women. Of special interest to writers is AFI's annual Television Writers Summer Workshop, held in L.A., which provides 2-4 weeks of intensive advanced training for 10 competitively selected writers, preferably new writers with media or theatre backgrounds who have no major commercial television writing credits; participants pay a fee of $475 and some scholarship assistance is available; interested writers should call (213) 856-7722 for guidelines and application information.

AMERICAN INDIAN COMMUNITY HOUSE

404 Lafayette St; New York, NY 10003; (212) 598-0100
Rosemary Richmond, *Executive Director*
Robert Kitson, *Director of Theatre*

American Indian Community House was founded in 1969 to encourage the interest of all U.S. ethnic groups in the cultural contributions of the American Indian, as well as to foster intercultural exchanges. The organization now serves the Native American population of the New York City region through a variety of social, economic and educational programs, and through cultural programs which include theatre events, an art gallery and a newsletter. Native Americans in the Arts, the theatre company of the Community House, is committed to the development and production of works by Indian authors, and presents staged readings, workshop productions and full productions. The Community House also sponsors several other performing groups, including Spiderwoman Theatre Workshop, the actors' group Off the Beaten Path, the Thunderbird American Indian Dancers, and the jazz-fusion and traditional singing group Pura Fe. A showcase for Native American artists is presented to agents and casting directors once or twice a year.

AMERICAN MUSIC CENTER
30 West 26th St, Suite 1001; New York, NY 10010; (212) 366-5260
Nancy S. Clarke, *Executive Director*
Eero Richmond, *Director of Information Services*

The American Music Center provides numerous programs and services for composers, performers and others interested in contemporary American music. The Jory Copying Assistance Program helps composers pay for copying music and extracting performance materials. The center's library contains more than 40,000 scores and recordings available for perusal by interested performers. The AMC provides information on competitions, publishers, performing ensembles, composers and other areas of interest in new music, and its publications *Contemporary Performing Ensemble Directory, Opera Companies and American Opera* and *Opportunities for Composers* are updated annually. Membership is open to any person or organization wishing to support the center's promotion of the creation, performance and appreciation of American music. Annual dues are $40 for individuals ($25 for junior members). Members receive the AMC's newsletter, discounts on AMC publications, monthly "Opportunity Updates" and the option of participating in group health insurance. New members receive a free packet of information and articles of interest to the American composer. All members may vote in the annual board elections and attend the annual meeting.

AMERICAN MUSIC THEATER FESTIVAL
2005 Market St; One Commerce Square, 18th Floor; Philadelphia, PA 19103;
　　(215) 851-6450
Marjorie Samoff, *Producing Director*

The American Music Theater Festival was founded in 1983 to foster the development of music-theatre as an American art form. The festival's primary purpose is to produce contemporary music-theatre in all its forms—musical comedy, opera, music-drama and experimental works—and to provide institutional support to creative artists doing innovative work in this field. Priority is given to work which takes risks and attempts to break new ground. The festival presents full productions with orchestra, showcases with instrumental ensemble, and workshop productions. Due to a full production calendar, the festival is not accepting unsolicited material in 1992–93.

AMERICAN TRANSLATORS ASSOCIATION (ATA)
1735 Jefferson Davis Hwy, Suite 903; Arlington, VA 22202; (703) 892-1500
Edgar Rugenstein, *Executive Director*

Founded in 1959, the ATA is a national not-for-profit association which seeks to promote recognition of the translation profession; disseminate information for the benefit of translators and those who use their services; define and maintain professional standards; foster and support the training of translators and interpreters and provide a medium of cooperation with persons in allied professions. Active membership is open to U.S. citizens and permanent residents who have professionally engaged in translating or closely related work and have passed an ATA accreditation examination or demonstrated professional attainment by other prescribed means. Those who meet these professional standards but are not U.S. citizens or residents may hold Corresponding membership; other interested persons may be Associate members. All members receive the monthly *ATA Chronicle* and a membership directory. Other publications include a *Translation Services Directory* containing professional profiles of Active members. ATA holds an annual conference and sponsors several honors and awards (see American Translators Association Awards in Prizes). Interested persons should write for a membership application. Annual dues are $75 for Active, Corresponding and Associate members; $40 for Associate-Students; $100 for institutions; and $150 for corporations.

MARY ANDERSON CENTER FOR THE ARTS
101 St. Francis Dr; Mt. Saint Francis, IN 47146; (812) 923-8602
P. W. Aberli, *Executive Director*
Terri J. Williams, *Information Assistant*

The Mary Anderson Center, founded in 1989, is a nonprofit organization dedicated to cultivating multidisciplinary exchange between artists and those who celebrate the artistic experience. Named after the 19th-century actress from Louisville who rose to become an international celebrity, the center is located on the 400-acre estate in southern Indiana bought for Mary Anderson by her uncle and guardian, a Franciscan priest. The center's goals include providing a place for artists to concentrate on their work and exchange ideas in a beautiful natural setting (see the organization's entry in Colonies and Residencies). In addition, the center presents performances and exhibitions of work by regional artists and those who have taken part in the residency program (artists participate in these presentations by invitation only). As part of its outreach effort to the Midwest and the nation, the center sponsors symposiums, conferences and other gatherings which explore, in a multidisciplinary mode, topics of major interest to society and to artists. Contributors to the center receive a quarterly newsletter featuring center activities and news of area artists.

ASCAP (AMERICAN SOCIETY OF COMPOSERS, AUTHORS AND PUBLISHERS)
1 Lincoln Plaza; New York, NY 10023; (212) 621-6234
Michael A. Kerker, *Director of Musical Theatre*

ASCAP is a nonprofit organization whose members are writers and publishers of musical works. It operates as a clearinghouse for performing rights, offering licenses that authorize the public performance of all the music of its composer, lyricist and music publishing members, and collecting license fees for these members. ASCAP also sponsors workshops for member and nonmember theatre writers (see ASCAP Musical Theatre Workshop in Development). Membership in ASCAP is open to any composer or lyricist who has been commercially recorded or "regularly published." Annual dues are $10 for individuals.

ASSITEJ/USA (INTERNATIONAL ASSOCIATION OF THEATRE FOR CHILDREN AND YOUNG PEOPLE)

c/o ITI/US; 220 West 42nd St, Suite 1710; New York, NY 10036; (212) 944-1490
Harold Oaks, *President*

ASSITEJ/USA is a nonprofit theatre agency which advocates the development of professional theatre for young audiences in the USA and facilitates interchange amoung theatre artists and scholars of the 45 member countries of ASSITEJ. ASSITEJ/USA sponsors festivals and seminars, operates an international playscript exchange and, with ASSITEJ/Japan, is founder of the Pacific-Asia Exchange program. Members are theatres, institutions and individuals concerned for the theatre, young audiences and international goodwill. Members receive *Theatre for Young Audiences Today* and priority consideration for participation in national and international events. Membership costs $50 a year for individuals, $25 for students and retirees, $100 for organizations and $30 for libraries. Write for membership application.

ASSOCIATED WRITING PROGRAMS

Old Dominion University; Norfolk, VA 23529-0079; (804) 683-3839
Gale Arnoux, *Director of Services*

Founded in 1967, AWP serves the needs of writers, college and university writing programs, and students of writing by providing information services, job placement assistance, publishing opportunities, literary arts advocacy, and forums on all aspects of writing and its instruction. Writers not affiliated with colleges and universities but who support collective efforts to improve opportunities are also represented by AWP. The *AWP Chronicle*, published 6 times annually and available for $18 a year, includes listings of publishing opportunities, grants, awards and fellowships; and *The AWP Official Guide to Writing Programs* (6th edition, $15.95 plus $2 postage and handling) offers a comprehensive listing of writing programs and an expanded section on writing conferences, colonies and centers. Write or call AWP for information on membership requirements.

THE ASSOCIATION OF HISPANIC ARTS

173 East 116th St; New York, NY 10029; (212) 860-5445
Jane Arce Bello, *Executive Director*

A nonprofit organization founded in 1975, AHA promotes the Hispanic arts as an integral part of this country's cultural life. It acts as a clearinghouse for information on all the arts, including theatre, and publishes a monthly newsletter *Hispanic Arts News* that provides information on playwriting contests, workshops, forums and other items of interest to Hispanic writers. AHA also provides technical assistance to Hispanic writers seeking funding.

ASSOCIATION OF INDEPENDENT VIDEO AND FILMMAKERS
625 Broadway, 9th Floor; New York, NY 10012; (212) 473-3400
Martha Gever, *Executive Director*

The association is a national trade organization of 5000 independent film and video makers. The independent producer's advocate in Washington and within the entertainment industry, AIVF offers members a subscription to *The Independent* magazine; group insurance for life and health, income disability and equipment; and other benefits. AIVF's educational arm, the Foundation for Independent Video and Film (FIVF), publishes *The Independent* as well as books related to the field, runs a festival bureau and conducts public events on practical and aesthetic problems of independent production.

BLACK SCREENWRITERS ASSOCIATION
Box 3558; Chicago, IL 60654; (312) 509-8521
Emma Young, *President and Co-Founder*
Rita G. Lewis, *Membership Chairperson*

Founded in 1990, the Black Screenwriters Association is an independent nonprofit membership organization formed to support work which reflects the creative and technical diversity of blacks in relation to the film and television industry. The association aims to foster the creation and perpetuation of positive black images in film and television; to establish itself as a "bank" on whose wealth of black writing talent industry leaders can draw, especially but not exclusively where black experience and culture are concerned; and to offer support to black filmmakers and their work. Activities include seminars and presentations by industry experts, readings of members' scripts, and viewings of television specials pertaining to blacks in the film and television industry. The association holds screenwriting workshops and arranges for studios and/or production companies to read members' scripts. Prospective members, who must show a strong commitment to screenwriting, should contact the membership chairperson for an application and additional information, and may attend one of the association's monthly general meetings. Annual dues are $50 for individuals, $25 for students, $500 for lifetime membership and $1000 for corporate membership.

BLACK THEATRE NETWORK
Box 11502, Fisher Building Station; Detroit, MI 48211; (313) 532-4709
Addell Austin Anderson, *President*
Gary Anderson, *Publicity Coordinator*

Black Theatre Network (BTN) is a national network of professional artists, scholars and community groups founded in 1986 to provide an opportunity for the interchange of ideas; to collect and disseminate through its publications information regarding black theatre activity; to provide an annual national forum for the viewing and discussing of black theatre; and to encourage and promote black dramatists and the production of plays about the black experience. BTN members attend national conferences and workshops and receive complimentary copies of all BTN publications, which include the quarterly *BTN News* listing conferences, contests, employment opportunities, BTN business matters and other items of interest from across the country; *Black Theatre Directory*, which contains over 750 listings of black theatre artists, scholars, companies, higher education programs and service organizations; *Dissertations Concerning Black Theatre: 1900–1991*, a listing of Ph.D. theses on black theatre; and *Minority Job Bulletin*, a quarterly listing of jobs in educational and professional theatre. BTN is collecting listings for a catalogue of works by black playwrights to be published in 1993. For further information and for a membership application contact the publicity coordinator. Annual dues are $75 for organizations, $40 for individuals, $25 for retirees and students.

BMI (BROADCAST MUSIC INCORPORATED)
320 West 57th St; New York, NY 10019; (212) 586-2000
Robbin Ahrold, *Vice-President, Corporate Relations*

BMI, founded in 1940, is the world's largest performing rights organization which acts as steward for the public performance of the music of its writers and publishers, offering licenses to music users. BMI monitors music performances and distributes royalties to those whose music has been used. Any writer whose songs have been published and are likely to be performed can join BMI at no cost. BMI also sponsors a musical theatre workshop (see BMI-Lehman Engel Musical Theatre Workshop in Development).

The BMI Foundation (President, Theodora Zavin) was established in 1984 to provide support for individuals in furthering their musical education and to assist organizations involved in the performance of music and music training.

BRITISH AMERICAN ARTS ASSOCIATION
116 Commercial St; London E1 6NF; England; (71) 247-5385
Jennifer Williams, *Director*

British American Arts Association acts as an information service and clearing-house for exchange between British and American cultural activities in all the arts fields. It provides information, advice, advocacy and technical assistance to professional artists, administrators and sponsors working in all arts disciplines throughout both countries.

CHICAGO ALLIANCE FOR PLAYWRIGHTS (CAP)
Theatre Building; 1225 West Belmont; Chicago, IL 60657; (312) 929-7287
Allan Chambers, *Board Member*

The Chicago Alliance for Playwrights is a service organization founded in 1990 to establish a network for Chicago-area playwrights and others committed to the development of new work for the stage. Founding members of the coalition include Chicago New Plays, Chicago Dramatists Workshop (see next entry), Columbia College New Musicals Project, New Tuners Theatre Workshop (see The New Tuners Theatre in Production), The Playwrights Center (see Development) and Writers Bloc. The alliance sponsors forums of interest to writers and intends to distribute nationally a catalogue of Chicago-area playwrights and their principal works. Write or call for membership details; annual dues are $15 for individuals and $75 for groups.

CHICAGO DRAMATISTS WORKSHOP
1105 West Chicago Ave; Chicago, IL 60622; (312) 633-0630
Russ Tutterow, *Artistic Director*

Chicago Dramatists Workshop is a developmental theatre organization which fosters original works and writers for the stage. It employs a variety of programs to advance the artistic and career development of both established and emerging Chicago-area playwrights. These programs include play readings, classes, workshops, symposiums, discussions, panels, productions, festivals, script consultation, talent coordination, marketing services, and referrals to producing theatres. Several of these programs are open to all Chicago-area playwrights. All programs are available to the workshop's resident playwrights. Although admittance to the Residency Program is selective, recruitment is ongoing. Interested Chicago-area dramatists are asked to attend the workshop's public events, and to interview with the artistic director, before submitting scripts.

COLORADO DRAMATISTS
Box 101405; Denver, CO 80250; (303) 972-8921
Patrick Gabridge, *President*

Founded in 1981, Colorado Dramatists is a service organization for playwrights at all levels of development. In addition to biweekly public readings, the organization sponsors private developmental readings, workshops, and group nights at the theatre. Members receive a monthly newsletter, and may use the group's reference library and rehearsal space, and make photocopies at a discount. Membership is open to all Colorado playwrights, and dues are $20 a year.

CORPORATION FOR PUBLIC BROADCASTING
901 E St NW; Washington, DC 20004; (202) 879-9600
Rick Madden, *Director, Radio Program Fund*
Don Marbury, *Director, Television Program Fund*

The Corporation for Public Broadcasting, a private nonprofit organization funded by Congress and by private sources, promotes and helps finance public television and radio. CPB provides grants to local public television and radio stations; conducts research in audience development, new broadcasting technologies and other areas; and publishes a biweekly newsletter *CPB Report*. The corporation helped establish the Public Broadcasting Service and National Public Radio (see entries in this section). It supports public radio programming through programming grants to stations and other producers, and television programming by funding proposals made by stations and independent producers.

THE DRAMATISTS GUILD
234 West 44th St; New York, NY 10036; (212) 398-9366
David E. LeVine, *Executive Director*

The Dramatists Guild is the professional association of playwrights, composers and lyricists, with more than 7000 members across the country. All theatre writers, whether produced or not, are eligible for Associate membership ($65 a year); writers who have been produced on Broadway, Off Broadway or on the main stage of a resident theatre are eligible for Active membership ($100 a year). The Guild offers its members the following activities and services: use of the Guild's contracts (including the Approved Production Contract for Broadway, the Off-Broadway contract, the LORT contract, the collaboration agreements for both musicals and drama, a stock tryout contract and a revue contract); advice on all theatrical contracts including Broadway, Off-Broadway, regional, showcase, Equity-waiver, small-theatre, dinner-theatre and collaboration contracts; a nationwide toll-free number for all members with business or contract questions or problems; advice and information on a wide spectrum of issues affecting writers; free or discounted ticket service; symposiums led by experienced professionals in major cities nationwide; a reference library; and a Committee for Women. (Also see The Dramatists Guild Fund in Emergency Funds.)

The Guild's publications are: *The Dramatists Guild Quarterly*, a journal which contains articles on all aspects of theatre and, in the spring and summer editions, an annual marketing directory with up-to-date information on agents, grants, producers, playwriting contests, conferences and workshops; and *The DG Newsletter*, issued 8 times a year, with announcements of all Guild activities and more immediate information of interest to dramatists.

Established by members of the Guild in 1981, The Foundation of The Dramatists Guild (Mary Rodgers, President) sponsors the Young Playwrights Festival (see Prizes).

THE FOUNDATION CENTER
National Libraries:
1001 Connecticut Ave NW; Washington, DC 20036; (202) 331-1400
79 Fifth Ave; New York, NY 10003; (212) 620-4230
Anne Borland, *Director of Public Services, New York Library*

Field Offices:
312 Sutter St; San Francisco, CA 94108; (415) 397-0902
1422 Euclid, Suite 1356; Cleveland, OH 44115; (216) 861-1933

The Foundation Center is a nationwide service organization established and supported by foundations to provide a single authoritative source of information on foundation giving. It disseminates information on foundations through a public service program and through such publications as *The Foundation Directory* and *Foundation Grants Index Annual.* Of special interest is *Foundation Grants to Individuals*, which lists scholarships, fellowships, residencies, internships, grants, loans, awards, prizes and other forms of assistance available to individuals from approximately 2021 grantmakers (1991 edition $40). The center maintains four libraries and a national network of more than 180 cooperating collections. For the name of the collection nearest you or for more information about the center's programs, call toll free (800) 424-9836.

HATCH-BILLOPS COLLECTION
491 Broadway, 7th Floor; New York, NY 10012; (212) 966-3231
James V. Hatch, *Executive Secretary*

The Hatch-Billops Collection is a nonprofit research library specializing in black American art and theatre history. It was founded in 1975 to collect and preserve primary and secondary resource materials in the black cultural arts; to provide tools and access to these materials for artists and scholars, as well as the general public; and to develop programs in the arts which use the collection's resources. The library's holdings include 1200 oral history tapes; theatre programs; approximately 300 unpublished plays by black American writers from 1858 to the present; files of clippings, letters, announcements and brochures on dance, theatre, art, film and TV; slides, photographs and posters; and over 3500 books and 1400 periodicals. The collection also presents a number of salon interviews and films, which are open to the public; and publishes transcriptions of its annual "Artist and Influence" series of salon interviews, many of which are with playwrights. The collection is open to artists, scholars and the public by appointment only.

HISPANIC ORGANIZATION OF LATIN ACTORS (HOLA)
250 West 65th St; New York, NY 10023; (212) 595-8286
Francisco G. Rivela, *Executive Director*

Founded in 1975, HOLA is an arts service organization for Hispanic performers and related artists. HOLA presents cold readings and staged readings of member playwrights' work, and provides information and referral services. The organization publishes a biennial *Directory of Hispanic Talent* and a newsletter, *La Nueva Ola*, that lists job opportunities, grants and contests of interest to Hispanic artists. Members pay annual dues of $40.

INDEPENDENT FEATURE PROJECT
132 West 21st St, 6th Floor; New York, NY 10011; (212) 243-7777
Catherine Tait, *Executive Director*

The Independent Feature Project (IFP), a nonprofit membership-supported organization, was founded in 1979 to encourage creativity and diversity in films produced outside the established studio system. The IFP produces the Independent Feature Film Market (IFFM), the premiere film event for independent cinema from both U.S. and international producers. The 1991 IFFM featured over 300 independent features, shorts, and works-in-progress and feature scripts. The IFP also publishes *The Off Hollywood Report*, a quarterly magazine, and sponsors a series of screenings, professional seminars and industry showcases. Group health insurance, a production insurance package, a Resource Program, publications, and a series of audio tapes of previous seminars and workshops are available to members. Membership dues start at $75 a year ($40 for students).

INSTITUTE FOR CONTEMPORARY EAST EUROPEAN AND SLAVIC DRAMA AND THEATRE

Graduate Center of the City University of New York; Box 355; 33 West 42nd St;
    New York, NY 10036-8099; (212) 642-2231, -2235
Daniel C. Gerould and Alma H. Law, *Co-Directors*

The Institute for Contemporary East European and Slavic Drama and Theatre, under the auspices of the Center for Advanced Study in Theatre Arts (CASTA), publishes annotated bibliographies of translations of Eastern European plays written since 1945. A bibliography of Hungarian, Czech, Yugoslav, Roumanian and Serbo-Croatian plays is currently in preparation and previously published bibliographies of Polish and Soviet plays are to be updated. The institute is interested in hearing of published or unpublished translations for possible listing in these bibliographies; translators may submit descriptive letters or scripts. A triquarterly journal published by the institute/CASTA, *Slavic and East European Performance: Drama, Theatre, Film,* is available by subscription ($10 a year) and includes articles about current events in the East European and Slavic theatre, as well as reviews of productions and interviews with playwrights, directors and other theatre artists.

INSTITUTE OF OUTDOOR DRAMA

CB #3240; NCNB Plaza; University of North Carolina;
    Chapel Hill, NC 27599-3240; (919) 962-1328
Scott J. Parker, *Director*

The Institute of Outdoor Drama, founded in 1963, is a research and advisory agency of the University of North Carolina. It serves as a communications link between producers of existing outdoor dramas and is a resource for groups, agencies or individuals who wish to create new outdoor dramas or who are seeking information on the field. The institute provides professional consultation and conducts feasibility studies; holds annual auditions for summer employment in outdoor drama; sponsors conferences, lectures and symposiums; and publishes a quarterly newsletter, as well as information bulletins. Writers should note that the institute maintains a roster of available artists and production personnel, including playwrights and composers. It seeks to interest established playwrights and composers in participating in the creation of new outdoor dramas, and to encourage and advise new playwrights who wish to write for this specialized form of theatre. On occasion the institute will read scripts by produced playwrights, who should send a letter of inquiry before submitting their work.

INTERNATIONAL CENTER FOR WOMEN PLAYWRIGHTS

c/o Department of English; 306 Clemens Hall; State University of New York at
    Buffalo; Buffalo, NY 14260
Akua Kamau, *Director*
Anna Kay France, *Secretary, International Communications*

The ICWP supports women playwrights around the world, continuing the work begun with the First International Women Playwrights Conference, held in

Buffalo in 1988. The center publishes a newsletter, edited by Elizabeth Page and Robin Grunder, and handles communications for the International Advisory Board, which determines the site and policy for future conferences. To become a member, send $10 (larger contributions welcome!) to the above address; checks should be made out to the Research Foundation of SUNY. The center may also be contacted by FAX: (716) 636-5980 or 831-3591.

The Third International Women Playwrights Conference will be held in Adelaide, Australia, in July 1994. The contact person there is Dr. Phyllis Jane Rose, Director; The Third International Women Playwrights Conference; c/o Drama Discipline, School of Humanities; The Flinders University of South Australia; Bedford Park, South Australia 5042; Australia; (618) 201-2460; FAX (618) 201-2556.

INTERNATIONAL THEATRE INSTITUTE OF THE UNITED STATES (ITI/US)
220 West 42nd St; New York, NY 10036; (212) 944-1490
Martha W. Coigney, *Director*
Louis A. Rachow, *Library Director*

Now operating centers in 76 countries, ITI was founded in 1948 by UNESCO "to promote the exchange of knowledge and practice in the theatre arts." ITI assists foreign theatre visitors in the U.S. and American theatre representatives traveling abroad. The ITI International Theatre Collection is a reference library which documents theatrical activity in 146 countries and houses over 12,000 plays from 92 countries. American playwrights frequently use the collection to make international connections; to consult foreign theatre directories for names of producers, directors or companies with a view to submitting plays abroad; and to research the programs and policies of theatres or managements. ITI answers numerous requests from abroad about American plays and also provides information on rights to foreign plays to American producers, directors and literary managers.

THE INTERNATIONAL WOMEN'S WRITING GUILD
Drama Consortium; Box 810, Gracie Station; New York, NY 10028-0082;
    (212) 737-7536
Hannelore Hahn, *Executive Director*

The International Women's Writing Guild, founded in 1976, is a network of women writers in the U.S., Canada and abroad. Playwrights, television and film writers, songwriters, producers and other women involved in the performing arts are included in its membership. Workshops are offered at events throughout the U.S. and annually at a week-long writing conference/retreat at Skidmore College in Saratoga Springs, NY. Members may also submit play scripts to theatres who have offered to read, critique and possibly produce IWWG members' works. *Network*, a 28-page newsletter published six times a year, provides a forum for members to share views and to learn about playwriting contests and awards, and theatre- and TV-related opportunities. The guild offers contacts with literary agents, group health and life insurance and other services to its members. Annual dues are $35 ($46 for foreign membership).

LATINO PLAYWRIGHTS READING WORKSHOP SERIES
267 West 89th St; New York, NY 10024; (212) 724-7059, 663-2777
Carla Pinza, *Artistic Director*

Founded in 1976, Latino Playwrights is a multicultural, nonprofit organization dedicated to developing the creative skills and culture of writers, directors and actors seeking employment within the English-speaking television, film and theatre mainstream. The organization sponsors a weekly workshop for writers, an annual Writers Forum and a spring Stage Reading Festival.

LEAGUE OF CHICAGO THEATRES/CHICAGO THEATRE FOUNDATION
67 East Madison, Suite 2116-2117; Chicago, IL 60603-3013; (312) 977-1730
Tony Sertich, *Executive Director*

Founded in 1979, the League of Chicago Theatres/Chicago Theatre Foundation is a trade and service organization for Chicago theatre companies, theatre personnel and freelance artists. It provides marketing, advocacy and membership services; and acts as an information clearinghouse, maintains resource files, conducts seminars and publishes a monthly newsletter and a *Theatre Chicago Guide* six times a year. Programs serving member theatres and individuals include the Visiting Artists/Observership Program, which provides airfare (in cooperation with USAir) to allow Chicago theatre professionals to work with colleagues around the country; and HOTTIX services. The league's individual membership program offers group health insurance, credit union services, and discounts to businesses serving the industry. Annual individual membership dues are $35.

LITERARY MANAGERS AND DRAMATURGS OF THE AMERICAS
Box 355–CASTA; CUNY Graduate Center; 33 West 42nd St;
    New York, NY 10036; (212) 642-2657

LMDA is the national network of American and Canadian literary managers and dramaturgs, founded in 1985 to affirm, examine and encourage these professions. Among the services it offers are a free 800-number telephone job line, insurance coverage, the LMDA Script Exchange, the quarterly *LMDA Review*, and the National Theater Translation Fund (see Fellowships and Grants). Activities include public panels, symposiums and workshops, as well as membership-only meetings and an annual conference. Associate membership is open to playwrights, artistic directors, literary agents and other theatre professionals interested in dramaturgy. Dues are $35 for voting members, $25 for associates, $15 for students and $75 for institutional memberships.

MEET THE COMPOSER
2112 Broadway, Suite 505; New York, NY 10023; (212) 787-3601
John Duffy, *Director*

Meet the Composer, a national composer service organization, was founded in 1974 to foster the creation, performance and recording of music by American composers and to develop new audiences for contemporary music. MTC awards grants for composer fees to nonprofit organizations that perform, present or commission musical works. Its programs include the Composers Performance Fund and Affiliate Network, an Orchestra Residencies Program, the Composer/Choreographer Project, the Meet the Composer/Reader's Digest Commissioning Program and the Meet the Composer/Rockefeller Foundation/AT&T Jazz Program (see Meet the Composer Grant Programs in Fellowships and Grants). Applications to all MTC programs are submitted by the nonprofit sponsoring organization, not the composer. Composers are selected by the sponsoring organizations. In addition to its ongoing programs, MTC has published two handbooks: *Commissioning Music* and *Composers in the Marketplace: How to Earn a Living Writing Music.*

MIDWEST RADIO THEATRE WORKSHOP
KOPN; 915 East Broadway; Columbia, MO 65201; (314) 874-1139
Diane Huneke, *Director*

MRTW is a national resource center for radio theatre in the areas of writing, directing, acting and sound design. Founded in 1979, it is a project of KOPN Radio/New Wave Corporation, a nonprofit community radio station serving central Missouri. MRTW holds an annual script contest (see MRTW Script Contest in Prizes) to identify and promote emerging and established radio writers. Winning scripts may be produced during one of a series of radio-theatre workshops held each year (see the organization's entry in Development). MRTW provides information and referral services and technical assistance to interested individuals and groups, distributes educational tapes and publishes an annual Scriptbook. In 1990 the workshop published its *National Directory of Radio Theatre Professionals and Audio Artists,* which lists radio-theatre series, trainers, writers and producers, and produced six educational tapes including "Writing for Radio." MRTW is also developing a radio-theatre talent bank to enable it to make referrals and identify potential new trainers and directors for its own and other organizations.

NATIONAL ACADEMY OF SONGWRITERS
6381 Hollywood Blvd, Suite 780; Hollywood, CA 90028;
(213) 463-7178 (in CA), (800) 826-7287 (outside CA)
Steve Schalchlin, *Managing Director*

Founded in 1973, NAS is a nonprofit organization dedicated to educating, assisting and protecting songwriters. Members may call a toll-free number for answers to questions about the music business, have songs evaluated by industry professionals, and, as proof of authorship, deposit songs in the academy's SongBank. NAS sponsors seminars and workshops, the latter in conjunction with the Lehman Engel Musical Theatre Workshop (see Development). Members receive the newspaper *SongTalk* and a listing of publishers and producers looking for new songs. Annual dues are $120 for Pro Membership (for those who have had at least one song commercially released and distributed), $75 for General Membership and $35 for Associate Membership.

NATIONAL ALLIANCE OF MUSICAL THEATRE PRODUCERS
330 West 45th St, Lobby B; New York, NY 10036; (212) 265-5376
Jim Thesing, *Executive Director*

The National Alliance of Musical Theatre Producers is an organization dedicated to supporting professional companies in their efforts to preserve and extend the American musical theatre as an art form. As part of its new works services, the alliance publishes a guide for composers, librettists and lyricists listing member theatre companies who produce and/or develop new musical projects, detailing submission procedures and special interests. The alliance also sponsors an annual Festival of First Stage Musicals in New York City, which aims to encourage further productions of the showcased works. Work to be considered for the festival should be submitted to member theatres, not to the alliance.

THE NATIONAL FOUNDATION FOR JEWISH CULTURE
330 Seventh Ave, 21st Floor; New York, NY 10001; (212) 629-0500
Mark Cohen, *Director, National Cultural Services*

NFJC coordinates programs and services for the field of contemporary Jewish theatre in North America. Its objectives are to foster the writing and performance of new plays about Jewish life and experience; to provide resources, information and consultation to theatres wishing to produce plays of Jewish interest; and to serve as an advocate and clearinghouse for contemporary Jewish theatre. Operating under the aegis of NFJC, the Council of Jewish Theatres serves as the forum for communication and interaction among individuals and groups involved in the field. NFJC publishes the catalogue *Plays of Jewish Interest.*

NATIONAL LEAGUE OF AMERICAN PEN WOMEN
1300 17th St NW; Washington, DC 20036-1973; (202) 785-1997
Mary Latka, *Secretary*

Founded in 1897, NLAPW is a national membership organization for professional women writers, composers and visual artists. Its local branches meet monthly. It holds annual State Association meetings, a National Biennial Convention and a National Art Show, and sponsors the biennial NLAPW Scholarships for Mature Women (see Fellowships and Grants). Members, who receive a monthly magazine, *The Pen Woman,* and a National Roster, pay dues of $25 a year.

NATIONAL PUBLIC RADIO
2025 M St NW; Washington, DC 20036; (202) 822-2399
Andy Trudeau, *Senior Producer, Cultural Programming Department*

National Public Radio is a private nonprofit membership organization which provides a national program service to its over 400 member noncommercial radio stations. It is funded by its member stations, the Corporation for Public Broadcasting and corporate grants. Among the programs available to member stations is *NPR Playhouse,* which presents 29-minute dramatic programs, series and serials. Writers should note that NPR does not itself read or produce plays. It acquires broadcast rights to produced packages. It will consider fully produced programs or works-in-progress on tape only.

NATIONAL THEATRE WORKSHOP OF THE HANDICAPPED
106 West 56th St; New York, NY 10019; (212) 757-8549
Ron Destro, *Dean of Studies*

Founded in 1977, the National Theatre Workshop of the Handicapped (NTWH) is a training, production and advocacy organization serving physically disabled adults who are talented in the performing arts. It is one of the very few places in the country where new dramatic literature on themes of disability is regularly tested and produced. In addition to offering professional instruction in acting, music, voice and movement, and playwriting, NTWH maintains a professional repertory theatre company which showcases the talents of its students. To help serve the interests of the 43 million disabled Americans, NTWH solicits the participation of both playwrights with disabilities and the playwriting community at large in its annual Festival of Short Works. Playwrights wishing to submit scripts to the festival should write for guidelines; submissions are accepted throughout the year. Artists with disabilities who are interested in participating in NTWH's training programs should contact the workshop for information.

NEW DRAMATISTS
424 West 44th St; New York, NY 10036; (212) 757-6960
Elana Greenfield, *Director of Artistic Programs*

New Dramatists is a service organization for member playwrights, which is designed to meet the varying needs of a large number of writers of diverse styles. Rather than producing plays, New Dramatists serves as a laboratory where writers can develop their craft through a comprehensive program which includes script-in-hand readings followed by panel discussions; a loan fund; a library; free tickets to Broadway and Off-Broadway productions; a monthly bulletin for members detailing grants, contests and opportunities; a biannual newsletter, *Readings,* whose subscribers include 5000 theatre professionals; exchanges with theatres in other countries; a national script distribution service, ScriptShare; and the Composer/Librettist Studio, a workshop exploring the composer/librettist relationship.
   Membership is open to all playwrights living in the greater New York area, and to those living elsewhere who are able to spend sufficient time in the city to use membership to their advantage. To apply for membership submit 2 copies of 2

full-length plays (no screenplays or adaptations), 2 large SASEs, a resume, a bio and a statement outlining what you wish to accomplish over the next few years and how New Dramatists would serve that purpose; inclusion of letters of recommendation and reviews is optional. If admitted, a playwright is eligible for all the organization's services for 7 years. *Deadline:* 15 Sep 1992; *notification:* May 1993.

Members of New Dramatists regularly offer classes to other playwrights; the fee for a 10-week session is currently $225. The organization also rents workspace with typewriters to writers. Write or call for further information.

New Dramatists administers the L. Arnold Weissberger Playwriting Competition (see Prizes).

NEW VOICES
551 Tremont St; Boston, MA 02116; (617) 723-9409
Stanley Richardson, *Artistic Director*

Founded in 1984, New Voices is a writers' theatre designed to find, develop and stage new plays. Together with the Public Media Foundation, New Voices is producing *The Radio Play,* a weekly series to be broadcast via National Public Radio's *NPR Playhouse* beginning in October 1992. In addition, selected plays will purchased by the BBC for broadcast in the United Kingdom. Both original work and adaptations that fit into a 30-minute format will be presented; New Voices is especially interested in receiving adaptations of American classics in the public domain. Writers are encouraged to send a query letter and obtain a style sheet from Stanley Richardson; *The Radio Play,* 74 Joy St; Boston, MA 02114.

THE NEW YORK PUBLIC LIBRARY
FOR THE PERFORMING ARTS
40 Lincoln Center Plaza; New York, NY 10023-7498; (212) 870-1639
Bob Taylor, *Curator, The Billy Rose Theatre Collection*

The Billy Rose Theatre Collection, a division of the Library for the Performing Arts, is open to the public (aged 18 and over) and contains material on all aspects of theatrical art and the entertainment world, including stage, film, radio, television, circus, vaudeville and burlesque. The Theatre on Film and Tape Project (TOFT) is a special collection of films and videotapes of theatrical productions recorded during performance, as well as informal dialogues with important theatrical personalities. Tapes are available for viewing, by appointment (call 870-1641), to students, theatre professionals and researchers.

NON-TRADITIONAL CASTING PROJECT
Box 6443, Grand Central Station; New York, NY 10163-6021; (212) 682-5790
Sharon Jensen, *Executive Director*

Founded in 1986, the Non-Traditional Casting Project is a nonprofit organization which exists to address and seek solutions to the problems of racism and exclusion in the theatre and related media, particularly as they relate to creative personnel: including, but not limited to, actors, directors, writers, designers and producers. The project works to advance the creative participation of artists of color and artists with disabilities through both advocacy and specific projects. NTCP holds national and regional conferences, maintains artist files and distributes educational materials, including a book *Beyond Tradition* and a videotape *Breaking Tradition.* In 1989 it published an Ethnic Playwrights Listing, containing contact information for, and a chronological listing of plays by, African-American, Asian-American, Latino and Native American playwrights. Playwrights of color and/or with disabilities, who are citizens or residents of the U.S. or Canada, write primarily in English, and have had at least one play given a professional production or staged reading, should contact NTCP to be included in a future expanded listing.

NORTHWEST PLAYWRIGHTS GUILD
Box 95259; Seattle, WA 98145; (206) 545-7955
Carl Sander, *Artistic Director*

Northwest Playwrights Guild is a member service organization which supports playwrights through workshops, staged readings, and information about play development opportunities. Currently the guild is concentrating on creating projects that bring playwrights together as artists, and putting less emphasis on the continuing problem of getting plays produced: less talk of contracts and copyrights, more work on dramatic action and good stagecraft. Membership dues are $25 for the first year, $15 a year thereafter.

OLLANTAY CENTER FOR THE ARTS
Box 636; Jackson Heights, NY 11372; (718) 565-6499
Pedro R. Monge, *Executive Director*

OLLANTAY's multidiscipline arts center has been serving the diverse Latin community of New York since 1977. The center provides a Traveling Theatre Program which tours plays by local writers, and an art gallery. The Literature Program is dedicated exclusively to the promotion of local writers, focusing attention on this unique community through conferences, and through panel discussions which are published by the organization's press. The center brings well-known Latin American authors to New York to teach an intensive playwriting workshop each season. Other publications of OLLANTAY Press include a writers' directory and an anthology of Hispanic one-act plays.

OPERA AMERICA
777 Fourteenth St NW, Suite 520; Washington, DC 20005-3287; (202) 347-9262
Marianne Harding, *Project Manager, Lila Wallace–Reader's Digest Opera for a New America*

OPERA America is the service and resource organization for professional opera companies in North America and abroad. Founded in 1970, OPERA America has a constituency of 123 members, and offers a wide variety of programs and services to its companies and their managers.

The goal of the Opera for a New America program is to strengthen the opera field by developing new works and broader audiences more representative of America in the late 20th century. The program's support of OPERA America's Professional Company Members and their commissioning/producing partners includes information provided through written and recorded materials, and consultations; and direct grants in support of selected costs incurred for the creation and production of new works and their use in reaching new audiences. The program backs the use of new works and creative productions of existing works as a way for opera companies to reach beyond their current audiences to embrace populations whose age or whose social, cultural, economic or educational status has served as a barrier to full participation in the artistic life of their communities.

Applications for grants provided through OPERA America are accepted only from its Professional Company Members. Individual artists and other organizations may request information about the program.

PEN AMERICAN CENTER
568 Broadway; New York, NY 10012; (212) 334-1660
Karen Kennerly, *Executive Director*

PEN is an international association of writers. The American Center is the largest of the 101 centers which comprise International PEN. The 2500 members of PEN American Center are established North American writers and translators, and literary editors. PEN activities include the Freedom-to-Write program; monthly symposiums, readings and other public events; a prison writing program; and a translator-publisher clearinghouse. PEN's publications include *Grants and Awards Available to American Writers*, a biennially updated directory of prizes, grants, fellowships and awards (1992–93 edition $8 postpaid); and *The PEN Prison Writing Information Bulletin*. Among PEN's annual prizes and awards are the Gregory Kolovakos Award, PEN–Book-of-the-Month Club Translation Prize and the Renato Poggioli Award (see Prizes); and Writing Awards for Prisoners, awarded to the authors of the best fiction, nonfiction, drama and poetry received from prisoner-writers in the U.S. The PEN Writers' Fund assists writers (see Emergency Funds).

PLAYMARKET
Box 9767; Wellington; New Zealand; (4) 382-8461
John McDavitt, *Executive Officer*
Susan Wilson, *Script Advisor*

Playmarket is a service organization for playwrights, established in 1973 as a result of a growing interest in plays by New Zealand writers and a need to find new writers. The organization runs a script advisory and critiquing service, arranges workshop productions of promising scripts, and serves as the country's principal playwrights' agency, preparing and distributing copies of scripts and negotiating and collecting royalties. Playmarket's publications include *The Playmarket Directory of New Zealand Plays and Playwrights*, and a script series *New Zealand Theatrescripts*.

PLAY WORKS AT TRY ARTS
623 South St; Philadelphia, PA 19147; (215) 592-8393
David Hutchman and Christopher J. Rushton, *Co-Artistic Directors*

The Play Works Company provides the theatrical talent, creative environment, and resources for the development of new plays and musicals for the American theatre. Programs for member playwrights include a carefully monitored system of private readings, improvisational play labs, public staged readings and workshop productions, with an annual showcase of original one-acts (see Play Works New One-Act Play and Theater Competition in Prizes); and the Producer "Plus" Program, a script and playwright referral service. Play Works is the resident theatre company at Try Arts, a center for new art. Emphasis is on Pennsylvania, New Jersey and Delaware playwrights. To apply for membership, playwrights should send a current script together with a resume. Annual dues vary from $20–75, depending on membership status.

THE PLAYWRIGHTS' CENTER
2301 Franklin Ave East; Minneapolis, MN 55406; (612) 332-7481
David Moore, Jr., *Executive Director*

The Playwrights' Center is a service organization for playwrights. Its programs include: developmental services (cold readings and workshops using an Equity acting company); fellowships; exchanges with theatres and other developmental programs; a newsletter; the Jones one-act commissioning program; PlayLabs (see Development); Playworks, a professional touring company performing for schools and community organizations; playwriting classes; and year-round programs for young writers. The center awards annually 6 Jerome Playwright-in-Residence Fellowships and 2 McKnight Fellowships, for which competition is open nationally, as well as 4 McKnight Advancement Grants open to Minnesota playwrights (see The Playwrights' Center Grant Programs in Fellowships and Grants). The annual Young Playwrights Summer Conference, open to playwrights grades 8–12, offers 2 weeks of workshops and classes for 40 young writers, with daily professional readings of students' work; participants, who are selected on the basis of writing samples and recommendations, receive college credit; scholarships available; *deadline:* 30 Apr 1993; *dates:* Jun 1993. A broad-based center membership is available to any playwright or interested person. Benefits of general membership for playwrights include discounts on classes, applications for all center programs, eligibility to apply for one-act commissions and script-development readings, and the center's newsletter. Core and Associate Member Playwrights are selected by a review panel each spring, based on script submission. Core playwrights have access to all center programs and services. Write for Membership brochure.

THE PLAYWRIGHTS FOUNDATION
Box 460357; San Francisco, CA 94114; (415) 777-2996
Norah Holmgren, *President*

The Playwrights Foundation provides ongoing developmental support to northern California playwrights. The foundation produces the annual Bay Area Playwrights

Festival (see Development). The Monthly Reading Series, for which scripts may be submitted by northern CA playwrights, presents staged readings of 1 or 2 scripts a month, possibly leading to production in the festival. The foundation's year-round programming also includes panel discussions and workshops led by established artists, and the publication of a newsletter *Re: Write.*

PLAYWRIGHTS THEATRE OF NEW JERSEY
33 Green Village Rd; Madison, NJ 07940; (201) 514-1787
John Pietrowski, *Artistic Director*

Founded in 1986, the Playwrights Theatre of New Jersey is both a service organization for playwrights of all ages and a developmental theatre. In addition to its New Play Development Program (see Development), PTNJ sponsors a state-wide playwriting-in-the-schools program; a playwriting-for-teachers project; adult playwriting classes; and "special needs" playwriting projects which include work in housing projects and with senior citizens, teenage substance abusers, persons with physical disabilities and court-appointed youth, as well as a playwriting-in-prisons initiative. Young playwrights festivals are held in Madison and Newark. Gifted and talented playwriting symposiums, hosted by well-known playwrights, provide intensive 2-day experiences for up to 60 students from various school districts. PTNJ also administers the Geraldine R. Dodge Foundation Theatre Program for Teachers and Playwrights.

PLAZA DE LA RAZA
3540 North Mission Rd; Los Angeles, CA 90031; (213) 223-2475
Gema Sandoval, *Executive Director*

Founded in 1972, Plaza de la Raza is a cultural center for the arts and education, primarily serving the Chicano community of East Los Angeles. Of special interest to playwrights is the center's Nuevo L.A. Chicano TheatreWorks project, designed to discover, develop and present the work of Chicano playwrights. Initiated in 1989 and recurring approximately every 4 years, depending on funding, as part of the Nuevo L.A. Chicano Art Series cycle (Visual Arts, Music, Dance and Theatre) the project develops 6 new one-acts through a 2-week workshop with director and actors, culminating in public readings; 3 plays are selected for subsequent full production. Chicano playwrights who are L.A. residents should contact the center for information on when and how to apply for the next round of the program. In addition to its playwrights' project, Plaza de la Raza conducts classes in drama, dance, music and the visual arts; provides resources for teachers in the community; and sponsors special events, exhibits and performances. Membership in Plaza de la Raza is open to all. Members, who pay annual dues of $10, receive the organization's newsletter *Plaza News.*

PROFESSIONAL ASSOCIATION OF CANADIAN THEATRES/ PACT COMMUNICATIONS CENTRE

64 Charles St East; Toronto, Ontario; Canada M4Y 1T1; (416) 968-3033
Catherine Smalley, *Executive Director*
Beverley A. B. Sweeting, *Administrator*

PACT is the national service and trade association representing professional English-language theatres in Canada. PACT was incorporated in 1976 to work on behalf of its member theatres in the areas of government advocacy, labor relations, professional development and communications. The members' newsletter *impact!* is published quarterly. PACT Communications Centre (PCC) was established in 1985 as the charitable wing of PACT in order to improve and expand communications and information services. PCC publishes: *The Theatre Listing*, a directory of English-language Canadian theatres which includes valuable information on festivals, rehearsal spaces, presenters, government agencies and arts service organizations; *Artsboard*, the monthly bulletin of employment opportunities in the arts in Canada; and *Canada on Stage*, an illustrated, fully indexed series of volumes documenting professional productions across the country. The 1986–88 edition is now available.

PUBLIC BROADCASTING SERVICE

1320 Braddock Pl; Alexandria, VA 22314; (703) 739-5000
Corporate Information

The Public Broadcasting Service is a private nonprofit corporation that distributes programs to its 344 member stations. The PBS Programming Department can advise independent producers about the development of specific projects. Information about the preparation, presentation and funding of projects can be obtained from PBS. Printed materials such as the *Producers Handbook* are also available.

During the 1981–82 television season, *American Playhouse* premiered on PBS. This drama series of classic and contemporary works by American writers is produced by Public Television Playhouse, Inc., a consortium of four public television stations: WNET/New York, KCET/Los Angeles, WGBH/Boston and the South Carolina Educational Television Network. For information about submissions, contact Lynn Holst, Director of Program Development; American Playhouse; 1776 Broadway, 9th Floor; New York, NY 10019; (212) 757-4300.

THE SCRIPTWRITERS NETWORK

11684 Ventura Blvd, #508; Studio City, CA 91604; (213) 848-9477
Ken Goldman, *Chairman*

Though the Scriptwriters Network, founded in 1989, is predominantly an affiliation of film, television and corporate/industrial writers, playwrights are welcome. Meetings feature guest speakers, developmental feedback on scripts is available, and staged readings may be arranged in conjunction with other groups. The network sponsors members-only contests and publishes a newsletter.

Prospective members submit a professional-caliber script and a completed application; there is a $10 initiation fee, and dues are $60 a year.

THE AUDREY SKIRBALL-KENIS THEATRE
9478 West Olympic Blvd, Suite 304; Beverly Hills, CA 90212; (310) 284-8965
Dennis Clontz, *Director of Programs*

Founded in 1989, the A.S.K. Theatre is an organization dedicated to new plays and playwrights, funding a number of programs across the country. Playwrights may deposit copies of plays that have been produced in southern California in A.S.K.'s special collection housed at the Los Angeles Central Library; for further information contact Tom Harris, c/o Unpublished Play Project, Literature/Fiction Department, 433 South Spring St, Los Angeles, CA 90013; (213) 612-3293. The organization's *L.A. Directory of Playwright Groups* may be obtained by sending a 6 x 9 SASE (75¢ postage) to A.S.K. Theatre; note in request whether or not you are a playwright. The group also circulates a biannual newsletter and an annual script-share publication featuring information on the more than 35 plays presented during the past year by A.S.K. Theatre (see the organization's entry in Development).

THE SONGWRITERS GUILD OF AMERICA
276 Fifth Ave, Suite 306; New York, NY 10001; (212) 686-6820
George Wurzbach, *National Projects Director*

Los Angeles Office:
6430 Sunset Blvd; Hollywood, CA 90028; (213) 462-1108
Nashville Office:
1222 16th Ave South; Nashville, TN 37212; (615) 329-1782

The Songwriters Guild is a voluntary national association run by and for songwriters; all officers and directors are unpaid. Among its many services to composers and lyricists, the guild provides a standard songwriter's contract and reviews this and other contracts on request; collects writers' royalties from music publishers; maintains a copyright renewal service; conducts songwriting workshops and critique sessions with special rates for members; provides a songwriter collaboration service; issues news bulletins with essential information for writers; and offers a group medical and life insurance plan. Full members of the guild must be published songwriters and pay dues on a graduated scale from $70–400. Unpublished songwriters may become associate members and pay dues of $55 a year. Write for membership application.

SOUTHEAST PLAYWRIGHTS PROJECT
353 Elmira Pl NE; Atlanta, GA 30307; (404) 523-1368
Jim Grimsley, *Executive Director*

Southeast Playwrights Project is a service organization for playwrights who live, or have lived, in the Southeast. Its programs fall into two general areas: script development (cold readings, rehearsed readings, staged readings and nonperformance workshops) and career development (dramaturgical advice, free theatre tickets, a mentor program, retreats and networking). Members of SEPP, who pay dues of $50 a year, receive the SEPP newsletter, are eligible for all career development services and for discounts on workshops, and can have their plays listed in a nationally distributed play catalogue. They can also participate in the Writers' Lab which meets twice a month to read and discuss scenes from members' works-in-progress. For full information send an SASE for the SEPP membership brochure.

S.T.A.G.E. (SOCIETY FOR THEATRICAL ARTISTS GUIDANCE AND ENHANCEMENT)
Box 214820; 4633 Insurance; Dallas, TX 75221; (214) 559-3917
Susan McMath, *Executive Director*

Founded in 1981, S.T.A.G.E. acts as an information clearinghouse for theatre artists and theatre organizations in the north Texas region. The society maintains a library of plays, theatre texts and resource information; offers counseling on agents, unions, personal marketing and other career-related matters; posts listings of miscellaneous job opportunities; and maintains an audition callboard for regional opportunities in theatre and film. S.T.A.G.E. runs the Playwrights Project, a program for regional playwrights which develops one-acts through private and public staged readings. Plays developed in the project are eligible for inclusion in the STAGES festival, one of several showcases produced by the society, which presents workshop productions of new one-acts each summer. Members of S.T.A.G.E., who pay annual dues starting at $45, receive a monthly publication, CENTERSTAGE.

THEATRE ASSOCIATION OF PENNSYLVANIA (TAP)
2318 South Queen St; York, PA 17402; (717) 741-1269
Lewis E. Silverman, *Executive Director*

TAP, founded in 1968, is a nonprofit professional association of theatres, theatre training programs, artists and educators, working cooperatively to encourage, foster, promote and aid all forms of quality theatre in Pennsylvania. The association serves as the central information agency for its membership; sponsors conferences and workshops; and administers the Philadelphia Small Theatre Program for the Pew Charitable Trusts, and two fellowship programs for the Pennsylvania Council on the Arts: The Pennsylvania Playwrights Project (for playwrights and solo performers) and the Pennsylvania Media Arts Scriptwriters Project (for film and television writers). Recipients of the playwriting fellowships can take part in TAP's Playwrights-in-Residence Program, which places playwrights on university campuses, and are also listed in *The Pennsylvania Playwrights Connection*, an annually updated, nationally distributed publication that introduces fellowship recipients and their work to theatres in seach of new plays. TAP's other publications include the bimonthly newsletter *TAP News and Notes*, *Pennsylvania Opportunities for Education, Training, and Experience in Theatre*, *TAP Vacancies* and an annual *Pennsylvania Theatre Directory*. Membership is open to all and annual dues start at $25.

THEATRE BAY AREA

657 Mission St, Suite 402; San Francisco, CA 94105; (415) 957-1557
Liza Zenni, *Executive Director*

TBA is a resource organization for San Francisco theatre workers whose members include 3200 individuals and over 200 theatre companies. Its programs include workshops, conferences and office referral services. Annual dues of $32 (out-of-state residents add $10 for 1st-class postage) include a subscription to *Callboard*, a monthly magazine featuring articles, interviews and essays by critics and playwrights from the Bay Area and elsewhere, as well as information on play contests and festivals, and listings of production activity, workshops, classes, auditions, jobs and services. TBA also biennially publishes *Theatre Directory of the Bay Area* (1991–92 edition $18/member, $22/nonmember, postpaid), which includes entries on organizations serving playwrights; profiles of local theatre companies; listings of rehearsal and performance spaces, classes, workshops, schools, agents and unions; and sources for commercial supplies and technical services.

THEATRE COMMUNICATIONS GROUP

355 Lexington Ave; New York, NY 10017; (212) 697-5230
Peter Zeisler, *Executive Director*

TCG, the national organization for the nonprofit professional theatre, was founded in 1961 to provide a forum and communications network and to respond to the needs of both theatres and theatre artists for centralized services. TCG's more than 300 Constituent and Associate theatres, as well as thousands of individual artists, administrators and technicians, are served through job referral services, management and research services, publications, conferences and seminars, and a variety of other information and advisory services. (For more information, see American Theatre and Plays in Process in Publication, and TCG Grant Programs in Fellowships and Grants.)

In addition to *American Theatre* magazine and *Plays in Process*, TCG publications of interest to theatre writers include *Theatre Profiles*, a biennial reference guide offering comprehensive statistical, historical and production information on more than 200 nonprofit theatres; *Theatre Directory*, which provides complete contact information for more than 350 theatres and related arts organizations across the U.S.; and *ArtSEARCH*, a biweekly bulletin of job opportunities in the arts. The "Opportunities" column of *American Theatre* supplements information provided in this *Sourcebook*. TCG also publishes other volumes of plays, play texts in *American Theatre*, and books dealing with all aspects of theatre. For further information, see Useful Publications, and Publications from TCG in the back of this book, or contact TCG for the current Publications catalogue.

UBU REPERTORY THEATER

15 West 28th St; New York, NY 10001; (212) 679-7540
Françoise Kourilsky, *Artistic Director*

Ubu Repertory Theater, founded in 1982, is a nonprofit theatre center dedicated to introducing translations of contemporary French-language plays to the English-speaking audience. In addition to producing several plays a year, Ubu commissions translations and schedules programs of readings, theatre-related film and video screenings, photography exhibits, seminars and workshops. Ubu publishes a series of contemporary French plays in English translation, distributed nationally by TCG, and houses a French-English reference library of published plays, manuscripts, audio- and videotapes.

VOLUNTEER LAWYERS FOR THE ARTS
1 East 53rd St, 6th Floor; New York, NY 10022; (212) 319-2787
Daniel Y. Mayer, *Executive Director*

Volunteer Lawyers for the Arts arranges free legal representation and legal education in the arts community. Individual artists and nonprofit arts organizations unable to afford private counsel are eligible for VLA's services; VLA can be especially useful to playwrights with copyright or contract problems. There is an administrative fee per referral of $30–50 for individuals, $50–100 for nonprofit organizations and $250 for nonprofit incorporation and tax exemption. VLA's education program offers biweekly seminars on nonprofit incorporation and evening seminars held regularly to educate attorneys and artists in specific areas of art law. Publications include the *VLA-Columbia Journal of Law & the Arts*, containing articles on legal aspects of the arts (annual subscription $35); and the *VLA Guide to Copyright for the Performing Arts* ($5.95 plus $2 postage and handling). For more information about VLA's publications and the 40 VLA affiliates across the country, contact the New York office; referrals can be made to volunteer lawyer organizations nationwide.

THE WOW CAFE
59 East 4th St; New York, NY 10003; (212) 460-8067 (service)
Lisa Kron, *Member*

The WOW (Women's One World) Cafe is a women's theatre collective producing the work of women playwrights and performers. WOW has no permanent staff and its members are encouraged to participate in all aspects of the group's operations. In lieu of dues, members volunteer their services backstage on fellow members' productions in exchange for the opportunity to present their own work. Each show is produced by the member who initiates it. Membership in WOW Cafe is open to all interested women.

WRITERS GUILD OF AMERICA, EAST (WGAe)
555 West 57th St; New York, NY 10019; (212) 767-7800
Mona Mangan, *Executive Director*

WGAe is the union for freelance writers in the fields of motion pictures, television and radio who reside east of the Mississippi River. The union negotiates collective bargaining agreements for its members and represents them in grievances and arbitrations under those agreements. It also makes credit determinations for the writing of its members. The guild gives annual awards, and sponsors a foundation which makes fellowships available to established documentary writer-producers and to beginning professional film and television writers; contact the guild for information. WGAe participates in reciprocal membership with the International Affiliation of Writers Guilds and with its sister union, Writers Guild of America, west. The guild publishes a monthly newsletter, which is available to nonmembers by subscription. Write for information on WGAe's registration service for registering literary material, or call (212) 757-4360.

WRITERS GUILD OF AMERICA, WEST (WGAw)
8955 Beverly Blvd; West Hollywood, CA 90048; (213) 550-1000
Brian Walton, *Executive Director*

WGAw is the union for writers in the fields of motion pictures, television and radio who reside west of the Mississippi. It represents its members in collective bargaining and other labor matters. It publishes a monthly newsletter, *The Journal.*

Epilogue

- **Useful Publications**
- **Submission Calendar**
- **Special Interests**
- **Index**

Useful Publications

This is a highly selective listing of the publications that we think most usefully supplement the information given in the *Sourcebook*. Note that publications of interest to theatre writers are also described throughout this book, particularly in introductions to sections, in Membership and Service Organizations listings, and on the Publications from TCG page in the back. Before ordering you would be wise to find out if the prices given in all listings still pertain.

We have purposely left out any "how to" books on the art of playwriting because we do not want to promote the concept of "writing-by-recipe." However, we do recommend David Savran's *In Their Own Words: Contemporary American Playwrights* (see Publications from TCG). We also recommend that you subscribe to the *Plays in Process* series. Writing can be an isolated activity, and playwrights scattered across the country tend to know very little about what their colleagues' work is like. An extremely important kind of cross-fertilization happens when playwrights read the work of other playwrights. To this end, we are providing a special discount order form for playwrights at the back of this book and we encourage you to use it.

American Theatre; Theatre Communications Group; 355 Lexington Ave; New York, NY 10017; (212) 697-5230. 1-year subscription (10 issues) $27, 2 years $50; single issue $3.95. TCG's monthly magazine includes an "Opportunities" column which updates *Sourcebook* information between editions, announcing new contests as well as the occasional revised competition. Performance schedules for some 200 theatres are listed every month, and productions nationwide are documented through pictures as well as reports. As part of its comprehensive coverage of all aspects of theatre, *American Theatre* regularly features articles and interviews dealing with theatre writers and their works, and publishes the complete texts of 7 plays a year.

Back Stage; 330 West 42nd St; New York, NY 10036; (212) 947-0020. 1-year subscription $59, 2 years $99; single issue $1.85, $4 by mail. This "complete service weekly for the communications and entertainment industry" includes a theatre section. Though the primary focus is on casting, theatres and other producers sometimes run ads soliciting scripts; workshops and classes for playwrights are also likely to be advertised here.

A Handbook for Literary Translators; PEN American Center; 568 Broadway; New York, NY 10012; (212) 334-1660. 2nd edition, 1991. 34 pp, free (send 52¢ business-size SASE) paper. Contents include "A Translator's Model Contract," "Negotiating a Contract," "Selected Resources" and "The Responsibilities of Translation."

Hollywood Scriptwriter; 1626 North Wilcox, #385; Hollywood, CA 90028; (818) 991-3096. 1-year subscription (12 issues) $44, 6 months $25; discount on renewals. This 12-page newsletter contains a "MARKETS for Your Work" section that includes "Plays Wanted" listings, as well as interviews and articles giving advice that is sometimes useful to playwrights as well as screenwriters. A list of back issues with a summary of the contents of each issue is available; call for information and a free sample.

The Individual's Guide to Grants by Judith B. Margolin; Plenum Press; 233 Spring St; New York, NY 10013; (212) 620-8051 or toll-free 1-800-221-9369. 1983. 276 pp, $19.95 cloth. This comprehensive guide to individual grantseeking, written by a former director of the New York library of the Foundation Center, offers detailed advice on each step of the process.

Literary Agents: A Writer's Guide by Adam Begley; Poets & Writers; 72 Spring St; New York, NY 10012; (212) 226-3586. 1992. 92 pp, $9 (plus $1.50 postage and handling plus sales tax where applicable) paper. This book contains several chapters exploring the functions of literary agents and the agent-writer relationship, and includes listings of 197 agencies which will consider unsolicited *queries* plus 37 more agencies which charge fees.

Literary Agents of North America; Author Aid/Research Associates International; 340 East 52nd St; New York, NY 10022; (212) 758-4213 or 980-9179. 4th edition, 1991. 262 pp, $29.95 (plus $3 postage and handling, $7 for priority mail, plus sales tax on NYS orders) paper. Profiles of more than 1000 U.S. and Canadian literary agencies include their areas of interest and policies regarding new writers and unsolicited manuscripts.

Literary Market Place 1992; R.R. Bowker; 121 Chanlon Rd; New Providence, NJ 07974; toll-free 1-800-521-8110, (908) 464-6800 in New Providence (may call collect). 1991. 1773 pp, $134.95 (plus 7% shipping and handling plus sales tax where applicable) paper. The "phone book" of American book publishing gives contact information for book publishers and those in related fields, and includes a "Names & Numbers" index over 450 pages long. The 1993 *LMP* is due out in November 1992.

The National Playwrights Directory; Phyllis Johnson Kaye, ed; O'Neill Theater Center; 305 Great Neck Rd; Waterford, CT 06385; (203) 443-5378. 1981. 507 pp, $20 (plus $3.50 postage and handling) cloth. With entries on 495 writers and an index of over 4000 plays, this book is still a useful source of information. A new edition is planned, but will not be out in the near future.

Playhouse America!; Feedback Theatrebooks; 305 Madison Ave, Suite 1146; New York, NY 10165; (212) 687-4185. 1991. 300 pp, $16.95 (plus $2 postage and handling) paper. This directory contains the addresses and phone numbers of more than 3500 theatres across the country; it includes a cross-reference to specialty theatres (e.g. Dinner Theatres & Showboats, Military Theatres).

The Playwright's Companion; Mollie Ann Meserve, ed; Feedback Theatrebooks; 305 Madison Ave, Suite 1146; New York, NY 10165; (212) 687-4185. 1991. 400 pp, $20.95 (plus $2 postage and handling) paper. This annual guide for playwrights publishes submission guidelines for more than 1300 theatres, contests, publishers and special programs. The *Companion* includes useful tips on query letters, synopses, resumes and submission etiquette. The 1993 edition is due out in December 1992.

Poets & Writers Magazine; Poets & Writers; 72 Spring St; New York, NY 10012; (212) 226-3586. 1-year subscription (6 issues) $18, single issue $3.95. Though primarily aimed at writers of poetry and fiction, this newsletter does include some announcements of grants and awards as well as other opportunities open to theatre writers. Poets & Writers also makes available reprints of selected major articles (write for list of titles; $2 plus SASE per reprint).

Professional Playscript Format Guidelines and Sample; Feedback Theatrebooks; 305 Madison Ave, Suite 1146; New York, NY 10165; (212) 687-4185. 1991. 18 pp, $4.95 (plus $1.50 postage and handling) paper. This 8½" x 11" booklet provides detailed instructions for laying out a script in a professional manner.

Publications of the U.S. Copyright Office; Register of Copyrights; Library of Congress; Washington, DC 20559; (202) 707-9100 for orders only (machine); 479-0700 for questions and advice. Call and ask for available free circulars, which include R1, "Copyright Basics." If you write for information instead, expect to wait a long time for a response.

Songwriter's Market; Michael Oxley, ed; Writer's Digest Books; 1507 Dana Ave; Cincinnati, OH 45207; (513) 531-2222. 1991. 528 pp, $19.95 (plus $3 shipping and handling) cloth. This annually updated directory, which lists contact information for 2000 song markets, includes a section on musical theatre. It also lists clubs, associations, contests and workshops of interest to songwriters. The 1993 edition is due out in September 1992.

Theatre Directory; Theatre Communications Group; 355 Lexington Ave; New York, NY 10017; (212) 697-5230. 1992–93 edition to be published October 1992. 89 pp, $5.95 (plus $2.00 postage and handling) paper. TCG's annually updated directory provides complete contact information on more than 300 nonprofit professional theatres—some of them such recent TCG members that they aren't included in this *Sourcebook*—and over 40 arts resource organizations.

Theatre Profiles 10; Theatre Communications Group; 355 Lexington Ave; New York, NY 10017; (212) 697-5230. 1992. 201 pp, $21.95 (plus $4 postage and handling) paper. Useful for finding out about this country's nonprofit professional theatres, the 10th volume of this biennial series contains artistic profiles, production photographs, 1990–91 financial information and repertoire information for the 1989–91 seasons of 229 theatres.

The Writer; 120 Boylston St; Boston, MA 02116; (617) 423-3157. 1-year subscription (12 issues) $27, 2 years $50, 3 years $74. This monthly magazine announces contests in a "Prize Offers" column, and publishes a special "Opportunities for Playwrights" section in the September issue.

A Writer's Guide to Copyright; Poets & Writers, 72 Spring St; New York, NY 10012; (212) 226-3586. 1990. 63 pp, $6.95 (plus $1.50 postage and handling plus sales tax where applicable) paper. This guide contains simply and clearly written information on copyright laws, authors' rights and the functions of the Copyright Office; it is illustrated with sample forms.

Writer's Market; Mark Kissling, ed; Writer's Digest Books; 1507 Dana Ave; Cincinnati, OH 45207; (513) 531-2222. 1991. 1008 pp, $25.95 (plus $3 postage and handling plus sales tax where applicable) cloth. This annually updated directory lists 4000 places to sell what you write. It includes many opportunities for playwrights and screenwriters. The 1993 edition is due out in September 1992 (price $26.95).

The Writing Business; Poets & Writers; 72 Spring St; New York, NY 10012; (212) 226-3586. 1985. 345 pp, $11.95 (plus $2.50 postage and handling plus sales tax where applicable) paper. This handbook is a compilation of articles filled with practical advice originally published in the Poets & Writers newsletter.

Submission Calendar

September 1992–August 1993

Included here are all *specified* deadlines contained in Production, Prizes, Publication, Development, Fellowships and Grants, Colonies and Residencies, and Membership and Service Organizations. Please note that suggested submission dates for theatres listed in Production are not included. There are always important deadlines that are not available at press time and so cannot be included here. The "Opportunities" column of *American Theatre* is one place to look for these.

September 1992

1 Bonderman IUPUI Competition for Young Audiences   *82*
1 Coe College Competition   *84*
1 Cunningham Prize for Playwriting   *85*
1 Dorland Mountain Colony (1st deadline)   *197*
1 Maxim Mazumdar Competition   *97*
1 Millay Colony for the Arts (1st deadline)   *200*
1 NEA Fund for U.S. Artists at International Festivals (1st deadline)   *173*
1 Stanley Drama Award   *106*

Contact for exact deadline during this month:

October 1992

November 1992

December 1992

January 1993

Contact for exact deadline during this month:
Border Playwrights Project   *136*
Frederick Douglass Center Workshops (2nd deadline)   *138*
Scholastic Writing Awards   *104*

February 1993

1 Asian Cultural Council (1st deadline)   *166*
1 Bay Area Playwrights Festival   *136*
1 Blue Mountain Center   *195*
1 Millay Colony for the Arts (2nd deadline)   *200*
1 Money for Women (1st deadline)   *173*
1 Mount Sequoyah New Play Retreat   *142*
1 National Music Theater Conference   *143*
1 NEA Fund for U.S. Artists at International Festivals
      (2nd deadline)   *173*
1 Source Theatre Competition   *105*
1 Texas Playwrights Festival   *152*
1 James White Review (2nd deadline)   *132*
13 Very Special Arts Young Playwrights Program   *109*
15 Jane Chambers Award   *83*
15 DC Art/Works Playwrights Competition   *85*
15 Southern Playwrights Competition   *106*
15 White Bird Contest   *111*
15 Wichita State University Contest   *112*
28 Hambidge Center residencies   *199*
28 Pleiades Playwright Grant   *102*

March 1993

1 Samuel Beckett Playwriting Internship   *194*
1 Camargo Foundation residencies   *195*
1 Cintas Fellowship Program   *168*
1 Cornerstone Competition   *85*
1 Discovery '93   *137*
1 Dorland Mountain Colony (2nd deadline)   *197*
1 Florida Studio Young Playwrights Festival   *25*
1 Lamia Ink! One-Page Play Competition   *95*
1 Love Creek One-Act Mini-Festival (May)   *96*

April 1993

May 1993

June 1993

July 1993

August 1993

1 Theodore Ward Prize   *109*
1 James White Review (4th deadline)   *132*
1 Yaddo (2nd deadline)   *206*
31 Marvin Taylor Award   *107*
31 Ten-Minute Musicals Project (2nd deadline)   *152*

Contact for exact deadline during this month:
Golden Gate Contest   *90*
Headlands Center for the Arts   *199*

Special Interests

Here is a guide to entries which indicate a particular or exclusive interest in certain types of material, or which contain an element of special interest to writers in certain categories. Under Theatre for Young Audiences and Media, we try to list every entry of interest to writers in these fields. In the case of adaptations, musicals, one-acts and translations, there are a large number of theatres willing to consider these types of material; we list here only those theatres and other organizations that give major focus to them. Under African-American, Asian-American, Hispanic/Latino and Native American Theatre, we have opted to include not only programs that specifically seek "works by minority writers," but also those that indicate an interest in, for example, "a multiethnic world view" or "works that reflect a multicultural society."

Adaptation

American Conservatory Theater *8*
Arden Theatre Company *9*
Chopstick Theater *17*
CSC Repertory Ltd.—The Classic
  Stage Company *21*
El Teatro Campesino *23*
Germinal Stage Denver *27*
Greatworks Play Service *123*
Indiana Repertory Theatre *32*
INTAR Hispanic American Arts
  Center *33*
Intiman Theatre Company *33*

L.A. Theatre Works *35*
New Jersey Shakespeare
  Festival *43*
Northlight Theatre *45*
Remains Theatre *53*
Roundabout Theatre
  Company *55*
The Shakespeare Theatre *59*
StageWest (MA) *62*
Three Rivers Shakespeare
  Festival *70*
West Coast Ensemble *72*

Experimental Theatre

Musical Theatre

Performance Art
(see also Experimental Theatre)

Theatre for, by and about People with Disabilities

Theatre for Young Audiences

Translation

Women's Theatre

Young Playwright Programs

Index

Remember the alphabetizing principle used throughout the book: Entries beginning with a person's name are alphabetized using the surname rather than the first name. Hence you will find the Mary Anderson Center for the Arts under A, the Alfred Hodder Fellowship under H, the Gregory Kolovakos Award under K.

A

About Theatre Communications Group

Theatre Communications Group is the national organization for the nonprofit professional theatre. Since its founding in 1961, TCG has developed a unique and comprehensive support system that addresses the artistic and management concerns of theatres, as well as institutionally based and freelance artists nationwide.

TCG provides a national forum and communications network for a field that is as aesthetically diverse as it is geographically widespread. Its goals are to foster the cross-fertilization of ideas among the individuals and institutions comprising the profession; to improve the artistic and administrative capabilities of the field; to enhance the visibility and demonstrate the achievements of the American theatre by increasing public awareness of the theatre's role in society; and to encourage the development of a mutually supportive network of professional companies and artists that collectively represent our "national theatre."

TCG's centralized services and programs facilitate the work of thousands of actors, artistic and managing directors, playwrights, literary managers, directors, designers, trustees and administrative personnel, as well as a constituency of more than 300 theatre institutions across the country that present performances to a combined annual attendance of nearly 19 million people.

Related TCG Publications

American Theatre
The national monthly theatre magazine containing news, features and opinion; includes complete texts of 7 plays a year.

Theatre Profiles
The biennial illustrated reference guide to America's nonprofit professional theatres.

Theatre Directory
The annual pocket-sized contact resource of theatres and related organizations.

New Plays USA 2
The second volume of this series of anthologies includes *Secret Honor* by Donald Freed and Arnold M. Stone, *Food from Trash* by Gary Leon Hill, *Mensch Meier* by Franz Xaver Kroetz, translated by Roger Downey, *Buck* by Ronald Ribman and *Mercenaries* by James Yoshimura.

New Plays USA 3
The third volume includes *Morocco* by Allan Havis, *Execution of Justice* by Emily Mann, *The Incredibly Famous Willy Rivers* by Stephen Metcalfe, *Between East and West* by Richard Nelson and *Cold Air* by Virgilio Piñera, translated and adapted by Maria Irene Fornes.

New Plays USA 4
Published in 1988, this volume includes *The Film Society* by Jon Robin Baitz, *Kind Ness* by Ping Chong, *T Bone N Weasel* by Jon Klein, *Tent Meeting* by Larry Larson, Levi Lee and Rebecca Wackler, and *The Colored Museum* by George C. Wolfe.

Plays in Process
A subscription service providing immediate circulation of new plays, translations and adaptations produced at theatres across America.

Between Worlds: Contemporary Asian-American Plays
Edited and with an introduction by Misha Berson, this volume includes *Nuit Blanche: A Select View of Earthlings* by Ping Chong, *The Wash* by Philip Kan Gotanda, *Tenement Lover: no palm trees/in new york city* by Jessica Hagedorn, *As the Crow Flies* and *Sound of a Voice* by David Henry Hwang, *And the Soul Shall Dance* by Wakako Yamauchi and *Pay the Chinaman* by Laurence Yep.

Coming to Terms: American Plays & the Vietnam War
This landmark anthology includes *Streamers* by David Rabe, *Botticelli* by Terrence McNally, *How I Got That Story* by Amlin Gray, *Medal of Honor Rag* by Tom Cole, *Moonchildren* by Michael Weller, *Still Life* by Emily Mann and *Strange Snow* by Stephen Metcalfe, with an introduction by James Reston, Jr.

On New Ground: Contemporary Hispanic-American Plays
Edited by M. Elizabeth Osborn, this volume includes *The Guitarrón* by Lynne Alvarez, *The Conduct of Life* by Maria Irene Fornes, *White Water* by John Jesurun, *Broken Eggs* by Eduardo Machado, *The House of Ramon Iglesia* by José Rivera and *Roosters* by Milcha Sanchez-Scott.

Out from Under: Texts by Women Performance Artists
Edited by Lenora Champagne, this volume includes texts by Laurie Anderson, Laurie Carlos, Lenora Champagne, Karen Finley, Jessica Hagedorn, Holly Hughes, Robbie McCauley, Rachel Rosenthal, Beatrice Roth, Leeny Sack and Fiona Templeton.

Plays of the Holocaust: An International Anthology
Edited by Elinor Fuchs, this volume includes *Eli: A Mystery Play of the Sufferings of Israel* by Nelly Sachs, *Auschwitz* by Peter Barnes, *Mister Fugue or Earth Sick* by Liliane Atlan, *Ghetto* by Joshua Sobol, *Cathedral of Ice* by James Schevill and *Replika* by József Szajna.

Strictly Dishonorable and Other Lost American Plays
Edited by Richard Nelson, this volume includes *Strictly Dishonorable* by Preston Sturges, *The Racket* by Bartlett Cormack, *The Ghost of Yankee Doodle Dandy* by Sidney Howard and *A Slight Case of Murder* by Howard Lindsay and Damon Runyon.

The Way We Live Now: American Plays and the AIDS Crisis
Edited by M. Elizabeth Osborn, this volume includes *As Is* by William M. Hoffman; *Zero Positive* by Harry Kondoleon; *Safe Sex* by Harvey Fierstein; *The Way We Live Now* by Susan Sontag, arranged by Edward Parone; *Andre's Mother* by Terrence McNally; *A Poster of the Cosmos* by Lanford Wilson; *Jack* by David Greenspan; and excerpts from *Angels in America* by Tony Kushner, *Laughing Wild* by Christopher Durang and *The Baltimore Waltz* by Paula Vogel; with an introduction by Michael Feingold.

The Gospel at Colonus *adapted by Lee Breuer*

Sister Suzie Cinema: Collected Poems and Performances 1976–1986 *by Lee Breuer*
Includes *Sister Suzie Cinema, Hajj, Red Beads, Lies!, The Warrior Ant* and *A Prelude to Death in Venice.*

Love & Science: Selected Music-Theatre Texts *by Richard Foreman*
Includes *Africanus Instructus, Hotel for Criminals, Love & Science* and *Yiddisher Teddy Bears.*

A Lesson from Aloes *by Athol Fugard*

Blood Knot and Other Plays *by Athol Fugard*
Includes *Blood Knot, Hello and Goodbye* and *Boesman and Lena.*

My Children! My Africa! *by Athol Fugard*

The Road to Mecca *by Athol Fugard*

Statements: Three Plays *by Athol Fugard with John Kani and Winston Ntshona*
Includes *Sizwe Bansi Is Dead, The Island* and *Statements After an Arrest Under the Immorality Act.*

Swimming to Cambodia *by Spalding Gray*

Approaching Zanzibar *by Tina Howe*

Coastal Disturbances: Four Plays *by Tina Howe*
Includes *Coastal Disturbances, Painting Churches, The Art of Dining* and *Museum.*

Peer Gynt *by Henrik Ibsen, translated by Gerry Bamman and Irene B. Berman*
(TCG Translations 2)

Self Torture and Strenuous Exercise *by Harry Kondoleon*
Includes *Self Torture and Strenuous Exercise, Christmas on Mars, The Vampires, Slacks and Tops* and *Anteroom.*

Through the Leaves and Other Plays *by Franz Xaver Kroetz, translated by Roger Downey*
Includes *Through the Leaves, Mensch Meier* and *The Nest.* (TCG Translations 1)

Reckless and Blue Window: Two Plays *by Craig Lucas*

The Floating Island Plays *by Eduardo Machado*
Includes *The Modern Ladies of Guanabacoa, Fabiola, In the Eye of the Hurricane* and *Broken Eggs.*

Four Plays *by Marsha Norman*
Includes *Getting Out, The Holdup, Third and Oak* and *Traveler in the Dark.*

The Secret Garden *book and lyrics by Marsha Norman*

Shimmer & Other Texts *by John O'Keefe*
Includes *Shimmer, Don't You Ever Call Me Anything but Mother* and *The Man in the Moon.*

New Music: A Trilogy *by Reynolds Price*
Includes *August Snow, Night Music* and *Better Days.*

The Rug Merchants of Chaos and Other Plays *by Ronald Ribman*
Includes *Buck, Sweet Table at the Richelieu* and *The Rug Merchants of Chaos.*

Assassins *by Stephen Sondheim and John Weidman*

Into the Woods *by Stephen Sondheim and James Lapine*

Pacific Overtures *by Stephen Sondheim and John Weidman*

Driving Miss Daisy *by Alfred Uhry*

Spunk: Three Tales by Zora Neale Hurston *adapted by George C. Wolfe*

People Who Led to My Plays *by Adrienne Kennedy*
An autobiographical scrapbook of words and images depicting the influences that have shaped the author's writing.

In Their Own Words: Contemporary American Playwrights *interviews by David Savran*

Catalogue available upon request

Notes

Notes

Notes

Notes

SPECIAL OFFER!
SAVE 25% ON *THEATRE PROFILES 10.*

This latest edition of TCG's biennial illustrated guide to America's nonprofit professional theatres provides comprehensive information on 229 theatres, featuring a statement of purpose from the artistic director, as well as production histories from the 1989–90 and 1990–91 seasons, listing playwright, director and designers for each play. Also included are production photos, names of artistic and managerial heads, telephone numbers, addresses, founding dates, performing seasons, seating capacities and types of stages, operating expenses and union contracts. Appendices include a complete name and title index, chronology of founding dates and a state-by-state breakdown. 8½x11, 200 pp, more than 225 photographs. Regular price: $21.95. *Theatre Profiles 10* is available to purchasers of *Dramatists Sourcebook* at the special price of $16.45.

. . . .

ORDER FORM

Yes! I would like a copy of *Theatre Profiles 10.*
Enclosed is a check or money order for $16.45.

Name _____

Address _____

City _____ State _____ Zip _____

Occupation _____

Make checks payable to Theatre Communications Group and mail with order form to TCG, 355 Lexington Ave., New York, NY 10017.

INTRODUCTORY OFFER!
NEW SUBSCRIBERS SAVE 25% ON
AMERICAN THEATRE.

Each issue of *American Theatre* provides comprehensive coverage of the dynamic, vital world of theatre, offering insight into the work of today's foremost theatrical innovators both in the United States and abroad.

Timely feature articles highlight important new developments in all aspects of theatre: acting, directing, design and playwriting, as well as developments in related art fields.

Regular monthly columns report news and updates on nationwide performance activity, international theatre events, playwriting contests, media highlights, theatre awards, book reviews, legislative and economic issues, fund-raising, trusteeship and management trends—plus performance schedules for some 200 theatres coast to coast.

In addition, complete texts of plays are published in the magazine seven times a year. These outstanding contemporary works reflect the diversity of interests and concerns among playwrights today, and their publication in *American Theatre* further enables readers to keep abreast of artistic trends in the stage repertoire.

Subscribe to *American Theatre* today and save 25% off the regular price of $27 for a one-year subscription. *Dramatists Sourcebook* purchasers pay only $19.95.

. . . .

ORDER FORM

Yes! I would like a subscription to *American Theatre* (10 issues a year). Enclosed is a check or money order for $19.95.

Name _____

Address _____

City _____ State _____ Zip _____

Occupation _____

Make checks payable to Theatre Communications Group and mail with order form to TCG, 355 Lexington Ave., New York, NY 10017.

SPECIAL OFFER!
SAVE 25% ON *PLAYS IN PROCESS.*

One of the best ways to grow as a writer is to read the works of other writers. *Plays in Process* is an annual subscription series of 12 new plays that have been produced professionally by TCG's member theatres. In addition to two important new scripts six times a year, a subscription to *PIP* includes six issues of our *Play Source* bulletin, containing synopses of over 150 more new plays, musicals and plays for young audiences.

Now, for purchasers of *Dramatists Sourcebook* only, *PIP* is being offered at a special discount price of $45 for a full year's subscription. *Plays in Process* offers its subscribers the most complete look at the current state of playwriting in America, and that's why, along with hundreds of theatres and producers across the country, more and more playwrights are beginning to subscribe.

Subscribe to *PIP* today and save $15. *PIP* is available to *Dramatists Sourcebook* purchasers for only $45 (regular price $60).

. . . .

ORDER FORM

Yes! I would like a subscription to *Plays in Process* (12 plays a year). Enclosed is a check or money order for $45.

Name _____

Address _____

City _____ State _____ Zip _____

Occupation _____

Make checks payable to Theatre Communications Group and mail with order form to TCG, 355 Lexington Ave., New York, NY 10017.